Basketball's Great Moments

Basketball's Great Moments

By Jack Clary

Foreword by Oscar Robertson

McGraw-Hill Book Company

New York   St. Louis   San Francisco   Auckland   Bogotá
Hamburg   London   Madrid   Milan   Mexico   Montreal
New Delhi   Panama   Paris   São Paulo   Singapore
Sydney   Tokyo   Toronto

This book is dedicated to all who have dribbled a basketball, swished it through a basket or even passed it behind their backs . . . and most especially to the players and coaches who have created the special excitement of this game—be it in a crowded college gym at Fordham . . . inside storied arenas like old Madison Square Garden . . . or within the mystique that surrounds the parquet in Boston.

Prepared and produced by Sammis Publishing, Inc.
Printed and bound by W.A. Krueger, Olathe, Kansas
Typeset by Midatlantic Photocomposition, Baltimore, Maryland
Designed by Alan Mogel

LCC: 88-13906
ISBN: 0-07-011138-3

Acknowledgments

The Naismith Basketball Hall of Fame in Springfield, Massachusetts was most helpful in the compilation of the great moments within this book. Joseph O'Brien, the executive director, and his staff, paticularly research specialist Wayne Patterson, were very generous with their time and expertise in helping in the accuracy of the telling graciously opening their research channels to pull together so much diverse material. The author also wishes to thank the various information specialists in college and professional basketball, namely:

Tom Hathaway, university of Cincinnati; Kit Klingelhofer, University of Indiana; Kevin Kelly, Rio Grande College; Greg Burke, Providence College; Jim Engelhardt, St. Bonaventure's University; Doug Vance, University of Kansas; Rick Brewer, University of North Carolina; Ken Krsolovic, St. Joseph's University; Bruce Woodbury, University of Utah; John Heisler, University of Notre Dame; Sweetie Aiwohi, Chaminade University; Mark Bockelman, North Carolina State University; Rick Rivers, University of Houston; Bobby Hall, Wayland Baptist University; Mike Treps, University of Oklahoma; Hunter Reid, Furman University; the sports information staff at the University of Kentucky; Harvey Pollack and David Coskey, Philadelphia 76ers; Joyce Syzmanski, Chicago Bulls; Bill Kreifeldt, Utah Jazz; Time Edwards, Indiana Pacers; Mike Caligiure, NBA office.

Special thanks for additional research help also goes to Alan Heim, former executive sports editor, Cincinnati Enquirer; Dick Forbes, Cincinnati Enquirer; Ray Meyer, former coach, DePaul University; and Jim McHale, Xavier '59.

Special photo credits go to Steve Lipofsky, Boston; Bill Fitzgerald, Wide World Photos; Scott Jahn, Bettmann News Photos; Jean Mulvancy, Boston Globe Library; and Photo Research Staff, Temple University Library.

Editorial and typing help came from John and Fred Sammis; Linda Sammis; Kathy Sammis; John Roman; Lori Stein; and Tom Quinn of McGraw Hill.

To all of those, and to the journalists who so diligently recorded many of the events contained within this book: Thank you.

About This Book

Basketball is the game born of America and its worn "Y gyms, its inner city cement playgrounds, the street sport that requires only the player to wear sneakers. No mitt, no racquet, no bat, no set of woods and irons, no spikes, no skates. A pick up game that begins when there are two and can grow to a dozen shooting for the rim, with or without netting.

There are those—I am one—who believe professional basketball demands more of its athletes than does any other sport. The pro in uniform must possess great strength, have endurance, speed, agility, eye and hand coordination, peripheral vision, team sense, the ability to go solo to the basket, to pass accurately, to dribble with either hand and to utilize these skills so economically they can be exercised on a hardwood floor that makes up a court severely limited in size. Two steps beyond the sidelines and a plunging player is in the lap of a courtside spectator.

Contrary to common belief, basketball is not just quickness and guile. It is a brutal contact sport, shoulders, elbows, knees and hips constantly crashing together with a ferocity overlooked by the viewer seeing the fluid moves of a Magic Johnson, a Michael Jordan, Larry Bird. Missed is the struggle of giant centers for position under the net that will yield the maximum in rebounds.

From this game as played at the College and pro level have come great moments which like the game itself, captivated millions and now beg a retelling as a part of basketball's legacy.

What we have compiled is intended as tribute to the game played to its optimum, these moments a celebration of the game's best and brightest, set down as a permanent record.

Such permanance, we feel, is necessary; the fast-moving nature of sports gives too little time for reflection. We tend to lose sight of the past in celebration of the now. To forget—worse—to ignore past greatness only lessens todays game.

CONTENTS

Introduction

Within the last few years, the nation has become wildly turned on to the game of basketball. The NBA championship series now is known as "The Finals," and millions watch during the sweltering days of early June. The NCAA championship simply is known as the Final Four, and millions who have no allegiance to any of the schools involved, become rapt followers over a three-week span during which nearly six dozen teams are pared down to the four who will, over a weekend, vie for the national title.

Before there are championships there are individual games, with great team and player performances that seem to be scene-setters for what is to come at season's end . . . great moments all, which have not begun only in the eighties, but which are an integral part of the sport's fabric.

What we have compiled is a tribute to the game played to its optimum, moments that are a celebration of the game's best and brightest. Such permanence is necessary; the fast-moving nature of competitive sports gives too little time for reflection. We tend to lose sight of the past in celebrating the now. To forget—worse, to ignore—past great moments only lessens today's game.

Selection of the sport's great moments over nearly a half century becomes an arbitrary procedure. Sadly, selection must omit some worthy moments: the two great duels which Bill Bradley and Cazzie Russell fought on behalf of their Princeton and Michigan teams in 1965; the magnificence of the Los Angeles Lakers' record-setting 33-game winning streak in 1972; the nail-biting excitement which the Celtics and Milwaukee Bucks produced in a double overtime playoff game in 1974; North Carolina's electric last-second victory in the 1982 NCAA championship game; the super-human efforts expended by Belmont Abbey College in 1983, playing a record eight overtime games; an equally exhausting seven-overtime game between Bradley and Cincinnati in 1981.

All of those—and many others—were moments worthy of more than a passing notice, and all were included in our semifinal list of one hundred moments. But our final selection was based on the games and people who, in our judgment, had a particularly lasting impact on the sport.

Great moments deserve to be cherished. It's my hope this book will help to serve that purpose.

Jack Clary
Stow, Massachusetts
July, 1988

Foreword

There always has been—and always will be—something special about the game of basketball. Certainly in my case, part of the reason is my association with the sport as a player for so much of my life. The other part is that I so admire the special skills which are used to play this game, and I can say without any fear of overstatement that some of the greatest athletes in the world become its stars.

Beginning with my high school days in Indiana, and continuing through my college career at the University of Cincinnati, and throughout my professional career, I have seen basketball players up close. Even after so many years of such close association I still am amazed and impressed at what the sport's best performers can do.

What is it that makes them so special?

Perhaps it is having a wide-open game played under control within a relatively confined area between the baskets on one side, and the sidelines on the other. Perhaps it is their marvelous athletic reactions, and their ability to perform so brilliantly under the most physically stressful circumstances. My reactions, I'm certain, are no different than others who have not played the game yet who watch and admire . . . whether in a small high school gym or in a huge arena where an NCAA title or an NBA championship is at stake.

Often, the beauty of the game is a combination of all of the above; or just the love of competition between a group of kids playing hour after hour in a schoolyard, or on a street where a basket has been nailed to a tree or a pole. Whatever, this is a truly American sport, invented and developed in this country, and copied with variation throughout the world. It embodies the mastering of physical skills which are unique to American athletes' use of the hands to control and throw the ball, as well as running, jumping, and in recent years, an ascent to athletic ballet that needs no music to enthrall.

Those feelings are even more underscored at special times when a player, or a team, rises above itself and performs the unbelievable. I need only recall my playing years with the Royals and Milwaukee Bucks to realize just how much our group of players could achieve under the most pressurized situations to fully appreciate the true beauty of this sport.

Some of the greatest players and teams are part of this book, and the recollection of these great moments stirs a variety of feelings because I played against many of the principals whose feats are celebrated within these covers. Perhaps I can appreciate better than most just what some of those players and teams did achieve, even though during a game there is not time to stand, watch and applaud the variety of talents involved. Ah, but afterward . . . the blur of the game slowed so that I often found myself wondering just how in the world certain plays ever could have occurred.

I hope the readers will share those same feelings as they recollect some of those great moments, on the college, professional, and Olympic levels. Everyone should appreciate, as a true work of athletic art, all that is a part of the game of basketball's legacy so that we will have even more capacity in future years to applaud great moments still to come.

Oscar Robertson
Cincinnati, Ohio
August, 1988

WHEN GIANTS CLASHED

March 6, 1945

Oklahoma A&M
vs.
DePaul

In the mid-forties, the big man in basketball was considered a sideshow freak, someone hired to bomb basketballs over the heads of his "normal" opponents. The game was not attuned to players some six feet nine inches or seven feet tall. It was a game of deliberate moves; size was secondary to agility, the ability to move quickly and get open for an uncontested shot. It was the day of the two-handed set shot artist who could bang away from the outside. If the shot missed, the rebound would likely fly back out past the key to be snatched by the nearest hands.

Terms such as power forwards and point guards were not part of the lexicon. A player was a forward, a center or a guard, and he was expected to play his position by strictly defined roles, working in patterns far less complicated than those employed in today's contests. Four decades ago basketball was just approaching the game of run and gun, of fly and soar, of blocked shots in your face that is now commonplace.

On the scene were coaches who intuitively sensed the game's future direction. One was Hank Iba, who coached the Oklahoma A & M squad; another was Ray Meyer of Chicago's DePaul. They realized the value of adding the big man who could run, jump, play dominating defense and, of course, shoot. It was no accident that the two preeminent big men of the mid-forties, Bob Kurland and George Mikan, had been picked up and coached by Iba and Meyer, Kurland playing for the Aggies and Mikan for DePaul.

Kurland was a seven-foot center who fit perfectly into Iba's defense-minded game plan. As a junior, Kurland had helped the Aggies win the NCAA championship. Iba loved ball control; Kurland made it work. Though slow, he was agile and used his height and strength to control the backboards, frustrating opponents near the basket. He was the Aggies' chief rebounder, who got the ball to a guard and then thundered upcourt behind his teammates' weave-type offense.

After Kurland worked into position under the hoop, he either got the pass for a shot or allowed a teammate to cut around him for a layup. Iba claimed that Kurland set screens better than any other college center he'd ever seen.

Actually, the big man's greatest contributions were on defense. He was a splendid shot blocker, so good he forced the NCAA into legislating rules to penalize goaltending. Without such rules to inhibit him, Kurland could knock the ball away just as it appeared to drop through for a goal, an easier defense blocking the ball on its upward arc.

In Kurland's final game for the Aggies, Iba decided to show his appreciation for the big man's willingness to play ball

*Laker center George Mikan blocks shot by Royals
guard Bob Davies, but Rochester beat the Lakers in
1951 Western playoffs.*

The Oklahoma A&M-DePaul Red Cross Benefit Game in 1945 at New York City's Madison Square Garden was the third—and last—such affair, a byproduct of the fund raising needs of World War II. This game, attended by 18,158 fans, produced some $50,000 for the Red Cross. One person paid $6,000 for the game ball, others chipped in for uniforms and other memorabilia.

However, that game was not the last in which New York fans saw Kurland play. The following season, he led Oklahoma A&M to its second straight NCAA title, beating North Carolina, 43-40, in the final at the Garden. Kurland, who also won his second straight MVP award, led all scorers with 23 points.

control and told him before the game to cut loose, to go all-out offensively. Freed from the tether of tight defense, Kurland tossed in 58 points against St. Louis University, the highest single-game total of his career.

George Mikan, on the other hand, always was a prolific scorer. In 1945 he too was a junior—some three inches shorter than Kurland—the forerunner of the point-making center who got into the game a decade later in the NBA. Mikan played an aggressive game, a believer in the efficacy of a sharp elbow when the opponent was in a perfect position to shoot.

"I've always considered George to be the ideal center," says his coach, Ray Meyer. "He was intelligent, competitive, and always consistent in his play. Sure he was big, but he had great court sense. Though he may have fooled some because he wore glassses, he always saw the whole court picture. That's why he had such ability to pass off the ball. Fans were more taken with his scoring talent, but in our multi-dimensional scheme of play, George was the center who got everyone involved."

Now, late March 1945, it was time for the climactic match-up of basketball's two big stars, the nation's best centers, one playing for the NIT champion, DePaul, the other for the NCAA champion, the Oklahoma Aggies. The occasion: the third annual Red Cross benefit game, to be played at the Old Madison Square Garden, on New York City's Eighth Avenue— the night the giants clashed.

Of the two prizes, the NIT was the more lustrous jewel in basketball's crown; the NCAA carried significance because it claimed to define the national collegiate champion. The crowd was there to watch Kurland, the giant of strength, versus Mikan, the giant who scored.

A preview of sorts had occurred early in the season when

Above left and right: *Mikan in action as a Laker and with DePaul*. Right: *Hank Iba receives NCAA championship cup from commissioner Tug Wilson. Kurland is behind both men.*

DePaul and the Aggies had met in Chicago. DePaul had squeaked by, 48-46; Mikan outscoring Kurland 15 to 8. "Kurland was the better defensive man," Meyer recalls, "but I thought Mikan did better all around."

Now it would be the game of the year. The oddsmakers agreed with Meyer and established DePaul as a 7-point favorite. A standing-room-only crowd of 18,158 was jammed to the Garden's rafters. Just a week before, Mikan had dazzled New Yorkers by scoring 53 points against Rhode Island State. In the NIT tourney's three games, Mikan had racked up a total of 120 points.

"GAME OF THE CENTURY," quietly announced the sports pages. Would it be muscle or shooting touch? This clash of giants making basketball history was, in actuality, a brief encounter, a moment of greatness in swirling exchanges, an Iba-conceived game of strength so effective that the skilled Mikan was in immediate foul trouble.

Ultimately, four DePaul performers were on the bench before the game ended, victims of the Aggies' strengths. Fourteen minutes into the first half, George Mikan had fouled out, gone for the duration, a zero factor. While he was in the game, Mikan had contributed brilliantly to help his team finish the half with the lead, 26 to 21, outscoring Kurland 9 to 7.

But the damage had been done. To begin the second half, the Aggies ran off nine points in a row, holding DePaul without a basket in the first five minutes of play. Neither of Mikan's replacements, John Phelan nor Gene Larochelle, could handle Kurland. With Mikan gone, Kurland became the difference. Although DePaul managed to cut the A & M lead to 47-44 with less than four minutes to play, Kurland grabbed a rebound from the defensive boards and sailed a long pass to Weldeon Kern. Kern's shot missed, but Cecil Hankins was there to pop in the rebound. The die was cast. It was the Aggies and Kurland's strength over the skills of Mikan and his DePaul five. Final score: Oklahoma A & M 52, DePaul 44.

This clash of giants, while brief, is considered the most significant of the several meeting between the two players. More than anything else, this game established the fun of watching big men head to head, an addition to the game that helped its popularity zoom by millions of enthusiastic fans.

Happily, as a humanitarian affair, the match met its fund goal for the Red Cross, raising a respectable $40,000.

Footnote: Kurland bypassed pro basketball for a career with the AAU's Bartlesville Oilers, and played on the triumphant U.S. Olympic squad, winning several gold medals.

March 6, 1945, at New York City			
Oklahoma A & M	G	F	Pts
Hankins	8	4	20
Kern	0	5	5
Kurland	4	6	14
Halbert	0	0	0
Williams	0	1	1
Parrack	3	0	6
Parks	3	0	6
Totals	18	16	52
DePaul			
Stump	5	2	12
Comerford	0	0	0
DiBenedetto	5	2	12
Furman	1	1	3
Mikan	2	5	9
Phelan	1	0	2
Allen	0	1	1
Niemiera	0	0	0
Kochan	2	0	4
LaRochelle	0	1	1
Halloran	0	0	0
Totals	16	12	44

Halftime: DePaul 26-21
Officials: Hagen Anderson & Pat Kennedy

2

THE WATER SHED GAME

April 22, 1947

Philadelphia
vs.
Chicago

Although the rim jammers, the slam dunkers, the sky-hookers were still in the future, at World War II's end pro basketball was ready to flourish. On April 22, 1947, the ABA Warriors of Philadelphia were scheduled to play the BAA champion Chicago Stags—the first championship game of the Basketball Association of America, just two years before the NBA was organized.

That April night in the old Philadelphia Arena set the tone for all that has occurred since. Since this contest, considered a watershed game in pro basketball's growth, more than 40 NBA champions have been crowned.

Before the Warriors-Stags encounter, two top quality squads had never clashed in a final match. Any number of pro "world championship" games had been played, but none were memorable. Such was the madcap nature of pro basketball in those years, two of the BAA division winners, the Stags and the Capitols (coached by Arnold Red Auerbach), played each other in the first round. Eventually, the Stags went on to meet Philadelphia, under coach Eddie Gottlieb.

The Warriors had the league's acknowledged star, forward Joe Fulks. Fulks had been a high school standout in Kuttawa, Kentucky, and a great scorer for Murray State College. His college days were cut short by two years of service with the Marines. Gottlieb admitted that he signed Fulks "more on his potential than on his record." The coach's hunch paid off; in that first season Fulks not only led the league in scoring with an unheard-of total of 1,557 points, but also had nine of the league's twelve best individual scoring performances.

A slim six-foot-five, weighing 190 pounds, Fulks had an unorthodox style—a twisting pivot shot, the forerunner of the jump shot. It earned him the nickname "Jumpin' Joe." Though not fast and never renowned for his defense, Fulks was the Larry Bird of that time, an instinctive player who had a great sense of exactly where and when to shoot. And he shot and shot and shot, with more tries than any other player in the league that year.

The Stags' star was Max Zaslofsky, ranked fifth in scoring. He played along with center Chuck Halbert (the Wilt Chamberlain of his time, not fouling out of a single game while causing those guarding him all kinds of headaches when they battled him on the boards) and guard Tony Janos. In fact, in the fourth of this best-of-seven series, both Fulks and Hillhouse of the Warriors had fouled out guarding Max.

For this fifth game, 5,000 fans were turned away at the gate, the Arena a sellout for the showdown. The old building had a posted capacity of 8,200, but the fire marshals must have

Warrior George Senesky drives for 2 of his 11 points in the championship game against Chicago in the crusty Philadelphia Arena.

"Jumpin' Joe" Fulks (10) goes for loose ball in championship game. Fulks led all scorers with 34 points in the game and 1,557 for the season.

taken the night off: some 10,000 crowded in to see if the Warriors could clinch the championship.

The packed house liked what it saw when the game began: The Warriors zoomed off to a 22-7 lead. The Stags, behind Janos and Halbert, then worked the score down to 40-38 at the half. Shortly after the second half began, Willie Kautz tied the game. From that point on, the match took on classic overtones. Chicago went ahead 48-47 for the first time on Chet Carlisle's shot, and the lead switched hands five more times in the third quarter.

Chicago appeared to jump on top for good when Don Carlson's long shot, a pair of fouls by Janos, and another field goal by Charley Gilmer gave the Stags a 68-63 lead at the start of the fourth quarter. The Stags stubbornly held that five-point spread until nine minutes remained to play.

"We had worked hard on defense against Zaslofsky to hold him in check during the game, or else we would have been out of it altogether," Senesky said later. "Max had burned us badly in Chicago and we were concentrating all of our efforts on stopping him. At that point, everyone was wondering if we would explode, as was our fashion, and get back into the game."

Which is exactly what did happen. Fulks hit a sideline shot for 2 of his game-leading 34 points. In quick succession, Angelo Musi, who had scored 9 points in a Warrior first-quarter breakout, got 2 more. Foul shots by Dallmar and Fulks finally put Philly back into the lead, 76-75.

Pro basketball in those days moved more slowly. With no 24-second clock, teams could patiently work for their best shot. That was Stags coach Olsen's style, and he signaled to Halbert to work into the middle for a 3-point play to give the Stags a 78-76 lead. The strategy worked, but Fulks came right back with a one-hander. Then Halbert got free in the middle again, and tied the score 80-80 with 80 seconds to play.

"Chicago really began to overplay Fulks, and that was dangerous because we were by far much more than a one-man show," Senesky noted.

Enter Howie Dallmar. Dallmar had hobbled through the first four games of the series painfully on calloused feet. This morning, he had gone to Dr. Pete Leanness and asked him to cut away the sorest spots from his left foot.

"No one expected him to play, perhaps not even to show up, after an operation like that," Coach Gottlieb observed. "He sat there, pestering me to let him in. When it came down to that point where I thought we might win the game, I sent him in and he was the ultimate difference."

After the Halbert goal that had tied the game, Dallmar on his sore feet led his team upcourt. Fulks, surrounded by Stags, flashed into the open, took a pass and launched a perfect one-hand shot, giving his team a two-point lead.

Chicago took possession, but in the next exchange Kaplowitz of the Warriors was fouled. His free-throw was good and the Warriors led 83-80. Again the Stags lost possession. This time, Petey Rosenberg of the Warriors gave what a courtside observer noted was "a great exhibition of dribbling to freeze the ball."

With time running out, Chicago fouled Petey, and as a final tribute to those younger and zanier days, Rosenberg allowed Kaplowitz to go to the foul line in his place, the officials seemingly unaware of the infraction. For the frosting on the bizarre moment, Kaplowitz missed. All of which was of no importance. The Warriors had taken the championship.

Each team split a total pot of $14,000. Fulks, who played all 48 minutes, led all scorers with 131 points for the playoff series. This did not make Fulks a one-man team, however. Dallmar as the team's best playmaker and George Senesky had given a marvelous balance to match up against the Stags' more college-oriented game geared around Max Zaslofsky.

In the end, the game served as the first true measure of the nation's best pro fives. Pro basketball had edged another inch toward the NBA millions—in dollars and in fans—of the present.

"Fulks is slow and he's not a great defensive player. How can he be a great defensive player when he takes so many shots? But I wish I had him. I'd sure build my team around him."

The comment came from Boston Celtics coach John (Honey) Russell after watching the Warriors' Fulks during his first season in the NBA.

Russell was correct. Fulks went on to a Hall of Fame career, finishing with an eight-season total of 8,003 points in an era when there were few 100-point final scores.

His greatest feat came in Philadelphia in 1949 when he scored a record 63 points against the Indianapolis Jets at a time when many teams didn't score 63 points in one game. In fact, it wasn't until ten years later that Elgin Baylor of the Lakers broke that record when he scored 64 points against the Celtics.

How did Fulks do it?

"They give me the ball and I shoot," he once said. "That's all there is to it."

April 22, 1947, at Philadelphia					
Chicago	FG-FGA	FT-FTA	A	PF	Pts
Carlisle	1-4	3-3	2	5	5
Halbert	3-19	2-5	0	1	8
Carlson	4-12	3-4	1	2	11
Zaslofsky	2-7	1-1	0	2	5
Gilmer	3-11	0-0	0	5	6
Seminoff	5-15	2-3	2	5	12
Davis	0-2	0-2	0	4	0
Janos	6-22	9-10	3	4	21
Kautz	5-19	0-2	0	4	10
Rotiner	1-6	0-0	0	1	2
Totals	30-117	20-30	8	33	80
Philadelphia					
Fulks	10-34	14-17	0	4	34
Musi	6-23	1-3	1	4	13
Dallmar	2-7	3-5	4	0	7
Senesky	4-14	3-5	1	4	11
Hillhouse	3-12	3-5	2	5	9
Kaplowitz	1-8	6-7	2	3	8
Fleischman	0-3	1-1	0	1	1
Rosenberg	0-0	0-0	0	0	0
Totals	26-101	31-43	10	21	83
Chicago	13	25	30	12	—— 80
Philadelphia	27	13	23	20	—— 83

Officials: Pat Kennedy & Eddie Boyle

3

WORDS THEY'D NEVER HEARD BEFORE

March 23, 1948

Kentucky
vs.
Baylor

March 26, 1949

Kentucky
vs.
Oklahoma A&M

March 27, 1951

Kentucky
vs.
Kansas State

I f one accepts the hyperbole, and one should, Adolph Rupp's coaching life was in itself a great basketball moment.

Rupp led his Kentucky teams to four NCAA championships within ten years. He retired as college basketball's all-time winning head, leaving his imprint on every facet of the sport. The way he built his teams, his playbook, his meticulous coaching of each individual player to reach his full potential, became "the Rupp Way."

Once a year, Kentucky pays brief attention to horses galloping around the Churchill Downs track in a race called the Derby. Put the Derby aside as an aberration and there is only one state pastime that counts, University of Kentucky basketball. A season without a Kentucky hoop championship is a julep without mint.

For 42 years Rupp dominated the Kentucky sports scene, earning the nickname "Baron" and all the questionable nuances of such a title. His first national championship came in 1948 with a team dubbed "Rupp's Fabulous Five." His last big win was in 1958 with a squad alliteratively nicknamed "The Fiddlin' Five." Both labels and titles were testimonials to his coaching skills, adding to his larger-than-life image, a man who dominated everyone who touched his world.

When he was at Kentucky, Rupp was more than the Baron—he was king of the hill. Football coach Paul (Bear) Bryant was then at Kentucky and received a gold watch for his championship season. Rupp got a new car for his NCAA title. Bryant couldn't take the competition for supremacy and left for Alabama, where he became college football's most successful coach. Everyone who followed at Kentucky in Bryant's footsteps felt the same long Rupp shadow and ultimately left, regardless of win-loss records.

Rupp began his basketball life on his family's farm in Kansas. The youngster used whatever he could find that would pass for a ball, flinging it into whatever would pass for a hoop. How basketball caught the lad's fancy on those prairie acres is anyone's guess.

Rupp attended the University of Kansas and played for renowned coach Phog Allen. He became a member of an unbeaten Jayhawks team, though as an ordinary member of the squad. Aiding and abetting Phog in coaching duties was Dr. James Naismith, inventor of the game. Between Naismith and Allen, Rupp became an ardent disciple of their teaching.

Graduated, Rupp was a determined man who told the Kentucky Board of Athletics in his job interview that he was "the best damned basketball coach in America." To back up

Top: *Kentucky center Ed Beck (34) blocks shot by Seattle's Elgin Baylor (22) in NCAA final.* Bottom: *Seattle's guard Charley Brown (45) and Wildcat forward John Crigler (32) fight for rebound.*

such modesty, Rupp had only his five-year stint as coach of the Belleville, Illinois, high school wrestling team; the basketball coaching job had already been filled. Rupp did, however, develop a state championship wrestling squad.

Given the job at Kentucky, Rupp wasted no time putting his theories into practice. He was relentless with players who believed that playing well was reward in itself. "If winning isn't the whole point, why in hell keep score?" Rupp roared. "Success is the builder of character; failure isn't!"

Rupp had no more respect for game officials than he had for his players. David Scobey, former Southeastern Conference official, recalled a game he worked between Kentucky and Mississippi.

"I hadn't been up and down the court more than two times," Scobey remembered, "when Coach Rupp hollered out at me, 'Is it going to be another of your nights, Scobey? Sure looks that way.'"

At one clinic, a young high school coach hoping for some tips from the master asked, "Mr. Rupp, I notice that every one of your players always shoots well. How do you account for that?"

"That is why they have scholarships," Rupp snapped.

At a freshman drill, Rupp watched the players battling for a rebound. He exhorted them thus: "Remember the Bible, men. It says, 'It is better to give than receive.'" The reference was not lost on the frosh, who immediately began using elbows, knees and hands to knock any opponent out of the way.

Fans and cheerleaders congratulate victorious Kentucky team after defeating Seattle for their fourth NCAA title.

Rupp often was accused of intimidating everyone around him, and sometimes of even going out of his way to build animosity. "He was unique," says Bill Spivey, his all-America center on the Wildcats' 1951 NCAA title team. "He wanted everyone to hate him—and often succeeded. He called us names some of us never heard before. That was the Rupp way. The player could quit or stay just to prove he could be as mean as Rupp."

Spivey, for one, felt Rupp's sting during the NCAA title game when he was outplayed by a six-foot-eight-inch Kansas center named Lew Hitch. Rupp tongue-lashed Spivey during halftime, then made him split the center duties with Cliff Hagen, who was a half-foot shorter. The result: Spivey caught fire in the second half, and Kentucky won the NCAA title.

Rupp always claimed to have a unique method of selecting his players, noting the door to his office was six-feet-two-inches high. "If they don't bump their head when they come in, I don't bother to shake hands." Not quite true, since some of Rupp's best players, such as guard Ralph Beard, were under six feet. To play safe, Frank Ramsey entered on tiptoe the first time he met Rupp.

While all of this was part of the Rupp coaching system, his basic approach stressed attack, a philosophy that was ahead of its time. Rupp employed three kinds of offense, depending upon what defense he faced. At all times he stressed the pressuring of the other team and wouldn't tolerate anyone who couldn't take return pressure and rise above it.

He detested zone defenses, and once swore he would never use one. When he did in his later years, he refused to call it a "zone." It was, he said "a stratified, transitional hyperbolic paraboloid."

Rupp's players were always the best prepared. Coach Ray Meyer of DePaul said he deliberately scheduled Kentucky early in the season "because Rupp would tell me what was wrong with my team, and backed it up by beating us." Red Auerbach loved to get Rupp's players on his Celtics teams because "they played my style of basketball, and were thoroughly grounded in the fundamentals of ball handling and floor movement."

Rupp won 879 games, 27 conference championships, 4 NCAA titles and 1 NIT title. He was voted No. 1 six times by wire service polls, appeared in 20 NCAA playoffs, and 31 of his players turned pro. And his starting 1948 team won an Olympic gold medal. The coach considered it one of his most cherished achievements.

Adolph Rupp, coach of the champion Kentucky Wildcats, receives victor's trophy after taking 1948 NCAA tournament.

Rupp's first NCAA title in 1948 really was not unexpected because the Wildcats had been a power for several years, winning one of three NIT finals and five consecutive SEC titles. In 1948, the Wildcats won 27 of 29 regular season games, and 4 more in the SEC playoffs before upending once-beaten Columbia and defeating NCAA champion Holy Cross in the first two games of the NCAA's Eastern finals.

This was Rupp's Fabulous Five—center Alex Groza, forwards Wallach (Wah-Wah) Jones and Cliff Barker, and guards Ralph Beard and Ken Rollins. There were no kids among this group, all veterans of Rupp's intensive training. Barker was a veteran of a bit more—he was 27 years old and had flown with the Eighth Air Force during World War II, spending 16 months in a prison camp after being shot down over Germany. There, a steady diet of volleyball helped him become a great ball handler.

Beard was the team catalyst, a ball-hawking guard who was a roadrunner in Rupp's fast-break offense, and possessor of an amazing long shot that made him a scoring threat from almost any place on the court. In 1948, the Associated Press selected its first collegiate All-America team and Beard was the top vote-getter, quite a feat for someone who came to Kentucky on a football scholarship, started one game, separated both shoulders, and quit.

Jones was the team's best athlete, earning 11 letters during his career at Kentucky. He was a starting wide receiver on the football team as well as one of the starting forwards for Rupp, and pitched for the baseball team as well. Jones used his football ability to good advantage with his strong rebounding and, along with Groza, helped control the middle.

Groza, whose brother Lou was a place-kicker and offensive tackle for the Cleveland Browns, was the team's top scorer and would have been the dominant player on any other team with less talent. As it was, he was MVP in the 1948 NCAA tourney, and also the leading scorer for the U.S. Olympic team's gold medal triumph later that summer.

In the NCAA final the Wildcats overmatched Baylor, a surprise winner in the Western regionals over Kansas State, and showed it by building a 7-0 lead in the first five minutes, upping that to 24-7 before Baylor carved the lead down to 44-35 during the second half while Rupp rested his regulars. Back they came and the Wildcats rolled on for a 58-42 victory.

A week later, the Wildcats beat Baylor again in the Olympic trials as they rolled through collegiate competition, before finally losing to the AAU champion Phillips Oilers and seven-foot center Bob Kurland, 53-40. So impressive were both

teams that their starting fives formed the nucleus of the U.S.
squad, and Rupp was one of the coaches. The team won all
eight games en route to its gold medal, and when the team
finally disbanded in late summer, Rupp was moved to call his
Fabulous Five "the greatest college basketball team of all
time."

It may have been, but those who saw the 1949 team
found it hard to draw any true distinctions because all but
Rollins returned, and Dale Barnstable ably filled his ball-
handling role. As a result, the team lost only to St. Louis
University in the early season, and then in the NIT to eventual winner, Loyola of Chicago.

After the NIT, Rupp took his top-ranked Wildcats home
and drilled them relentlessly to regain the marvelous balance
they had attained after he moved Barker from forward to
guard, and used either Barnstable or Jim Line at forward. In
the end, the postgraduate course was very necessary because
Kentucky had to overcome a 30-point performance by Villanova's Paul Arizin in the first NCAA game. Groza scored 30
for Kentucky, Line got 21 and Barker 18 in an 85-72 victory.

Next came a relentless 76-47 win over Illinois in a
breathtaking display of passing during which 16 of Kentucky's
field goals were layups.

Kentucky flew to Seattle for the NCAA final against
Oklahoma A & M, where Hank Iba still preached muscular
defense first and deliberate offense. His big weapon was center Bob Harris, who matched Groza's height. Iba's strategy
misfired. Groza was quicker, and time and after time, he beat
Harris to the hoop and forced him to foul out early in the
second half.

At one practice, Rupp caught
one of his players hesitating
on a layup, allowing the shot
to be blocked. He whistled
practice to a halt.

"You get the ball like
this," he told the offender,
freezing him with his pa-
tented stare that humbled All-
Americans and reserves alike,
as he hefted an imaginary
basketball slowly over his
head. "Then you say, 'Our Father Who art in Heaven, hal-
lowed be Thy name; Thy
kingdom come; Thy will be
done. I am now going to
shoot the damn basketball.'"

Adolph Rupp's basketball coaching career at a glance: Winningest collegiate basketball coach in history, with 879 victories and 190 losses for 82.2 percent.
Four NCAA champions: 1948, 1949, 1951, 1958.
One NIT champion (1946), 27 Southeast Conference championships, national champions in poll rankings five times, five Sugar Bowl tournament titles and 13 crowns as host team in Kentucky Invitational Basketball Tournament.
25 players named to All-America teams, 52 as all-SEC performers, 31 became pro players, 7 won Olympic gold medals.
20 appearances in the NCAA championship playoffs.
Coach of the Year four times. Elected to Naismith Basketball Hall of Fame in 1959.

While Rupp loved his go-go offense, his defense often went unrecognized. In this game, he matched his friend Iba defensive ploy for defensive ploy, while allowing Groza to carry on with his offense. The strategy worked as Groza won a second straight MVP with his 25 points before fouling out in the final minutes; the defense held the Aggies scoreless for minutes at the start of the second half to get a 35-23 lead. Oklahoma A & M cut it to 39-32, but Groza slammed in two quick baskets, and the Wildcats romped to a 46-36 victory.

Rupp celebrated his back-to-back NCAA titles with a little jig in the dressing room after the game, bid farewell to his great team (which would form the Indianapolis Olympians of the NBA a year later) and looked for bigger fields to conquer.

His next significant triumph didn't come until 1951 when he celebrated the opening of a 12,000-seat arena on Kentucky's campus with a third NCAA title. This was won by an entirely different cast of characters, led by Spivey, Cliff Hagen, and Ramsey, who compiled a 28-2 record. Incredibly, Kentucky lost the SEC playoffs but the conference had decided before the season that its regular season winner would go to the NCAA tourney. In yet another close call in that event, Kentucky needed a 28-point, 16-rebound performance plus a crucial steal in the final seconds by substitute guard C. M. Newton (later a distinguished coach at Alabama) to slip past Big Ten champion Illinois, 76-74.

Kentucky then met Kansas State for the title, the Wildcats having beaten second-ranked Oklahoma A & M. Iba told Rupp he didn't believe Kentucky could beat Kansas State, but Rupp was unruffled until he saw that Spivey was being outplayed by Lew Hitch, the six-eight K-State center. Rupp unloaded on Spivey at halftime, and took Hagen off the bench—and off the sick list—to rally the Wildcats. Spivey responded with 22 points, 21 rebounds, and a 68-58 victory.

Afterward, Rupp acknowledged that "Spivey was the difference—*after* he went to work."

Rupp had another set of concerns in 1958 with a team which he claimed was a group of "fiddlers."

"They're pretty good fiddlers, and they'd be okay at a barn dance," he said. "But I tell you, you need a violinist to play in Carnegie Hall, and we don't have any violinists."

Thus was born the "Fiddlin' Five," a team without a dominant player, or even an SEC all-star, let alone an All-American. But they had Rupp, and he was more determined than ever to get a title. All his genius was required in an early-round game to salvage a 2-point win over Temple. With the Owls ahead 60-59 and 23 seconds to play, Rupp called time out and instructed his team to give Vern Hatton the ball. The six-three senior guard promptly drove for the winning basket, and a 61-60 win.

In the championship game, Kentucky faced Seattle University and its star, Elgin Baylor, a great offensive player who, Rupp believed, might be unstoppable. To compensate, Rupp sent Ed Beck, and then John Crigler, a quick six-three forward, at Baylor time and again. Elgin kept a good offensive game going, carrying his team to a 29-18 lead in the first ten minutes, but he also accumulated three personal fouls. Baylor got his fourth foul with Seattle ahead 44-38 early in the second half and had to curtail his natural aggressiveness. Rupp then turned loose his offense, led by Johnny Cox, who scored 16 points in the final 15 minutes. His long shot tied the score at 56; then Don Mills put Kentucky ahead for good at 61-60 with a hook shot, touching off an 8-0 run that sealed the unlikeliest of the Wildcats' four NCAA titles with an 84-72 victory.

Fourteen years later, Kentucky made Rupp retire at the age of 70. He went kicking and screaming. Five years later he succumbed to a long battle against cancer, in a Lexington, Kentucky hospital only a mile from his beloved school. Ironically, Rupp's death occurred only moments after Kentucky's team, coached by one of his former players on the 1948-49 team, Joe B. Hall, defeated his old school, Kansas, on "Adolph Rupp Night" in the Phog Allen Field House. Naturally, it was located on Naismith Avenue.

Of all the great teams Adolph Rupp produced at Kentucky, which was the most special?

Until the day he died in 1977, Rupp always said it was the 1958 NCAA champions.

"These were just a bunch of ugly ducklings," he said. "Not one of them made the all-conference team.

"And," he added in perhaps the most telling of all statements, "I didn't get a single vote for coach of the year, so I know it wasn't me."

THE MIRACLE DOUBLE

NIT Championship
March 15, 1950

CCNY
vs.
Bradley

NCAA Championship
March 29, 1950

CCNY
vs.
Bradley

olf and tennis have their grand slams, horse racing its Triple Crown. And once, basketball had a two-crowned championship team, a shining moment that will never be repeated.

The year: 1950. The double win: the NIT and the NCAA. The team: the CCNY Beavers.

It happened this way. In the fifties, the NIT tourney was held in New York's Madison Square Garden, the venerable, aging arena in mid-Manhattan. The best college teams stood in line hoping to be chosen for this event. It was fitting that the scene was New York. Other cities had their ball fields, their tennis courts, their pools, their golf courses. New York had its cement playgrounds, its rusted, netless hoops and its passion for the game of basketball. If the tourney took place in the Big Apple, it had to be the best. Quite often it was.

Back then the NCAA deferred to the NIT, holding its tournament after the New York event. Before the 1950 NCAA tournament got underway, there was a stalemate among the district selection members. Was the final place to be filled by CCNY, by Duquesne or by St. John's? Why not, it was suggested, wait and invite the team among the three that went the furthest in the NIT contest? As it turned out, CCNY got to the finals, defeating Duquesne on the way, while St. John's lost to Bradley.

The Beavers were in.

Earlier, when the NIT was beginning to line up its bids, CCNY was close to the bottom of the invitational list. Granted, veteran coach Nat Holman had done a fine job with his predominantly sophomore squad, but there had been a midseason slump after the Beavers had gained a national ranking of seventh. Sure, Holman had reversed the momentum, but was that enough? Ultimately, the bid came because CCNY had defeated all the other local teams.

When the NIT got underway, Bradley was the favorite and CCNY was unseeded, a fact that did not go unnoticed in the sports pages. In general, it was agreed that the Beavers had little chance of making headway in this prestigious event.

Bradley, on the other hand, had rolled through its season as Missouri Valley champion with an NCAA invitation already in hand and a 17-3 record that made the Braves a pre-tourney favorite. The team was led by Gene Melchiorre and Paul Unruh as the front guys in an up-tempo offense designed by coach Fordy Anderson.

Bradley was given a first round bye, then easily defeated St. John's and Syracuse to get to the finals and be established as a seven-point favorite to take the title.

Above: *CCNY forward Irwin Dambrot grabs rebound from Bradley center Chuck Grover. Left: Dambrot (5) and reserve Jim Kelly fight for rebound in 1950 NIT struggle.*

The betting scandals which rocked college basketball in 1951 were a long-time brewing, but when they became public, the nation was shocked to disbelief that anyone—let alone the CCNY team that had achieved the amazing Grand Slam less than a year before—would sully the sport in such a manner.

In 1945, five Brooklyn College players admitted they had accepted bribes to throw their game with Akron University, which was never played. From then, until the scandals broke six years later, the rumors never stopped.

In 1949, a George Washington University player reported he had been approached by gamblers asking that he "do business" with them.

The scandal finally burst in 1951 when a Manhattan College player, Junius Kellogg,

Below: *A less-than-sophisticated program cover for the NCAA finals.* Bottom right: *Coach Nat Holman holds one of the two trophies his predominantly sophomore Beavers won in 1950.*

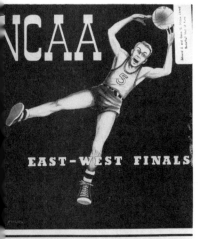

BRADLEY UNIV. vs. CITY COLLEGE
NO. CAROLINA ST. vs. BAYLOR U.
MADISON SQUARE GARDEN   MARCH 28, 1950
25¢

CCNY did it the hard way. First, the Beavers defeated defending champion San Francisco, then dumped another favorite, Kentucky, 89-50, one of the most embarrassing losses ever for an Adolph Rupp-coached team. It was Duquesne in the semifinal round, and Homan's young sophs, led by Ed Warner (who already had amassed 71 points) and Ed Roman, swept ahead for a stunning win.

Now it was the finals and somehow there was CCNY. It seemed obvious that the grand march to glory would end here when the two teams took the floor, and in the first minutes of play nothing challenged that assumption. Led by Melchiorre, Unruh and Bill Mann, the veteran Bradley five rolled to a 29-18 lead.

Holman began to wonder whether getting out of a sick-bed with a 103-degree temperature really was worth it and decided it was time to try and cure the misery. Holman ordered in a substitute, Norman Mager, who had been used only sparingly during the season. Mager immediately flagged down a rebound—something that starters Warner, Roman, Floyd Layne and Irwin Dambrot had failed to do—and snapped the Beavers out of the doldrums. They immediately tightened up their defense and held Bradley without a point for the final seven minutes of the half, carving the Braves' lead to just 30-27.

In the second half, Warner, Roman and Dambrot got back their rhythm. In a furious battle during which there were six ties and seven lead changes, CCNY finally got a 57-56 advantage at the fifteen-minute mark, and never trailed again. Bradley didn't go easily, Aaron Preece, the replacement for Melchiorre (who fouled out at 10:40) brought his team back to within 2 points with just two minutes to play. Warner then gave CCNY a 4-point lead, and again Mager came on to make a couple of key defensive plays in the closing seconds to allow the Beavers to win 69-61.

After the game, Bradley went back home and defeated

Kansas for the District Five berth in the NCAA. CCNY, now invited to play in the NCAA, moved uptown to practice for the tourney. Ironically, the NCAA would take place on the same Madison Square Garden floor two weeks later.

If Bradley was bothered by having its 14-game winning streak broken in the NIT, it hardly showed. The Braves routed UCLA and then struggled past underrated Baylor to win the West and earn another flight back to the Garden. CCNY, as in its NIT competition, again did it the hard way, first beating the nation's second-ranked team, Ohio State, as field goals by Mager and Layne late in the game got them a 56-55 victory. Holman's team then won the East title by beating fifth-ranked North Carolina State, thanks to a pair of field goals by Warner and a pair of fouls by Layne in the final two minutes for a 78-73 victory.

Thus, CCNY and Bradley, which had never even played each other until the NIT, were matched again, the fifth and sixth teams to compete in both the NIT and NCAA tourneys in the same year (rules and scheduling practices made this impossible after 1952). Holman was totally confident that his team could win again.

"The team has just seemed to arrive," he said before the NCAA tourney. "I don't think we've just been lucky, we've simply found ourselves. If we stay hale and hearty, I believe we can beat anyone, and that includes Bradley."

For three quarters of the game, the Beavers easily handled Bradley's zone defense and held a 58-47 lead with ten minutes to play. Then the Braves switched to a pressing man-for-man defense, even though four of their starters each had four personal fouls. The press worked against the jittery sophs; with a minute to play, CCNY led by only 69-63, a lead that almost disappeared as Melchiorre twice stole the ball for easy layups and Joe Stowell sank a foul shot. City's lead was cut to just one point.

Madison Square Garden, whose spectators had eagerly cheered the hometown team during its early going, now was in bedlam. Nearly all of the 18,000 fans were standing. When Melchiorre again stole the ball and headed for the go-ahead field goal, the place exploded. Incredibly, Dambrot picked the ball off the Bradley guard's hands as he attempted a shot from the top of the key. In almost the same motion, Dambrot lofted an arching pass downcourt for Mager, a bit woozy after a collision early in the game cut a gash tha required five stitches to close. Nevertheless, Mager scored the clinching field goal for a 71-68 CCNY victory.

"This is one of the proudest days of my life," Holman told

reported he had been offered $1000 to control the point spread of a game. Two of his teammates and three gamblers were arrested. Soon the scandal spread across the country, touching 17 states.

The greatest shock centered around revelations that Kentucky's 1949 NCAA championship team and CCNY's 1950 Grand Slam teams were involved. It was revealed that Kentucky players tried to shave points against Loyola of Chicago in the 1949 NIT, and lost that game, 67-56. They later beat Oklahoma A&M for the NCAA title.

CUNY coach Nat Holman found out his team was involved en route back to New York City by train from Philadelphia where the Beavers had just defeated Temple.

"The kids were having such a good time celebrating their victory," Holman once recalled. "As we neared New Brunswick (N.J.), a gentleman approached me, apologized and said, 'I have some bad news for you, Nat. I've got orders to pick up some of your boys. But I don't want to make a scene.' The gentleman was from the New York District Attorney's office."

When the players arrived at New York's Pennsylvania Station, Holman took each of them aside and told them, "When they speak to you, tell them the truth. If your conscience is clear, you have nothing to fear."

As it turned out, there was plenty to fear.

NIT Championship, March 15, 1950, at New York City

CCNY	FG-FGA	FT-FTA	Ast	PF	Pts
Dembrot	10-19	3-4	3	3	23
Warner	6-23	4-9	3	1	16
Roman	9-17	1-3	3	5	19
Galiber	0-0	1-2	0	0	1
Roth	0-4	0-5	4	1	0
Cohen	0-1	0-1	1	0	0
Mager	2-6	0-0	1	3	4
Layne	2-6	2-4	1	3	6
Totals	29-76	11-28	16	16	69

Bradley					
Grover	3-16	0-2	1	3	6
Preece	2-7	0-1	2	3	4
Unruh	7-12	1-2	5	1	15
Schlictman	1-4	0-0	1	3	2
Chianakas	0-1	0-0	0	1	0
Behnke	6-10	3-3	2	3	15
Kelly	0-3	2-3	0	0	2
Mann	4-10	0-0	1	5	8
Melchiorre	2-8	5-7	4	5	9
Totals	25-71	11-18	16	24	61

Halftime: Bradley 30, CCNY 27

Officials: Nucatola & Anderson

NCAA Championship, March 29, 1950, at New York City

CCNY	FG-FGA	FT-FTA	Ast	PF	Pts
Dembrot	7-14	1-2	2	0	15
Roman	6-17	0-2	1	5	12
Warner	4-9	6-14	3	2	14
Roth	2-7	1-5	3	2	5
Mager	4-10	6-6	2	3	14
Galiber	0-0	0-0	0	1	0
Layne	3-7	5-6	1	3	11
Nadell	0-0	0-0	1	1	0
Totals	26-64	19-35	13	17	71

Bradley					
Grover	0-10	2-3	3	3	2
Schlichtman	0-3	0-0	0	2	0
Unruh	4-9	0-0	2	5	8
Behnke	3-10	3-3	2	4	9
Kelly	0-1	0-2	0	0	0
Mann	2-7	5-5	1	5	9
Preece	6-11	0-0	0	5	12
D. Melchiorre	0-0	0-0	0	0	0
G. Melchiorre	7-16	2-4	5	4	16
Chianakas	5-7	1-3	1	4	11
Stowell	0-0	1-1	0	0	1
Totals	27-74	14-21	14	32	68

Halftime: CCNY, 39-32

Officials: Eisenstein & Gibbs

thousands of cheering students at the CCNY campus the following day after they had nearly drowned New York City with their "Allagaroo" cheers. The enormity of this feat even caught up some of the school's more staid professors, one of whom called it "the greatest thing that ever happened in the 102-year history of this venerable institution."

The celebration and the glory had a gloomy postscript. A year later, some CCNY players, including Warner, MVP in both games, Roman and Alan Roth, as well as three Bradley players including Melchiorre, were arrested for fixing or altering the point spread of nearly 75 games. So were more than two dozen other players from another half dozen schools across the country, including some from Kentucky's two-time NCAA champions.

The players were banished from collegiate and NBA competition. Many of them wound up leading very productive lives. Roman got his doctorate in psychology and counseled high school students in New York City for many years before his death in 1988.

Scandal aside, basketball's only Miracle Double still belongs to the Allagaroo Kids from CCNY.

5

THE LONGEST GAME

January 6, 1951

Indianapolis
vs.
Rochester

How much is too much?

On the night of January 6, 1951, 3900 viewers at the Edgerton Sports Arena in Rochester, New York, sat through a total of 78 minutes of play that included six overtimes as the Rochester Royals battled the Indianapolis Olympians. The game length set a record, pro and college, that most believe will stand forever.

In 1951 there was no 24-second pro clock and no 45-second college clock to prod players into taking their shots. Teams could do what they wanted with the basketball for as long as they wanted. If no one wished to shoot—twice in the longest game, not a single scoring attempt was made in a five-minute stretch—there were no whistles, no penalties. Scoreless play continued until the ball was put through the hoop.

There is no doubt in any basketball historian's mind that this six-overtime contest inspired the pro swing over to clock control. In fact, it took three years for Danny Giascone, then the owner of the Syracuse Nationals, to convince his fellow owners that the pro game needed such pacing. As it turned out, the change revolutionized the game.

In 1951, the rules favored the ball handlers, not the shooters. Two-handed dribbling was permitted, and a good ball handler could control the game by himself for endless minutes.

The Rochester Royals (later the Cincinnati Royals, the Kansas City Kings and the Sacramento Kings) had these two-handed dribblers in Bob Davies and Red Holtzman, later the distinguished coach of the New York Knickerbockers. Davies, a first-team All-Star, was a great ball handler and behind-the-back passer in the mold of Bob Cousy, who had just joined the Boston Celtics.

Davies' backcourt mate at Rochester was Bobby Wanzer; together they made up the best in the NBA. Both could hit from the outside and drive, typical of the pro players who attended Eastern colleges. This group was quick and savvy, rather than big. The style was give-and-go, the players a product of coaches from the New York City area whose gospel was so widely accepted in the East in those times. They also were good set shooters who could stand back 20 or 25 feet from the basket and fire the ball with two hands in long, arching shots that soared over their opponents' heads.

NBA teams whose rosters were stocked with players from the Southeast and Midwest were bigger, more physical teams, and more suited for rough, rollicking inside play. They didn't try to outslick anyone, though they had their share of talented ball handlers who could get the ball inside and set up the big men.

The Indianapolis Olympians represented a combination of both styles of play. The entire team had been coached in college by Adolph Rupp of Kentucky, where the stress was on attack-type basketball, grounded heavily in finely-tuned fundamental ball handling, rebounding, passing, and shooting. All were given equal importance in the Rupp system.

This style proved tremendously successful in the late forties and early fifties. Kentucky players were widely sought by the pros. A group of Indianapolis businessmen approached the NCAA champion Kentucky Wildcats when their 1948-49 season was completed and asked them to come en masse into pro basketball. This was the team comprised of Alex Groza, Ralph Beard, Wah-Wah Jones, Joe Holland and Cliff Barker,

Arnie Risen takes rebound from Knick Harry Gallatin in NBA finals played three months after longest game.

Risen takes hook shot over Dick McGuire of Knicks. In the six overtime game three months earlier, Risen led all scorers with 26 points.

who became a player-coach. This squad had just won their second straight NCAA title and were considered invincible.

The NBA owners were as mesmerized by the Kentucky mystique as was the general public. Hoping that the squad would provide instant drawing power for their new league, the owners allowed the five to enter intact, each player being given an ownership share in the team. Trading on their gold medals from the 1948 Olympic basketball title (the team also went to the Games in London after winning the 1948 NCAA title), the owners dubbed them the Olympians.

They didn't do that badly, either, winning the NBA's Central Division title in 1950 as Groza finished second to George Mikan of the Lakers in scoring.

Coming to the game January 6, the Olympians were going against a team that had won seven straight. No one in the Arena had illusions that Rochester might win, however. It was simply fun to be inside watching the famous do their stuff.

The Olympians, as expected, raced to a 20-10 first quarter lead and were ahead at the half, 38-33, comfortable enough not to worry.

In the fourth quarter, the Royals mounted a spectacular defensive show, holding the Olympians to just eight points. Miraculously, at the end of regulation play, the score stood tied at 65-65.

"At that time," says Red Holtzman, "the team that held the ball until a high percentage shot opportunity arose was the team that won. Discipline was the name of the pro game. When this game went into overtime, everyone slowed down. No one wanted to make a foolish mistake. We were determined to try only shots we thought had a good chance of going in."

In the first five-minute overtime, each team scored two points. In the second overtime, not a point was put on the board. In the third, again each team scored once. In the fourth, it was zip again. Incredibly, neither team even got off a shot.

In the fifth overtime, Arnie Risen, Rochester's big center, got two baskets, one when he seemingly was stopped by Groza, only to step around for a layup. Beard then matched those points for Indianapolis, but Risen sank a hook shot for a 73-71 lead. Groza got a field goal to tie the score at 73 all.

In the sixth overtime, Rochester controlled the ball for three-and-a-half minutes. Coach Les Harrison then called time-out to discuss strategy. Harrison's idea failed when the wily Olympians forced Risen into a desperation shot with four seconds to play. He missed, and so did his rebound attempt, which was then grabbed by Paul Walther.

While Risen was missing, Ralph Beard raced toward the other basket, and Walther spotted his teammate at the other end of the court. He heaved a perfect pass to Beard, who dribbled once and then arched a beautiful shot through the hoop with one second left.

Beard's basket not only won the game for Indianapolis, 75-73, but also was the only score in that sixth overtime period. In three of the six overtimes, Rochester hadn't scored a point.

"Such a game will never occur again," Holtzman says. "The 24-second clock forces a team to shoot, and shooters now are so good that it is very tough for any team to get past one overtime period."

The game ran so late the Olympians missed a train connection to Chicago en route to a match the next night in Moline, Illinois. Instead, the team went to Detroit and slept for five hours, after which player-coach Barker put Beard, Walther, Groza, Leo Barnhorst and Mal MacMullen aboard a chartered plane (that's all the plane would hold) so they could get to Moline in time for their game. Barker and the rest of the players made their way by train and arrived five minutes after the Olympians had been upset 83-79 in regulation time.

That was the last season for most of the Kentucky contingent. Later that year, basketball was rocked by betting scandals involving collegians who had shaved points or thrown games in the late 1940's. Some of the Olympians were implicated and were banned from the game forever.

The Rochester Royals were no strangers to overtime basketball. In fact, early in the next season, the Royals played three straight overtime games; and the year after that, they played in a dozen durng an entire season, two of them going four extra periods.

The season record for most overtimes belongs to the 1950-51 New York Knicks, which played in 13 . . . and the record for frustration belongs to the Golden State Warriors, which lost all eight of its overtime games in 1979-80, and to the Baltimore Bullets of 1952-53 which lost ten of the 12 they played in 1952-53.

January 6, 1951, at Rochester, N.Y.				
Indianapolis	FG	FT	PF	Pts
Barnhorst	4	1	3	9
MacMullen	2	3	2	7
Holland	0	0	0	0
Groza	8	1	0	17
Lavoy	6	1	3	13
Beard	8	1	1	17
Barker	0	0	0	0
Walther	4	4	1	12
Totals	32	11	10	75
Rochester				
Johnson	0	1	1	1
McNamara	2	0	0	4
Holtzman	1	1	0	3
Saul	3	0	2	6
Risen	11	4	3	26
Coleman	7	1	2	15
Wanzer	3	0	0	6
Calhoun	6	0	1	12
Totals	33	7	9	73

Indianapolis	20	18	19	8	2	0	2	0	4	2 --	75
Rochester	10	23	20	12	2	0	2	0	4	0 --	73

6

A GRAND IDEA

March 2, 1951
January 21, 1954
January 21, 1958
January 17, 1961
January 16, 1962
January 13, 1965
January 12, 1971
January 16, 1972
February 13, 1977
February 10, 1985
February 9, 1986
February 8, 1987
February 7, 1988

East All-Stars
vs.
West All-Stars

In 1950 Walter Brown, who owned the Boston Garden and the Boston Celtics, had a grand idea—not exactly original, but grand nonetheless in the context of the newly-formed National Basketball Association.

Why not an annual All-Star Game?

Baseball's All-Star Game had been a smashing success for nearly two decades and pro football had just reinstated its Pro Bowl. Wasn't matching a league's best players against each other for one game a marvelous way to promote the league, the sport, and the greatness of the players themselves?

From its humble beginnings on March 2, 1951, when an underdog Eastern Division team trounced the West 111-94 before more than 10,000 at Boston Garden, to the rather contrived current three-day extravaganza complete with Old Timers' Game, Slam Dunk, and Three-Point shooting contests and the All-Star Game itself, this event has become something special to the game of pro basketball.

Regardless of the surroundings—including a strike threat, airline problems, blizzards, and the giant egos of its stars—the game has achieved its purpose: to become a showcase for its great stars.

The event has produced three thrilling overtime games; great individual performances by Bob Cousy, Bob Pettit, Oscar Robertson, Wilt Chamberlain, Bill Russell, Elgin Baylor, Jerry West, Kareem Abdul-Jabbar, Julius Erving, Magic Johnson, Larry Bird, and Michael Jordan; and always the style of basketball that seems to allow each player a measure of creative freedom that he doesn't enjoy during the regular season.

"It has been an evolving institution within pro basketball," says Tom Heinsohn, who has played in, coached and broadcast more than a dozen of the games. "At one time, creativity had to mesh with fundamentals. Now it is a bit looser, with more freedom for the players to jump in and out of the game and do what they do best for as long as they are in."

Heinsohn points to Magic Johnson, the All-Pro Laker guard. "Magic is the creator for his own team's offense, and he uses that same style when he joins the All-Star team. Look what he's done for players like Ralph Sampson and Tom Chambers."

What Magic did was to help make both of them Most Valuable Players in two All-Star Games with his great skills as a playmaker.

In 1985 Sampson had perhaps his best day ever as a pro as he got pass after pass from Johnson (Magic had 15 assists in the game) and scored 24 points to lead his team to a 140-129

victory over the East. "He was going good, so I stayed with him," Johnson said after the game. For his part, Sampson never seemed to have enjoyed himself as much as he did in this game. He made 10 of his 15 field goals and led all rebounders and scorers.

IN 1987 Chambers made the Western Conference All-Stars only because Sampson had injured his knee the previous week and had to withdraw. The event was staged in Seattle, before Chambers's own fans. But the previous day, he had performed poorly in the Slam Dunk contest, and he held out little hope of anything more than a perfunctory appearance in the game.

When Chambers got in, Johnson was directing the West's offense, and the two of them formed an immediate bond, so much so that Chambers wound up leading all scorers with 34 points. Time after time, Magic penetrated the East's defense, and when it converged on him, he simply dished off the ball to Chambers or Orlando Blackmon, as the West got the game into overtime and won it 154-149 in the extra period.

"Magic made it all happen," Chambers said. "He deliv-

Left: Rolando Blackman of Dallas makes a free throw to tie score in fourth quarter of 1987 game. Right: In front of home fans, Tom Chambers dunks ball on way to being named Most Valuable Player.

How soon they—all of them—forget!

Kareem Abdul-Jabbar played for the Milwaukee Bucks for six years before his trade to the Los Angeles Lakers. He returned to his old city to play in the 1977 All-Star Game under strange circumstances, to say the least.

First, he forgot his Lakers warmup suit and was introduced to the Milwaukee crowd wearing a Bucks warmup uniform, which delighted the hometown fans.

But before that occurred, he tried to enter the arena at the employees' entrance but was turned away, though he had come through that very gate hundreds of times during his stint with the Bucks.

"They changed people and no one recognized me," he said.

Larry Bird isn't fond of NBA All-Star Games though he has been selected every year he has played in the NBA. But he loves the Three-Point shooting contests. Why not? He won the first three.

In 1986, the first year the event was held, Larry flat out told the seven other participants that he was going to win even before the shooting began. "I just want to know, which of you thinks he is going to come in second?" he asked the others.

When he reached the finals with Craig Hodges of Milwaukee, Larry congratulated him for finishing second and then hit 11 consecutive three-point shots within the one-minute shooting period to win the contest.

ered the ball every time, and all I had to do was put it in the basket."

The game also demonstrated that the competitive nature of those great players is as much in evidence in an exhibition of skills as it is during the most intense regular season and playoff games. Orlando Blackmon had a pair of free throws to shoot with no time left in regulation play and his West team trailing, 140-138. Two East players, Isiah Thomas of the Pistons and Julius Erving of the '76ers, walked past him, suggesting strongly that he was going to miss at least one of the shots.

"I was calling him a sissy, chump, punk—whatever I could think of," Thomas said. In fact, Isiah was so persistent in his needling that Magic Johnson had to push him away from Blackmon.

Erving then chimed in, "Make the first one and brick the second."

Blackmon made both . . . and Johnson became the All-Star Game's all-time assists leader, passing Bob Cousy's record of 86.

Cousy was a perfect example of a great player who is capable of winning a game on his own, as he demonstrated in the All-Star Game's first overtime thriller, a 98-93 East victory in 1954. This was the first All-Star Game ever played in New York's Madison Square Garden, and the old joint on Eighth Avenue was jammed. Fans were on their feet screaming as the Lakers' George Mikan sank a pair of free throws at the buzzer to force the overtime—the 13th tie of the game. Just five seconds before, Cousy had put the East ahead with one of his patented set shots.

In the overtime, Cousy simply took the game for his own. He opened with another set shot and then scored the last eight of his team's 14 points in that period. In between, he had the crowd cheering with a dazzling display of the dribbling that was such a key part of his game. The West simply had to foul him to get control of the ball, and he made six free throws as a result. Fittingly, he also was named the game's Most Valuable Player.

Cousy did it again four years later while playing in his eighth Al-Star Game, pacing his East team to a 130-118 victory with 16 points in the second half, all the while taking a back seat in the individual stats department to Bob Pettit, who scored a then-record 28 points and set a rebound mark with 26 against the Celtics' Bill Russell.

Pettit was a great All-Star Game performer. In the 1961 game, he not only led his Western Division team to a smashing 153-131 upset but also broke his own scoring record with

In 1987 Larry had to survive a first-round shootoff to advance, but in the finals against Detlef Schrempf of Dallas, he made his first 8 shots. Schrempf missed 9 of his first 11, got back in the groove and on his last chance, he had an opportunity to tie Bird. His final shot bounced out.

In 1988 Bird made only 5 of the first 15, but with the money on the line, he zapped 8 of his last 10, the last one coming with the score tied . . . and it didn't even hit the rim. It was worth $12,500.

Wilt Chamberlain (13) played in All-Star games for both East and West, and had some great games and not-so-great.

47

Top: *Adrian Dantley wrestles with Jeff Malone (24) for control of the ball during 1986 game.* Above: *Isiah Thomas is stonewalled by Kareem Abdul-Jabbar in Dallas.*

29 points. The following year he won his fourth MVP title and broke his rebound record with 27 boards. West coach Fred Schaus had taken him out of the 1962 game with a few minutes to play, but when he learned Pettit could set the rebound mark, he put him back in—a great gesture in front of Pettit's own fans in St. Louis, where his Hawks team then played.

Jerry West of the Los Angeles Lakers was another player who dominated All-Star Games. In the 1972 contest, his 21-foot jump shot with one second to play provided a spectacular finish to the West's 112-110 victory. Jerry had played in rather unspectacular fashion during the first three quarters of that game. In the fourth quarter he became a defensive demon and made five steals or deflections in the final eight minutes. His last one came with just under three minutes to play and gave his team a 9-point lead. The East team came right back, led by John Havlicek's shooting, cut the lead to 2 points with half a minute to play and then tied the score on Dave Cowens's basket with eleven seconds left. After a time out, West got the ball and, working against guard Walt Frazier of the Knicks, one of the NBA's best defensive players at that time, Jerry took the shot from the top of the key and hit it cleanly for the win—and for the MVP award.

Kareem Abdul-Jabbar, playing then for Milwaukee as Lew Alcindor, had a similar game the previous year when his fall-away jump shot with 48 seconds to play hung on the rim for a second or two and then rolled into the basket to help the West to a 108-107 victory. Ironically, he was fed by West, who had penetrated toward the basket and drawn the defense to himself before feeding the big center. The field goal broke a 105-105 tie, and Kareem tacked on a foul that offset a basket by Jo-Jo White in the final seconds.

Few players ever had a better debut than Julius Erving in 1977. He had played in five all-Star games in the American Basketball Association before joining the 76ers of the NBA when the league merged, and it seemed as if he had been saving up some of his special court magic for this showcase event in Milwaukee.

In 30 playing minutes, he scored 30 points, 13 in the fourth quarter, and three of his dozen field goals were his patented "house calls" of soaring, gliding, hang-forever-in-the-air swoop shots. On the first, he beat Rick Barry down the floor, then flew over Abdul-Jabbar to jam the ball through the basket. On another, he took a between-the-legs pass from Pete Maravich of the New Orleans Jazz and swiveled his way over and around some West defenders for another jam.

In addition to his scoring (his team lost 125-124), Erving also was the leading rebounder with 12, and he handed out three assists.

"I had heard about his spectacular play in the ABA," Heinsohn said, "but in that game, he showed me that all the great words were true. And he did it while playing some good defense, for which he never received much credit."

Yet with all this offensive show, it was a great defensive play by Paul Westphal of the West team that preserved the victory. With six seconds to play, Maravich tried to drive to the basket, but Westphal slapped the ball away and recovered it to save the victory. Still, Erving was chosen the game's Most Valuable Player, noting afterward that he had never received that honor in his five ABA All-Star Games.

As Cousy, West, and Westphal proved, stardom in the All-Star Game is certainly not reserved for the big players. Isiah Thomas, six-one, underscored that fact in winning the 1986 game's MVP award when he scored 30 points, had 10 assists and added 5 steals, the East winning, 139-132. Thomas, who also had been an MVP in the 1984 game, got it done in the last quarter by scoring 12 points to blunt a West surge that had given them a 128-121 lead with less than four minutes to play. Just the day before, five-foot-seven-inch Spud Webb of Atlanta had shocked some of the NBA's high flyers by winning the Slam Dunk contest, and after the East's victory, Lakers' coach Pat Riley noted, "They gave hope to everybody under six-five that you can play, that you don't have to be six-six or six-seven. Those guys showed that if you've got heart, you can play."

The All-Star get-together also proves that the teams come to this special game to play defense, when necessary, just as much as they come to show off their offensive talents. Bill Russell of the Celtics proved that early in the series when he played hard enough to foul out of a couple of games, and nearly every year, some player has come up with a key defensive play to either turn a game around or decide it.

Then, of course, there are the unselfish players who come to play for their team, not for individual glory, even though they may not particularly like All-Star Games. Larry Bird of the Celtics is one of those players. He enjoys the individual competition events such as the Three-Point contest, which he won in 1986-88, but he seemed to get a bigger thrill helping Michael Jordan of the Chicago Bulls win the MVP award before his hometown fans in 1988.

"I don't like All-Star Games," Bird says, "because you set a pick for somebody and he ends up going the other way.

Top: *The pressure of Artis Gilmore (53) forces Robert Parish to lose control of the ball.* Above: *Thomas manages a layup in spite of some rather impressive defense.*

There's no set pattern. You just get the ball and go."

Bird agrees with Heinsohn when he notes that players such as Erving and Magic Johnson thrived in All-Star Games because they are one-on-one players, "and if their shots are falling they're going to look good. But I've never been a one-on-one player."

Bird has been a team player, and he gladly stepped aside to allow Jordan to star in 1988. So did Thomas of Detroit, but that was more of a payback than anything else after Isiah, believing the Chicago player had been "too arrogant" during the All-Star weekend, conceived a "freeze out" of Jordan during Michael's rookie season All-Star Game appearance. In the 1988 game, Thomas went all out to make amends on the

From left, an All-Star Game's All-Stars: Jerry West, Tom Heinsohn, Bob Cousy, Len Wilkens, and Elgin Baylor. Cousy once scored 8 of his team's 14 overtime points.

court, consistently feeding the ball (he had 15 assists) to Jordan, who finished with 40 points as the East won, 138-133.

In evaluating the All-Star spectacle, as Heinsohn noted, point-scoring often is secondary to winning. "In 1963 the West team had Chamberlain, Pettit and Walt Bellamy on the front line, Pettit the little guy at six-nine. Elgin Baylor, who was six-six, was in the backcourt with Jerry West, both 20-points-per-game players, so everyone said that team would score 200 points and blow us out.

"We won the game, 115-108, and in the process, we kicked the hell out of them. It was great."

It is also why the game is played.

7

FIRST OF THE DYN- ASTIES

April 13, 1949

Minneapolis
vs.
Washington

April 12, 1954

Minneapolis
vs.
Syracuse

The Minneapolis Lakers of Mikan & Co. were the NBA's first dynasty—champions in five of the league's first six seasons, a team that had power and talent in every facet of the game as it was then played. Moreover, the Lakers were interlopers. They had won the National Basketball League title in 1948 and then joined the Basketball Association of America later that summer, along with the Rochester Royals, the Fort Wayne Pistons, and the Indianapolis Jets. Before the 1949 season began, the NBL—then the nation's oldest continuous pro league—and the BAA merged to form the National Basketball Association.

As. so often seems to happen when the "other guys" join the so-called establishment, those "other guys" tend to upset the status quo. In fact, the Lakers that first season set the standards by which all other NBA teams were measured until the Boston Celtics were deep into their own dynasty in the sixties.

The Lakers star, and the No. 1 player in all of basketball at that time, was George Mikan. The six-foot ten-inch star from DePaul had played professionally for the Chicago Gears of the NBL for a couple of years, helping the team to win the league playoffs in 1947, before Minneapolis took over the defunct Detroit franchise in 1948. He came to the Lakers, along with Jim Pollard and Arnie Ferrin, and soon thereafter such other key players as Vern Mikkelsen, Slater Martin, and Bob Harrison joined the squad.

Mikan was the essential aggressive center who battled anyone coming into his area with his massive body and a sharp pair of elbows. He had a great hook shot and was also an excellent passer—in short, a player around whom to build a team.

He was perfectly complemented by Pollard, who joined the Lakers in 1948. Known as "The Kangaroo Kid," he had great leaping ability and used it to launch a feathery jump shot. But most of all he was marvelously consistent, giving equal attention to all parts of his game. Along with Mikkelsen, who came in 1950, and Mikan, the Lakers had the best front court trio in basketball . . . which is why they dominated opponents for so many years.

Beginning in 1950, the Lakers also had one of the NBA's best guards in Slater Martin, a five-ten, 170-pounder from the University of Texas. He was the first of the breed now known as the point guard because he directed the Lakers' offense. He also was their spiritual father, who thought only in terms of helping the team.

Once, after scoring 42 points in a game against the

Mikan hooks successfully over Knick Nat (Sweetwater) Clifton during fourth game of championship series for NBA crown. Clifton was the first black to play in NBA.

Mikan gets 2 of his pro tournament record 40 points against the New York Rens at Chicago Stadium, April 11, 1948.

The Minneapolis Lakers certainly attracted some great players during their dynasty years from 1949 through 1954, but at the time, none of them ever expected that one of their teammates would become one of the NFL's finest football coaches.

Bud Grant, who had such a spendid coaching career with the Minnesota Vikings, played with the 1950 NBA champions and also on the 1951 team. He was a three-sport letter-winner at the University of Minnesota and was also the number one pick of the Philadelphia Eagles of the NFL, where he played for several seasons while also playing for the Lakers.

Pistons, he was signing autographs when some fan yelled, "Hey, Martin, you were lucky tonight."

"The harder I work, the luckier I get," he told the guy, and that, says Mikan, was how he approached his role. He carried it into the locker room. At the start of every season, he made his only speech when the rookies came together for the first time.

"Have all of you signed your contracts?" he'd ask, and after he saw all the heads nodding affirmatively:

"Do you want to know how to make even more money?"
Again the heads bobbed up and down.
"Well, you win a title, that's how you do it," he would say.
"And do you know how you do that?"
This time there were some blank stares.
"You feed Mikan," he said.
"No wonder I loved the little guy," Mikan says.
Martin wasn't around to "feed Mikan" in 1949 when the Lakers ended the NBA's first season by whipping Red Auer-

bach's (yes, *that* Red Auerbach) Washington Capitols four games to two in the championship series. Minneapolis won the deciding game 77-56, the low score reflecting the way the game was played back then, Mikan dominating at both ends of the court. He also scored his game-leading 29 points despite playing with a fractured wrist that was encased in heavy tape, with just enough room for his fingers to flex and enough room at the elbow to allow him some flexibility to get off his shots.

In 1950 coach Johnny Kundla had established all of the ingredients of the dynasty. Mikkelsen, a six-seven, 230-pound center from tiny Hamline College, became the prototype of the power forward only because Kundla did not have room for two talented centers and needed Mikkelsen in his lineup. So he created the center duties in a forward's position, allowing Mikan more freedom in the middle. With his holdovers, plus guard Bob Harrison, Martin and Mikkelsen, the Lakers easily defeated the Syracuse Nationals in five games, splitting up the munificent sum of $19,500 for their second straight title.

Mikan scored 40 points in that game, matters getting so heated that three fights spiced the contest. When Pollard and Paul Seymour of the Nats got into it, the police had to intervene. Syracuse's player-coach, Al Cervi, was banished in the third quarter, and the Lakers finished with just seven players because of fouls from the rough play—but they were more than enough to win the deciding game, 110-95.

Such was the game style that the 110 points represented only the eighth time that entire season that Minneapolis topped the 100-point mark. The next time the Lakers won, in 1952, such was the state of the game that their opponents, the New York Knicks, played their championship game in a downtown Manhattan armory that seated about 5,500 people, instead of in 18,500-capacity Madison Square Garden, the

Part of a future dynasty meets the present one as Bob Cousy (14) drives against Jim Pollard of the Lakers.

mecca of American indoor sports. It seems the circus was in town and pro basketball had not yet usurped the circus in the hearts of the Garden accountants.

The 1952 series went seven games. Minneapolis showed it could play defense just as well as it played offense, and won the deciding game, 82-65. The Lakers held New York to just 10 field goals in the first three quarters, getting a gritty performance from Pollard, who had missed two previous games because of a back injury. He scored all 10 of his points in the last quarter to help hold off the Knicks.

In 1953 Mikan recalls his team taking a 3-1 lead against New York after playing in Minneapolis, and hearing the Knicks players boasting that things would be different when the series returned to the armory (yep, the circus was in town again!) in New York City. In the end, the Lakers won, 91-84, though it became a bit of a struggle as New York closed to within 1 point with 40 seconds to play, helped in part by Minneapolis managing without Mikan for more than half the game because of foul trouble.

"As so often happens when a key player goes out, everyone seems to play harder to make up for the loss," Mikan said. "That's what happened with us. I went out in the second quarter the first time, and then after a fourth foul, I had to sit out most of the second half. The Knicks threw an all-court press at us and little by little that got them back into the game."

With Minneapolis ahead 85-84 and 40 seconds to play, Mikkelsen's foul shot gave the Lakers a 2-point lead, and a few seconds later Mikan followed with a 3-point play that secured the victory . . . and its bonus pot of $16,500.

The last jewel in the Laker's dynasty crown came the following year in 1954, again a seven-game set against Syracuse. The clinching game belonged to Pollard, who scored 21 points in the 87-80 victory. Nine of those points came on a third-quarter scoring burst that opened up a 16-point lead, sending the Lakers to their fifth NBA title in six seasons.

Was it difficult to sustain that level of excellence?

"We never were bored with winning," Mikan said. "Each title seemed to be more thrilling than the last one, but when you consider that we also had won the National Basketball League's playoffs in 1947 and 1948 against some of the competition that came into the NBA, then it really was seven titles in eight years."

That's a dynasty!

Opposite: *Jim Pollard, "The Kangaroo Kid," uses his leaping ability to thwart a Knick attack.* Above: Mikan, *truly a giant of his day, poses for a publicity session.*

8

A PAIR OF 100-POINT MOON WALKS (1955)

February 4, 1954

Rio Grande
vs.
Hillsdale

February 13, 1954

Furman
vs.
Newberry

An individual player who scores 100 points in a game is basketball's equivalent of a man walking on the moon because the feat is truly unbelievable . . . only twice (actually thrice, but we'll get to that later) in college basketball history.

Oddly enough, these two feats came just nine days apart back in 1954, first by a six-foot-nine-inch almost-fictional character named Clarence (Bevo) Francis; and then by Frank Selvy, a machine-gun-like scorer who all but destroyed the NCAA record book during his career at Furman University.

About the only thing each of these players had in common, in the public's mind at least, was the fact that each had scored 100 points in a game. Selvy was an established national star when he knocked in his 100 against Newberry College on February 13, 1954, while Francis was almost considered a mistake . . . as one some felt was an aberration in the sport when he got 133 points against Hillsdale College on February 4, 1954.

Oh, there was a bit of common ground. Selvy was raised in Corbin, Kentucky, in the coal-mine Applachia region, and his Furman team represented a small school away from the publicity glare of big city areas. But such were the numbers he put up game after game that his feats were cheered everywhere.

Francis was from the northeastern part of Ohio, but his school, Rio Grande, with less than 150 students, was located in the mining region of southeastern Ohio. He too accumulated giant gobs of points in game after game, often against major college competition in the 1954 season. There seemed to be, however, a question, a hestitation to accept his feats as real.

This was nothing new to Francis. He had grown up in Hammondsville, Ohio, and was well over six feet when he entered high school. He decided to transfer to nearby Wellsville High, and from that moment on, his entire basketball career was played under a cloud.

First, the Ohio High School Athletic Association declared him ineligible for a year, though they never proved recruiting irregularities. As Francis was about to play his first game as a sophomore, he was told the suspension still hadn't been lifted, though evidence of impropriety had still not surfaced. So Bevo played with town and area teams and began building a great reputation. Finally, he was allowed to play in his junior season, though he preferred football to hoops and went out for that sport instead.

Wellsville then had a new basketball coach, an energetic

self-promoter named Newt Oliver, who had been a star at Rio Grande College in the late forties. He chased Francis off the football field and onto the basketball court, where Bevo averaged 33.1 points per game, second highest in Ohio to Robin Freeman, who later became a star at Ohio State. Bevo's top game that year was 57 points, and on eight occasions he either tied or outscored the opposing team.

"I had more than 60 scholarship offers after that season because I had used up my high school eligibility because of age [he had repeated a year of grammar school because of illness], and by this time I was married and the father of a child. But I had a burning desire to play college basketball."

Many thought he would pick the University of Wyoming to enjoy the outdoor life, and because Oliver had done his graduate work there.

But Newt had other ideas. He had made a deal with Rio Grande that he would bring in Bevo if they made him coach, and together they would put the school on the map. Getting

The free throw good, Bevo Francis of Rio Grande breaks the one-season national collegiate scoring record of 970 points.

Regardless of level, and against whatever competition he played, Bevo Francis was amazing. Consider some of the highlights of his career:

In 20 of his 68 games, he scored more than 50 points, and in 9 games against major college competition, he never scored fewer than 28 points.

In all games in his two seasons at Rio Grande, his team had a 61-7 record and played before 244,000 persons. The largest crowd was 13,800 at Madison Square Garden, the smallest, 62 persons at Rio Grande's gym. The biggest single game gross was $34,500; the smallest was $19.20.

Bevo average 50.1 points in his first season at Rio Grande against small college competition, and 48 points per game in his second season against a predominantly major-college schedule, when he had five of his top nine single-game scoring figures.

Nothing really came easily, because in most games he was double- and triple-teamed. In one game, the opposition refused to shoot the ball, so two Rio players went to the bench and began playing cards. A fan walked onto the floor and asked Bevo for an autograph . . . and still the opposition wouldn't shoot.

on the map wasn't as important to the school's president, Dr. Charles Davis, as surviving, because dwindling enrollment—to the point where just 92 students attended the school—had caused the American Baptist Church to withdraw support.

Oliver had become a second father to Bevo, so he went along with his coach, and together they lifted a team that had won just four games the previous season to a 39-0 record in 1952-53. They did it partly in the school's gym, a ramshackle auditorium aptly dubbed the "Hog Pen" because plaster fell from its ceilings and pots and pans caught rainwater from a leaky roof. Spectator seating was a couple of hundred folding chairs, and this certainly didn't jibe with Oliver's visions of thousands coming to see his team play. Nonetheless, he established his star and his team, but he couldn't shake off the skepticism and disdain which accompanied the victories.

"It was unfair, despite Newt's obvious penchant for self-publicity," says Dr. Carl Benner, who was the trainer for that team and later chairman of the mathematics and science department at Wright State University in Dayton. "Newt went out and got kids to play with Bevo and they were all class people. They were team-oriented, and they had to be because Bevo's scoring achievements were no one-man-gang kind of feat."

His biggest scoring success that first season was his 116 points against Ashland Junior College in the 17th game. To that point, Rio Grande's victories had been against small two- and four-year schools in Ohio and western Pennsylvania, but the explosion against Ashland suddenly brought a torrent of publicity about Bevo and his school—a torrent, by the way, that was pumped at the start by Oliver, who spent an entire day contacting every major news outlet in the country to call attention to the feat.

It worked, because the final game of the season was played before 10,000 persons in Cleveland Arena, and Rio Grande defeated John Caroll University of Cleveland, 109-55, and earned the 26th place in the final Associated Press poll—one notch ahead of a UCLA team coached by John Wooden.

Bevo averaged more than 50 points per game that season, but the cloud that hovered during his high school career reappeared in the form of a ruling by the NCAA that erased all scoring records achieved against any but four-year schools—and made it retroactive to the previous season, meaning his 116-point game against Ashland was off the books. The ruling also called into doubt his other scoring feats and the legitimacy of Oliver's basketball program at Rio Grande.

Undaunted, Oliver decided the only way to cure the

problem was to play against major college competition, so he scheduled his team into Madison Square Garden, Boston Garden, Philadelphia's Palestra, Buffalo's Municipal Auditorium, and the Cincinnati Gardens. He lined up games against such major college teams as North Carolina State, Wake Forest, Boston College, Providence College, Villanova, Creighton (twice), Arizona State, and the University of Miami. He abandoned the "Hog Pen" and played every game off campus.

The big publicity plum, of course, was playing against Adelphi College in Madison Square Garden in December 1953. For the first time, Bevo Francis and Rio Grande (and, of course, Newt Oliver) would get the national treatment. On the day of the game, Francis recalls being awakened at 5 a.m. for an appearance on the *Today Show* and then having an interview of some kind every hour on the hour until he went to the Garden.

No wonder his team lost 83-76 before nearly 14,000 of the curious, though Bevo scored 32 points, 26 in the first half. After that, the Redmen defeated Providence, Miami, Wake Forest, Butler, Creighton, and Arizona State, averaging more than 92 points a game. Bevo cracked the NCAA record book with a 46.5 per game scoring average against the four-year schools, despite the fact that he basically played away from the basket and took most of his shots from the nine- to twelve-foot range. He scored 1,318 points, and made the AP's second All-

Francis fights for a shot against Creighton. His 114 points against Ashland were declared a non-record by NCAA.

Nothing came easy off the court, either, once he became a star. In a day and a half, *Life* magazine took over 1,000 pictures for a story, even waking up his baby to pose, and then wanting to get a few of him while he slept.

Even those who should have supported him seemed to make his life miserable, such as the night in 1953 when the team was honored as "Most Improved Team in the Country," and a special Saturday night dinner was held at nearby Gallipolis with Notre Dame football coach Frank Leahy in town to make the presentation.

During the dinner, Francis was summoned by one of the school's religion professors, who demanded that a course requirement of speaking at Sunday worship service be fulfilled right then. She yanked him from the banquet and they drove most of the night to Dayton to complete the project.

America team, just missing the first team by 17 points.

Of course, his biggest moment was the 113 points he scored against Hillsdale. Oliver still seethed about the expunged scoring mark against Ashland, and he plotted one last chance to get his star that heady number. Francis wanted it too, so Hillsdale, with a very poor team, was the designated target.

The game was played at the nearby Jackson High School gym, with the court set up on a stage and hundreds of people crammed into the small hall to watch. They weren't disappointed, because Bevo pumped in 43 points in the first half, after which Oliver directed that every shot had to be taken by his star. When a couple of players decided to score themselves, he yanked them from the game.

In the second half, Francis—who wasn't told he would get the ball on every play for a shot—was even hotter. The Redmen played a pressing defense and just stripped the ball time after time from the undermanned Hillsdale players; or if they didn't, then they fouled them to get possession. Bevo scored 31 points in the third quarter (teams played 10-minute quarters back then) and exploded with 55 points in the final 10 minutes, as Rio Grande won, 134-91.

"I still can't believe it," he says. "I didn't know I had gotten 113 points until I was coming out of the shower after the game and a couple of players told me. I knew I'd been shooting well, but getting 113 points! I had no idea."

Sadly, Bevo faded away after that season, again at the hand of Oliver who, Francis says, talked him into signing a contract with promoter Abe Sapperstein to play with the Boston Whirlwinds (Oliver was the coach) as part of the Harlem Globetrotters tour. That lasted a couple of years, and a career with the Cleveland Pipers of the old American Basketball League in the late fifties was even shorter. The team was owned by George Steinbrenner, but Francis was cut because the club had to keep the players signed to no-cut contracts—and he wasn't one of those.

Since that time, Francis has worked in a steel mill and a rubber plant in Ohio, but more importantly, he has regained his hero status back at Rio Grande, where he participates each year in the annual Bevo Francis Classic, a two-day tournament . . . and where he also was the recipient of an honorary degree from his school.

For Frank Selvy, there were no such rocky roads. Selvy had established himself at Furman in the early fifties and then just tore through opponents with his great shooting. By mid-February of 1954, he had an opportunity to break the four-year scoring record set by Jim Lacy of Baltimore Loyola in 1949 of 2,154 points . . . but he needed one big game to get him there.

That game came on a rainy night at Textile Hall in Greenville, South Carolina, home of Furman, before more than 4,000 fans, including Selvy's mother, who had never seen Frank play a college game. She had come to Greenville with several hundred citizens from Corbin to honor Selvy, and so big was the moment that a local television station arranged for the game to be telecast statewide, the first live home telecast of a Furman game.

Selvy was always up for such games, but he got some unexpected help that night when Bobby Bailey of Newberry, charged with guarding him, fouled out after just 2 minutes and 43 seconds. That was one indication of how good Selvy was, and how difficult it was for anyone to hold him in check.

After that, Selvy scored 24 points in the first quarter, and 13 in the second, and that halftime total of 37 points set a school mark . . . that lasted just one half.

As happened with Bevo Francis—and which really must happen for any collegiate player to hit 100 points—Selvy's teammates began feeding him on nearly every play. Newberry cooperated by trying to keep pace, so the game roared along at breakneck speed. Selvy scored 26 points in the third period and hit the 100-point mark with 37 in the final 10 minutes.

However, it was a rush to the wire. His final three field

Francis shows perfect form as he scores his first basket in his last game of the 1954 season.

The date February 13 is a big one in the Selvy family.

Frank Selvy established his 100-point game on February 13, 1954, as Furman defeated Newberry, 149-95.

Exactly 10 years later, on February 13, 1964, at a 10-year anniversary celebration of that feat, Furman pulled off one of the biggest upsets in its basketball history by defeating Lefty Driesell's fourth-ranked Davidson team, 70-55. There were no 100-point scorers that night, but Frank Selvy flew into Greenville, South Carolina, for the game and watched his younger brother David score 17 points.

And Lyles Alley was the winning coach in both of those February 13 masterpieces.

Francis breaks Butler's zone defense as Rio Grande defeated the Bulldogs in 1954 contest. Francis broke the Butler Field House scoring record.

goals came in the game's last 30 seconds, and the 99th and 100th points came on a high, arching shot from the top of the key *at the far end of the court*—a desperation shot for 100 points—just 2 seconds before the final buzzer.

"It was my night, because that ball went right through the basket and hit nothing but net," Selvy said. "It was one of those shots where more luck than skill was involved, but when a player scores 100 points, there has to be plenty of both."

Probably true, but Selvy still hit 41 of 66 field goal tries and 18 of 22 fouls in Furman's 149-95 victory; and more than three decades later, no one has come within 20 points of matching his feat.

February 4, 1954, at Jackson, Ohio

Rio Grande	FG	FT	Pts
Wiseman	1	2	4
Barr	1	0	2
Ripperger	2	5	9
Francis	38	37	113
McKenzie	0	0	0
Vyhnalek	0	0	0
Moses	1	0	2
Gossett	0	1	1
Weiher	1	0	2
Myers	0	1	1
Totals	44	46	134
Hillsdale			
Lowry	4	1	9
Helsted	6	7	19
Kincannon	0	3	3
Wagner	1	0	2
Davis	7	11	25
Sewell	0	3	3
Fake	0	2	2
Neff	4	4	12
Check	1	1	3
Allinder	1	2	4
Thiendeck	1	0	2
Tallmen	1	1	3
Vushan	2	0	4
Totals	28	35	91

Halftime: Rio Grande, 69-52

February 13, 1954, at Greenville, South Carolina

Furman	FG	FT-FTA	Pts
Bennett	0	1-1	1
Floyd	12	1-1	25
Fraley	3	0-2	6
Poole	0	0-0	0
Thomas	5	1-1	11
Kyber	0	0-2	0
Roth	0	0-0	0
Gordon	0	0-0	0
Selvy	41	18-22	100
Deardorff	1	1-1	3
Wright	0	0-0	0
Jones	0	1-1	1
Gilreath	1	0-0	2
Totals	63	23-31	149
Newberry			
Boland	0	0-0	0
Warner	2	0-4	4
Leitner	6	4-7	16
Bailey	0	1-2	1
Blanko	14	7-10	35
Cone	1	0-0	2
Roth	0	3-4	3
McElven	1	0-0	2
Davis	13	6-7	32
Totals	37	21-34	95

Furman	19	25	22	29 -- 95
Newberry	38	39	32	40-- 149

9

THE UNBEAT- ABLE DONS

March 19, 1955

San Francisco
vs.
LaSalle

March 24, 1956

San Francisco
vs.
Iowa

Winning streaks are pure joy for the sports fan. The enthusiasm translates into tickets at the box office and the cash support that builds new stadia and better teams.

Joe DiMaggio's 56 consecutive game hitting streak gave baseball buffs immediate identification with greatness and statisticians a reference that appears in every record book.

A team winning streak is perhaps the most difficult to achieve—coach and players must be in perfect harmony game after game. No college basketball team had ever come close to winning 50 games in a row. In fact, no one imagined that it might happen until the year of the San Francisco Dons. It might well never have happened then if Bill Russell had lost any more time trying to find his way to the office of the San Francisco head coach Phil Woolpert.

This unlikely scenario had firm plot lines. First, the Bill Russell who nearly wasn't a Don had never started a basketball game until his senior year at McClymond's High School in Oakland, California, where his family had moved. Second, only the perseverance of a former player on San Francisco's 1949 NIT champions, Hal DeJulio, persuaded Woolpert to extend a trial scholarship to Russell. There was little other than a hunch to back up DeJulio's recommendation. Russell was a gawky six-foot-seven, growing physically and emotionally, totally unpolished in the nuances of basketball.

Third, Woolpert had never seen Russell play. He had to ponder Russell's first statement when the interview began. "Coach, I intend to become an All-American," Russell declared, without bombast but deadly earnest. Fine with me, Woolpert thought, his fingers crossed. What the hell, let's give the man a try.

With Russell aboard, the next plot twist leading to the San Francisco Dons' 55-game winning streak happened when the freshman Russell and the sophomore K. C. Jones became roommates and friends.

Jones travelled a route to San Francisco much like Russell's. Jones' angel had been his high school history teacher, Mildreth Smith, who pestered Woolpert until he yielded. On Smith's word, he offered K. C. a scholarship. Actually, Woolpert had more to go on in the case of Jones, who had been selected to regional all-star teams in football and basketball.

Jones appeared on campus a year ahead of Russell and, like Russell, had difficulty finding the school and Woolpert for his first meeting. In fact, he missed his appointment altogether. Strictly on a hunch, Woolpert sent a squad member

to Jones's home to escort K. C. back the following day.

In his freshman year Jones proved to be a hot shooter but lacking in overall teamwork and defense. A reflective young man, K. C. took stock of himself after the season and decided that his best skills lay in defense, setting the stage for the arrival in September of gawky Bill Russell, who walked into K. C.'s dorm room and announced that he was the new roommate.

Thus the final plot elements fell into place. K. C. and Bill, overcoming an innate Russell shyness, became friends. Bill's shyness soon evaporated, and the two learned to innately communicate on court and off. There wasn't a subject they didn't want to discuss, their obvious prime target being the game they both loved.

Together they concocted every possible situation that could happen on a court, developing their own means of coping, establishing a system of signals to use in all game conditions. The more they practiced and played, the more

Top: *Iowa's Carl Cain (21) grabs rebound from Harold Perry, but Dons won the game, 82-71.* Above: *K.C. Jones, unable to play the semi-final against SMU, lends encouragement to Bill Russell.*

Russell watches his shot through the hoop. He led his team to 1956 semi-final victory over SMU, putting the Dons into the final against Iowa, where they kept their record intact.

intense their collaboration became until each knew absolutely what the other would do at any time.

Basketball life at San Francisco at this time was far from big time. There was no campus gymnasium; practice was held at nearby St. Ignatius High School, or at a neighborhood boys' club, or sometimes in a parish hall. Yet in 1954 the team managed a 14-7 record, mostly without Jones, who missed all but the first game of the season because of an appendix so badly ruptured his life was in danger.

Russell, minus K. C., became obsessed with improving his playing skills. He spent hours working with assistant coach Ross Giudice, and just as many more playing one-on-one with Hal Perry, a quick, smallish teammate.

The 1955 season opened with Jones fully recovered and Russell a polished player. Thus the Dons were poised for the beginning of greatness, though it didn't seem that way when they lost their third game against UCLA and a future dynasty maker, coach John Wooden. When, a week later, the two teams met again, Woolpert put Perry into the starting lineup and the Dons won.

After that game, San Francisco rolled through the season, winning the All-College tournament in Oklahoma City. This moved the Dons into the number-one spot in the polls in early January, where they stayed right into the NCAA championship. During the season, Russell had brought a new dimension to the game—his shot blocking and intimidation. He was cobra-quick in timing his leap to reject shots as they left the shooter's hand, redirecting the ball toward a teammate. Defense like Russell's was unheard of in college basketball. Suddenly, the opposition's best shooters hesitated to go for the hoop, fearful that Russell would loom in their way.

When the Dons faced defending champion LaSalle in the NCAA finals, they needed all of Russell's skills. The LaSalle Explorers were led by their great Tom Gola. Woolpert decided to put Jones on him, allowing Russell to spend more time near the basket. It was a masterful move; Jones limited Gola to 16 points (Tom had averaged 24 a game during the season) and scored 24 himself.

Russell was the ultimate difference in this game. No one kept figures on blocked shots in those days, but it seemed that shot after shot by LaSalle close to the basket was batted away. Russell also grabbed 25 rebounds and scored 23 points, including 18 in the first half when the Dons broke the game open to lead 35-24. It was no different in the second half, and San Francisco easily won, 77-63.

That was only act one of a two-part drama. In 1956, the

Dons kept right on rolling, which was as much a tribute to Woolpert and his coaching style as it was to his players' talents. Jones says of his college coach, "Woolpert engendered a goal-oriented team success; he made every player feel valuable and important to the team. He gave his squad a pattern to follow and let each of us use our skills to modify or change that pattern as needed, and he capped this style with a steadfast belief in the overall ability of his players."

The Dons never let Woolpert down; the team rolled through the season unbeaten, crashing through the supposedly impregnable barrier of 40 consecutive wins halfway through the season with a 33-24 victory over the University of California. The Dons beat a slow-down pace ordered by Cal coach Pete Newell, a college teammate of Woolpert's and the man who preceded him as head coach at San Francisco.

The Dons tagged on 15 more victories before the year was ended, but they had to play their NCAA tournament games without Jones. He had been allowed to return for a fifth season in 1956, but the one game he played in his sophomore season before succumbing to the ruptured appendix made him ineligible for the playoffs. He was the team captain, its quarterback, and now he had to sit on the bench and watch while his team capped its great season. Woolpert moved Gene Brown, a sophomore—a better outside shooter but not in K. C.'s class as a defensive player—into Jones's spot.

Now Russell was surrounded by Perry and forwards Carl Boldt and Mike Farmer. This was enough to propel the Dons back into the finals for the second straight year, facing Big Ten conference champion Iowa, which had five players who scored in double figures. As strategy, Iowa coach Bucky O'Connor ordered his six-seven center, Bill Logan, to position himself at the free throw line to draw Russell away from the basket.

The move worked early in the game as the Hawkeyes raced to a 15-4 lead, forward Carl Cain exploiting any openings. Finally, Woolpert called time out.

"We didn't have a forward quick enough to stay with Cain," Perry said, "so Phil put Brown at forward to use his quickness, and put Warren Baxter at guard."

Baxter was just five-eight and Brown a smallish guard trying to cope with a bigger forward, but the change worked. Russell clamped down on Logan, Brown stymied Cain and soon the Dons were back in front. They led 38-33 at the half and won going away, 83-71.

And Russell?

After watching San Francisco center Bill Russell during the 1955 NCAA championship series, Kansas coach Phog Allen, one of the game's great coaches and pioneers, was asked his opinion of Russell's performance.

"I'm introducing legislation to raise the basket to 20 feet," he replied.

K.C. Jones leads the Dons to victory in 1955. K.C. scored a team-high 24 points against LaSalle in the NCAA finals, but called teammate Bill Russell the best.

He scored 26 points, grabbed 17 rebounds and held Logan, a 36-point scorer in the semifinal game against Temple, to just 12 points to help the Dons finish a 29-0 season and become only the third team ever to win back-to-back NCAA titles.

Bill did miss one last accolade; he did not get the MVP award for the tournament. That went to Temple's Hal Lear, who had scored 48 points in a consolation game victory over SMU—the most by any player in tournament history—after a 32-point performance against Iowa in the semis.

From a perspective of three decades later, the MVP was a gross oversight; there is little doubt that Bill Russell was the best player in that tournament—and in the country. You have K. C. Jones's word for it.

March 19, 1955, at Kansas City				
San Francisco	FG	FT-FTA	PF	Pts
Mullen	4	2-5	5	10
Buchanan	3	2-2	1	8
Russell	9	5-7	1	23
Jones	10	4-4	2	24
Perry	1	2-2	4	4
Wiebusch	2	0-0	0	4
Zannini	1	0-0	0	2
Lawless	1	0-0	0	2
Kirby	0	0-0	1	0
Totals	31	15-20	14	77
LaSalle				
O'Malley	4	2-3	1	10
Singley	8	4-4	1	20
Gola	6	4-5	4	16
Lewis	1	4-9	1	6
Greenburg	1	1-2	4	3
Blatcher	4	0-0	1	8
Maples	0	0-0	0	0
Fredericks	0	0-0	0	0
Totals	24	15-23	12	63
Halftime: San Francisco, 35-24				

March 24, 1956, at Evanston, Illinois				
San Francisco	FG	FT-FTA	PF	Pts
Boldt	7	2-2	4	16
Farmer	0	0-0	2	0
Preaseau	3	1-2	3	7
Russell	11	4-5	2	26
Nelson	0	0-0	0	0
Perry	6	2-2	2	14
Brown	6	4-4	0	16
Baxter	2	0-0	0	4
Totals	35	13-15	13	83
Iowa				
Cain	7	3-4	1	17
Schoof	5	4-4	3	14
Logan	5	2-2	3	12
George	0	0-0	0	0
Scheurman	4	3-4	2	11
Seaberg	5	7-10	1	17
Martel	0	0-0	0	0
McConnell	0	0-0	0	0
Totals	26	19-24	10	71
Halftime: San Francisco, 38-33				

10

QUIGG'S DREAM

March 23, 1957

North Carolina
vs.
Kansas

Once there was a young, gawky, seven-foot-one-inch Philadelphian who traveled west to the flat wheat fields of Lawrence, Kansas, to play basketball for the Kansas Jayhawks.

And once, far to the east of Lawrence in the softly rolling lush hills of Chapel Hill, the common joke on campus was that the New York subway must have somehow been extended to end just short of the North Carolina field house. How else to explain the dozen Northerners, speaking with accents harsher than the soft Carolina drawl, who had come to make up much of the Tar Heel basketball team?

How had these transformations occurred? The more cynical say that the young Philadelphian had come to Lawrence because of the unopened superhighway stretching alongside the school where he could freely race his new sports car that, these cynics claim, had mysteriously appeared on his signing to play.

Easier to explain the young men from the North at Chapel Hill. Tar Heel coach Frank McGuire was a New Yorker who knew every high school in the five boroughs where he could scout undiscovered talent among the swarms of eager basketball players. It had been easy, listening to the persuasive McGuire, to become convinced that life at Chapel Hill would be a pleasant change indeed from the choked streets of home.

Down they came with that special New York cool the big-city-bred acquire, growing up to the certainty that they can take whatever life is about to dish out. In short, these young basketball players came South believing that they were winners.

And so it was that in the year 1957, the Kansas Jayhawks led by Wilt Chamberlain would meet the North Carolina Tar Heels in the NCAA championship finals at Kansas City. The 18,000-odd who packed in to see the game would leave knowing that they had witnessed a classic struggle and would go home with memories to be recalled and relished of a long winter's night.

The odds makers, seeing that Kansas and North Carolina were in the opposite halfs of the draw, figured the two would meet at the end and set their betting lines. Was the collective cool of the Tar Heels squad enough to overcome the devastating offensive and defensive play of the man from Philadelphia, this Wilt Chamberlain yet pro years away from the loving sobriquet of Wilt the Stilt? Wilt's play for Kansas had been phenomenal.

The legendary Phog Allen, who had once coached

Adolph Rupp at Kansas, was the most convincing of more than 200 college coaches from every part of the nation who had sought Chamberlain, but he never had a chance to coach Wilt because he was forced to retire at age 70. "We could win the championship with Wilt, two sorority girls and a pair of Phi Beta Kappas," Allen told everyone, and then turned his job over to long-time assistant Dick Harp.

Wilt, fighting back the pressure of his celebrity, was everything the fans expected in his sophomore season as Kansas won 21 of 23 games. Wilt smoothly integrated himself into Harp's system, averaging almost 30 points per game, pulling down over 500 rebounds and making 63 percent of his foul shots. The toughest game was an overtime, second-round NCAA playoff win against Southern Methodist. In the semifinals against the defending NCAA champion, University of San Francisco, Wilt helped destroy the Dons (without the graduated Bill Russell), 80-56.

All of that was pretty much expected, but in Chapel Hill,

Left: *Lennie Rosenbluth, North Carolina's big man, Player of the Year in 1957.* Above: *Tar Heels carry their jubilant coach Dick McGuire off the court after stunning victory over Kansas Jayhawks.*

there was a bit of magic on the march. McGuire, who had coached at St. John's University in Brooklyn and whose team lost to Kansas in the 1952 NCAA championship, had his own great player, Len Rosenbluth, but without all of Chamberlain's publicity. Rosenbluth really was the product of the parts that McGuire used to build his team—those New York imports like the coach and the star who operated on their own wavelength and who believed that it was just as possible to outpsyche opponents as it was to outrebound them.

This is exactly what McGuire planned for Kansas—an almost ridiculous ploy whereby he would send out five-foot-eleven-inch guard Tommy Kearns to take the opening tap-off of the championship game against Chamberlain. The fact that Kearns was the shortest of the Tar Heels starters was part of this deliberate plan.

"I told him that if he jumped high enough, he might reach Wilt's stomach," McGuire said. "I also told him we probably wouldn't get the tap anyhow, so why waste a big man like Joe Quigg (six-nine). The big thing was that Wilt looked freakish standing there so far above our man, and I knew it would get to him because he still was a kid, albeit a pretty big one, and kids are kids in how they react to certain situations."

Much of McGuire's planning involved psyching out Kansas. At one point he told his team that Chamberlain was so good, "maybe we better not show up." On another occasion, he said to them that Wilt might stuff some of them through the basket with the ball and that North Carolina didn't have a chance "unless our entire team defensed him at all times" and "he'd still probably beat us so badly it would be embarrassing to go home."

"Of course," he said later, "I was kidding them in one sense, and they knew it, but I also was psyching them up and loosening them up at the same time. I didn't want them all tightened up, and I tried to keep a balance that this was just a game, not the end of the world."

For their part, McGuire's players allowed their New York cool to direct their own emotions. Though they all admit today they were as psyched up for that game as for any they played that season, they certainly were not awestruck, and Wilt Chamberlain didn't throw any chills into them. In fact, most say they never doubted they could beat him and his team.

Kansas was just as concerned with Rosenbluth, who had averaged 28 points per game that year, as the Tar Heels were with Chamberlain and decided to confront him with a box-and-one defense—four players in a zone and one following Rosenbluth. But when Quigg didn't show up for the opening tap, the Jayhawks were shaken and fell out of synch.

They became more shaken when Quigg, instead of playing the middle as he usually did, stepped to the corner. He wanted Chamberlain to follow him, but Wilt stayed close to the basket. Quigg, who was not a good outside shooter, then popped in two straight shots from that spot, and Pete Brennan's 3-point play sent Carolina off to a 9-2 start.

On defense, Quigg fronted Chamberlain to prevent him from getting easy passes, and the two forwards, Rosenbluth and Brennan, formed a wall to keep him from the basket. It took Wilt nearly five minutes to get his first points, while the Tar Heels, meticulously working the ball to open spots, hit their first seven shots and led 19-7 before Harp finally abandoned his defensive scheme and went man-to-man.

That worked fine for McGuire's team because whenever Quigg went to the corner, Chamberlain followed him, leaving the middle open. Rosenbluth thrived and scored 14 points, helping his team to a 29-22 halftime lead.

Harp's message to his team at the halftime break was basically, "Don't panic, play your game and we'll still win." He was convinced the Tar Heels could not continue at a 64-percent shooting clip, while his team was bound to improve on its dismal 27-percent pace.

He was correct. The game became a tremendous battle. Ever so gradually the Jayhawks closed the edge until they took the lead, 46-43 with less than two minutes left, and felt

Below left: Wilt Chamberlain shows his power in Big-8 game against Colorado. Below right: Rosenbluth drives past Wilt for layup in Tar Heels one-point victory in 1957 NCAA championship.

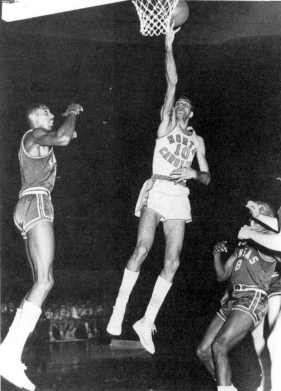

The 1957 North Carolina Tar Heels. Among the players are Danny Latz (33), Ken Rosemond (11), Bob Cunningham (32), Joe Quigg (41), and Gehrmann Holland (31).

secure as Rosenbluth fouled out after scoring 20 points. However, Quigg cut the deficit to a point with a field goal, and, after a Kansas turnover, Kearns tied the score 46-46 with a foul shot just before the end of regulation time.

Bob Young, replacing Rosenbluth, got Carolina ahead early in the overtime, but Chamberlain matched it, and neither team scored again in that session, nor during a second overtime period. Caution was the byword as each team held the ball, looking for an opening but never really finding one.

Kearns finally did, early in the third OT, first with a field goal and then with a pair of foul shots. North Carolina led, 52-48. Chamberlain answered with a 3-point play, and Maurice King retied the game by sinking one of two fouls.

Again, the Tar Heels played for the final shot, but with half a minute to play, John Parker of Kansas flicked the ball away from Quigg and into the hands of forward Gene Elstun. Kearns knocked him down, and Elstun was awarded two foul shots. He made only one.

Kearns got the ball, and when he tried to drive around Chamberlain, Wilt batted the ball away—but directly into the hands of Quigg, who was trailing the play. Quigg went up for the shot and was fouled. Two shots, his chance to win the game, the culmination of a dream he'd had the night before, though then it was by sinking a jump shot as the final buzzer sounded.

Outside Municipal Auditorium in Kansas City, a big clock in the city had just struck midnight; in the arena six seconds remained in Quigg's real-life drama as he stepped to the foul line. He sank both shots, and the Tar Heels were ahead, 54-53.

Kansas had one last chance, a long, arching pass for an alleyoop shot to Chamberlain. But there was Quigg with his dream again. This time, he batted away the ball and, sure enough, the buzzer sounded, ending the longest game in NCAA championship history.

The difference, McGuire later said, was that "we had the better team. In point of fact, we played Wilt, not Kansas, and we beat Kansas, not Wilt Chamberlain."

If that subway *had* reached beyond the Hudson River, it would have been a happy nickel ride home for a victorious group of New Yorkers gone South.

March 23, 1957, at Kansas City					
North Carolina	FG-FGA	FT-FTA	Reb	PF	Pts
Rosenbluth	8-15	4-4	5	5	20
Cunningham	0-3	0-1	5	4	0
Brennan	4-8	3-7	11	3	11
Kearns	4-8	3-7	1	4	11
Quigg	4-10	2-3	9	4	10
Lotz	0-0	0-0	2	0	0
Young	1-1	0-0	3	1	2
Totals	21-45	12-22	36	21	54
Kansas					
Chamberlain	6-13	11-16	14	3	23
King	3-12	5-6	4	4	11
Elstun	4-12	3-6	4	2	11
Parker	2-4	0-0	0	0	4
Loneski	0-5	2-3	3	2	2
L. Johnson	0-1	2-2	0	1	2
Billings	0-0	0-0	0	2	0
Totals	15-47	23-33	25	14	53

North Carolina	29	17	2	0	6 -- 54	
Kansas	22	24	2	0	5 -- 53	

Officials: Conway & Anderson

11

THE FIRST IS ALWAYS THE SWEET- EST

April 13, 1957

Boston
vs.
St. Louis

April 9, 1960

Boston
vs.
St. Louis

April 18, 1962

Boston
vs.
Los Angeles

April 28, 1966

Boston
vs.
Los Angeles

May 5, 1969

Boston
vs.
Los Angeles

F irst, there was Auerbach.
Next, there was Cousy.
Then, there was Russell.
Finally, and not coincidentally, there was what some believe to be professional sports' greatest dynasty: the Boston Celtics.

Also not so coincidentally, there came that wondrous bit of basketball theater called "The Seventh Game."

The dynasty, with its amazing legacy of success in the seventh and final games of NBA finals, began in 1957 its official run of 11 NBA championships in 13 seasons, including 9 in a row, later adding another 5. The green and white NBA championship banners hang in bunches from the ceiling of Boston Garden, evidence of the greatness of this franchise and the genius of one man, Red Auerbach.

A bit of history: the dynasty really began the day in 1950 when Walter Brown hired Auerbach as his head coach. Like the team itself, Red was a charter member of the NBA (formerly the BAA), having coached at Washington and Tri-Cities. He took over a Celtics team that had never been to the playoffs, and then never missed post-season play during his 16-year coaching tenure, though it took him seven seasons before his team won its first title.

The second thing that Auerbach did as Celtics coach— picking Bob Cousy's name from a hat in a dispersal of Chicago Stags players—proved to be one of his greatest accomplishments. The first thing he did—bypassing Cousy earlier that year in the draft—could have been his worst move because under Auerbach, Cousy established the famed Celtics "style." For the next five years, Auerbach went about perfecting that style and fitting it with the proper people. In 1956 he made his third, and final, significant move, picking center Bill Russell of NCAA champion San Francisco in the draft. With Russell signed, Red's last major building block was in place, all the parts perfectly compatible with each other.

In 1957 the Celtics had warmed up for their first title by eliminating the Syracuse Nationals and then finding themselves in the seventh and deciding game of their first NBA championship series against the St. Louis Hawks. Russell had joined the team in December after winning an Olympic gold medal and melded with another rookie, Tom Heinsohn, and such veterans as Cousy and Bill Sharman, who ran the backcourt; and later in the season, the first of Auerbach's famed "Sixth Men," Frank Ramsey, who had just finished fulfilling his military obligations.

In the seventh game of the final, the teams ended regu-

Bill Russell, defensively dominating and the cornerstone of the Celtic's dynasty, was, according to Red Auerbach, "the greatest ever."

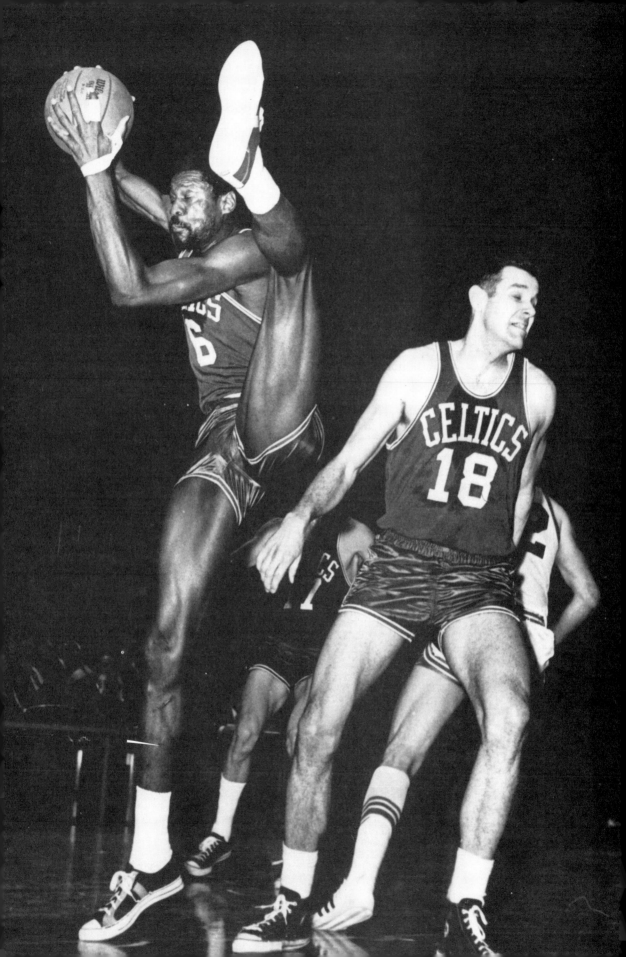

lation play tied 103-103 and were tied at 113 at the end of the first overtime as Heinsohn and Jack Coleman of the Hawks each hit field goals in the final 15 seconds. In the second overtime, Ramsey broke a 121-121 tie with 3 points in 20 seconds, but the Hawks got a couple of fouls to close the gap to 124-123 with 23 seconds to play.

Following a turnover, Jim Loscutoff sank a foul for a 125-123 Boston lead with one second to play. The Hawks had one last dash to try. Player-coach Alex Hannum, putting the ball into play, whipped a court-long pass that bounced off the backboard and into the hands of teammate Bob Pettit. Incredibly, Pettit, one of the NBA's most accurate shooters and the leading scorer in this game with 39 points, saw his shot roll around the rim and out.

Boston had won its first title, 125-123, a two-overtime drama. Russell patrolled the boards, accumulating 32 rebounds, scoring 19 points and blocking innumerable shots (no official stats were kept of blocks in those years). He also

Below: Russell sets a successful pick for John Havlicek against Lakers. Opposite: Elgin Baylor drives the basket on way to 61-point performance in 1962 title game, which Boston won in overtime, 110-107.

What was the single biggest deal that made the Boston Celtics?

Some say it was Red Auerbach pulling Bob Cousy's name out of a hat. (Actually, it was the only slip left in the hat after two other teams had made picks of three Chicago Stags players in a dispersal draft.) But without doubt, it was a deal in which Auerbach sent Ed Macauley and the rights to 1953 No. 3 draft pick Cliff Hagin to the St. Louis Hawks for the draft right in 1956 to Bill Russell. Macauley was picked by Auerbach in a 1950 dispersal draft of players from the St. Louis Bombers and was one of Red's two best players—the other being Cousy—during Auerbach's first six seasons as Boston's head coach.

Just as the 1956 playoffs ended, Macauley's year-old son was stricken with spinal meningitis and placed in hospital care in St. Louis, Macauley's home town. A few weeks later, Celtics owner Walter Brown called and asked Macauley if he would mind a trade to the Hawks, by which the Celtics could acquire Russell's draft rights.

"The move seemed just the right thing for me because I could stay at home and be near my son, and also play in my home town," Macauley said.

So the deal was made . . . along with the Celtics dynasty.

Oh, yes, there is one P.S. The number 22 that hangs among the retired jerseys in Boston Garden is Macauley's number . . . the highest honor that can be paid to any Celtics player.

underlined why Auerbach had made him the key player—"the greatest ever to play the game," Red said. He had great scores and added the dimension of defense, rebounding, and shot-blocking. (Actually, Russell's great talent for redirecting those blocked shots to his teammates was of even greater assistance in keying the Celtics' famed fast break.) In effect, Russell changed the way pro basketball was played as he controlled the area under his basket, the Celtics simply moving traffic in this direction, where the threat of intimidation made cowards of dozens of NBA shooters.

On offense, Cousy was a magician with the basketball, passing and directing the offense and deadly either driving or shooting from long range. Heinsohn was the battler, and prolific scorer, who seemed to revel in the melees under the basket as much as he did when he fired his no-arc, line-drive hook shots. Russell, while not expected to be an offensive dynamo, still got out on the fast break and was always there to work the offensive boards, or to get a stuff shot. In one game during his early career, he blocked a shot near his own basket and wound up scoring on the break from that play—all within four seconds!

Russell played in ten seventh games, including some semifinal rounds and five with titles on the line, and he never lost, the greatest individual record in NBA history.

The second of the title games came in 1960, again against the Hawks, and also in Boston. In this game, Boston broke out to a 1-point lead after the first quarter, added 8 quick points at the start of the second period and rolled to a 122-103 victory. Russell had 35 rebounds and 22 points, and Ramsey, in his sixth-man role (Auerbach developed the role to get a fresh pair of legs running when the other team was tired) led the scoring with 24 points. The Celtics' superiority was underscored with their total of 78 rebounds, compared with just 39 for St. Louis, which had a couple of six-foot nine-inch players in Pettit and Clyde Lovellette along its front line.

Two years later, Russell did it again with a 44 rebound effort as Boston defeated the Los Angeles Lakers 110-107 in overtime. This, say many Celtics experts, including Auerbach himself, was the game that really established the dynasty, the Celtics coming five-eighths of an inch—the width of a basketball rim—from having their nine-game run interrupted.

Frank Selvy was the culprit—and the near-hero who forever has been answering questions about "the shot that almost went." But before he took that one, he also had brought his team from a 100-96 deficit to a 100-100 tie, and then became the central figure as the Lakers called time out with five seconds to play. Elgin Baylor was the popular choice for the final shot because he was en route to a 41-point game—after a record 61 in the fifth game that had given Los Angeles a 3-2 series edge—but Auerbach switched his defense and sent Russell to guard Baylor. K. C. Jones guarded Jerry West, Ramsey had Hot Rod Hundley and Cousy got Selvy. Baylor and Rudy LaRusso set screens for West and Selvy, and Hundley was to get the ball to the open shooter.

In five seconds that seemed like an eternity to Celtics fans, Hundley found West covered, thought about taking the shot himself, then looked and saw Selvy open in the corner

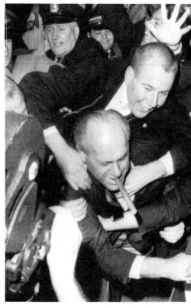

Opposite: *Russell hooks off the famed Boston parquet.* Top: *Happy Hairston grabs rebound from John Havlicek, the "best sixth man in basketball."* Above: *Auerbach, victory cigar in place, celebrates 1966 win over Royals to gain Eastern Division finals.*

83

and whipped the ball to him. The shot was made for Selvy, one he made seven out of ten times, but he was aware of the clock, too, and he hurried his jumper. The ball hit the front rim, then the back rim, and trickled to the floor as the buzzer sounded.

Thus was born another tradition—give the Celtics life after apparent death, and pay the consequences. Sam Jones's 3-point play broke a 102-102 tie early in the overtime, and Boston went on to win, 110-107.

There were other hair-breadth finishes as well, such as Auerbach's final game as head coach when, with the Celtics ahead 95-85 and just 30 seconds to play, thousands milled about the Boston Garden floor, ready to salute him and the Celtics. Suddenly, West canned two quick baskets in 14 seconds to cut the lead to 6 points, but Auerbach was satisfied and he allowed Gov. John Volpe to light his famous "victory cigar."

That was a signal for crowd hysteria, and the game went completely out of control for the Celtics, who in the next 16 seconds committed *four* turnovers. Their lead shrank to 2 points when, with six seconds to play, Leroy Ellis of the Lakers sank a jump shot. Auerbach, at this point, was just about swallowed up in the crowd and had no control over his team, nor the game. But K. C. Jones and John Havlicek controlled the inbounds pass against the desperate LA team, and the Celtics won, 95-93.

"I never came closer to disaster," Auerbach said.

But the disaster didn't happen . . . the Celtics won their ninth straight playoff, and Russell got two more as head coach, the last in equally dramatic fashion with a desperation shot by Don Nelson in the 1969 finals at the Forum in Los Angeles. With 77 seconds to play in the game, the Celtics led 103-102 when Havlicek had the ball deflected out of his hands by Keith Erickson of the Lakers—and directly into the hands of Nelson. With just a couple of seconds left on the shooting clock, Nelson rushed a jumper, and the ball hit the rim, bounced some 15 feet into the air and then plopped through for the 2 points that insured a 108-106 Celtics victory.

Just another seventh game for the Celtics—and another title—and the continuation of a legacy that lasts to this day. And for Auerbach, which was the best?

"The first championship is always the sweetest. There will never be another one for me like '57."

There is little doubt that former Celtics coach Bill Russell was the greatest "playoff player" in NBA history—and not simply because he appeared in the most games.

"If you ever hear anybody say I'm in the playoffs only for the money, you can tell them they're dead wrong," Russell once said. "I get up for the playoffs because I like being part of a world championship team.

"I always want to be part of a world championship team because I always want to win one more time.

"I like the taste."

Opposite: *Cousy splits St. Louis Hawks defense.* Above: *The Hall-of-Fame guard gets hug from Bill Russell after Celts won their fifth straight NBA crown in Cousy's last game.*

12

A TIME OF FES-TIVALS

March 19, 1938

Temple
vs.
Colorado

March 22, 1958

Xavier
vs.
Dayton

March 25, 1961

Providence
vs.
St. Louis

March 20, 1977

St. Banaventure
vs.
Houston

March 24, 1980

Virginia
vs.
Minnesota

The National Invitation Basketball Tournament was born when playing in New York's old Madison Square Garden was just coming into vogue. Any game in that long-gone Eighth Avenue arena was a big deal and, in those days, there was no bigger deal than being asked to play in the NIT.

From the immediate postwar era until the late sixties, New York and the Garden represented the best in basketball. Its schools may not always have been among the nation's top-ranked teams, but the country's focus was always on the teams playing in the Garden, and a team or a player could make a lasting reputation in that arena. Playing in the NIT could rivet reputation in place.

The NIT was a ten-day basketball festival, with doubleheaders every other day that drew thousands of fans. Coincidentally, the semifinals and the finals always fell within the week of the St. Patrick's Day holiday—New York City's version of the Mardi Gras—and this heightened the hoopla.

During those years, the NIT was college basketball at its best played in a city that prided itself on its sophistication. The tournament was a festival of youthful exuberance that brought young people from every part of the country and ignited the city. The result was that the NIT, more than any single event, helped to propel the college game to the heights it now enjoys.

The NIT forced the NCAA to expand further in order to gather the best teams for its own event. Through a combination of muscle and membership, the NCAA gradually eroded the NIT's drawing power to the point where today the NIT really is a two-day festival in New York City after a series of elimination rounds elsewhere in the country, and is played in the shadow of the giant nationally televised NCAA carnival.

There are those who will declare that in its heyday, the NIT was bigger and better than any other college basketball event because it had everything that New York City demands of its entertainers: good theater, drama, the unexpected, heroes and villains and, at all times, anticipation and excitement.

The NIT began in 1938, the year before the NCAA tournament, and Temple was its first champion after beating Colorado 60-36. As part of the basketball promotion cooked up by Ned Irish, a former New York City sportswriter, that first tournament was national in scope, with Bradley and Oklahoma A & M joining the two winners as well as two local schools, NYU and Long Island University.

It didn't take long for the NIT to begin showcasing what

Left: *Early NIT action at the old Madison Square Garden.* Below: *Providence's Ray Flynn, later to be mayor of Boston, gets 1963 NIT MVP award.*

college basketball is about. A battle of the unbeatens was settled the second year when LIU defeated Loyola of Chicago 44-32; LIU then became the first school to win a pair of NIT's with a 56-42 win over Ohio University in 1941. The first major upset occurred the next year when eighth- and last-seeded West Virginia defeated Western Kentucky. In 1944 St. John's University was the first team to win back-to-back tournaments, beating Toledo University in 1943 and DePaul in 1944.

Big names and great teams began to dominate after the war when George Mikan and his DePaul team each set ten records in the Blue Demons' 71-54 win over Bowling Green. Kentucky and its legendary coach, Adolph Rupp, won their first—and only—NIT the next year when Ralph Beard sank a free throw in the final seconds for a 46-45 victory over Rhode Island. Ernie Calverly of Rhode Island had become a folk hero in New York a few nights before by heaving a 55-foot shot at the buzzer to beat Bowling Green.

When City College defeated Bradley in 1950 as part of its

Providence plays Miami during NIT in days when the New York tournament was more important than the NCAA championships.

double championship, the NIT was in full bloom, and even the subsequent revelations about point shaving and thrown games involving that team didn't dampen the enthusiasm for the unexpected and the underdogs that delighted New York's fans. That was the case in 1952 when freshman Tom Gola led LaSalle to the title and in the early sixties when an unheralded group of Providence College players delighted spectators with their tenacious play and their fans' unbridled enthusiasm.

More than a few poignant moments occurred during NIT play. One was Dayton finally winning the NIT after nine unsuccessful tries, including five losses in the finals. Another was St. John's unsettling Villanova 55-51 in the 1965 game to give famed coach Joe Lapchick a victory in his final game.

There were surprises as well, but none more startling than Southern Illinois, the nation's No. 1-ranked small college team, coming up with the 1967 title behind a relatively unknown guard named Walt Frazier. New York fans would take him to their bosom the following year, when he became the Knicks' No. 1 draft pick. He would be a favorite for two championship seasons in the seventies.

Other games that stand out: Providence College's 1961 title game victory over St. Louis University. With the Friars down by seven points and ten minutes to play, a five-foot-eight-inch blond sparkplug named Vinnie Ernst, who grew up across the Hudson River in Jersey City, took the game away from the favored Billikens with a dynamic display of ball-hawking and floor leadership. Though he scored just four points in the game, Ernst assisted on seven baskets, most of them in the final minutes when Providence came on to win, and he capped that performance by stealing the ball and setting up the Friars' go-ahead basket with three minutes to play. His leaping one-hander from close range bounced off the rim, but center Jim Handnot slammed home the rebound. Ernst was named the tourney's MVP, and he and his affable coach, Joe Mullaney, were immediately engulfed by their enchanted fans.

In 1977, a flamboyant left-handed shooter named Greg Sanders, who had convinced St. Bonaventure University to give him a scholarship when no other school was interested, made the gamble pay off when he tossed in a 22-foot jump shot with just 66 seconds to play (his 40th point of the game) to help defeat Houston and also to win MVP honors. It was the kind of shot NITs are famous for, one that makes coaches cringe and brings a sold-out Garden to its feet.

"It wasn't the best shot in the world," Bonnies coach Jim

Satalin said. "I looked at it after Greg released the ball and thought, 'No-no-no,' and suddenly found myself leaping in the air yelling, 'Yes!'"

In this game, as in so many other NIT finals, the last minute was perhaps the best, because Houston trailed only 90-89 with 20 seconds to play and had a golden chance to retake the lead when St. Bonaventure lost the ball. But Ken Williams blew a shot for the Cougars before his team got new life when the Bonnies' Tim Waterman missed the second of two free throws. Houston still had an opportunity to tie or win the game in the final seconds until Glenn Hagan got the rebound of Waterman's missed foul, was fouled himself and made the shot for a 92-89 lead with 12 seconds to play. One more Bonnies' score cushioned a closing basket by Otis Birdsong of Houston for an eventual 94-91 victory.

In 1980 another battle of the big men occurred; Ralph Sampson of Virginia against Kevin McHale of Minnesota. Sampson and the Cavaliers came out on top, 58-55. Officially, Virginia guard Jeff Lamp scored the final four Virginia points for the victory margin, but Sampson's defense—his intimidation, rebounding and blocked shots—really was the difference.

Virginia led 54-53 with 33 seconds to play when Sampson snapped up a missed foul shot by teammate Terry Gates and passed the ball back to Lamp. Lamp was fouled and made both shots for a 56-53 lead with 19 seconds to play. Although

The NIT has attracted its share of diverse personalities from among players who have gone on to distinguish themselves in other fields. Georgetown coach John Thompson was the center for Providence College's 1963 NIT champions. That game's Most Valuable Player was one of the Friars' forwards, Ray Flynn, mayor of Boston in the 1980s.

Flynn wasn't the only politician to have played in the NIT. Stewart Udall, a future Secretary of the Interior, played for the University of Arizona in the 1946 tournament. His team lost in the first round.

Providence big man John Thompson proves a formidable barrier. Thompson went on to tremendously successful career as the coach of Georgetown and U.S. Olympians.

Above: *Hank Stein leads his Xavier team to NIT win over Dayton in 1958 NIT tourney. Opposite: Bonnie's Essie Hollis goes for dunk in 1977 NIT championship.*

Sampson had only a 5-for-15 shooting night, his overall play won him the MVP award by unanimous vote.

The NIT now was being played in the newer Madison Square Garden, and it did not always attract the top teams. Though Virginia had finished fifth in the Atlantic Coast Conference that year and Minnesota was tied for fourth in the Big Ten, the level of play was of championship caliber, the enthusiasm of 14,000 fans undimmed.

Similar circumstances seemed not to affect the tourney as late as 1988 when the University of Connecticut, last in the Big East, defeated Ohio State, fourth in the Big Ten, for the title, the 51st NIT. UConn forced a dozen second-half turnovers to take the win, 72-67.

Of all the games, all the upsets, all the stars, sung and unsung, perhaps the game and team that best captured the spirit of the NIT was the highlight of the 1958 tournament: an unheralded, unappreciated Xavier University team from Cincinnati that came to New York and won the first overtime championship game, 78-74, over second-seeded University of Dayton.

If ever a team stunned the basketball world, it was that band of musketeers. They had lost to Dayton twice during the regular season and had slumped so badly after a 10-1 start that even the students on campus pelted the bus with snowballs as the team left for the tournament.

Jim McCafferty, the engaging Xavier coach, was more upbeat. "I brought two clean shirts because you never go to New York City with less than that," he joked. "I used them up after we beat Niagara and Bradley, and said, 'Now what do I do?' But none of us wanted to go home, so I laundered them myself."

McCafferty's team had lost top rebounder Cornelius Freeman to scholastic problems at midseason and then lost six of its last seven games, before McCafferty rearranged matters, allowing Joe Viviano and guard Hank Stein to become catalysts for a group of players who suddenly found themselves energized. Frank Tartaron, the team's center and captain, played his best basketball of the season in those four NIT games. The team's spiritual leader was forward Tony Olberding, their top rebounder, who fired up his team against Bradley and, in the minds of most, really set the stage for their astounding championship victory that followed an easy semifinal win over St. Bonaventure.

"Our kids came to New York as the 12th seed in a 12-team field, and that seemed to give them all the incentive they needed," McCafferty said. "Heck, if we had made our foul shots, we could have won that game by 15 points in regulation time instead of having to drag it out in overtime."

In the overtime, Stein was unstoppable, his shooting sending Xavier ahead to stay.

"We played our best game all-around in the final, but what probably won the tournament for us was overcoming the 41-point performance by Boo Ellis of Niagara in the first game. When we did that, we knew we were special," Mc-Cafferty said.

Festivals thrive on special performances, on the unseeded blossoming into champions. This, indeed, was the NIT of its glory years.

13

HOLD ON THE GOLD

September 10, 1972

United States
vs.
USSR

July 27, 1976

United States
vs.
Yugoslavia

I t once was said that the United States could put together eight Olympic basketball teams in any one year and any of them could win a gold medal—a bit jingoistic, but an apt description of the U.S. talent and coaching resources. With the rules now being pushed to allow *all* basketball players, pro and college, to compete in future Olympics, that belief may be more correct than ever.

With the exception of the debacle in the 1972 Olympic Games in Munich, the U.S. is without peer as the king of Olympic basketball, and much of any discussion about basketball and American participation pretty much boils down to trying to decide which team was the greatest.

The first Olympic final, between the U.S. and Canada in 1936, was played on an outdoor clay and sand surface tennis court. It rained that day and the players found it difficult to dribble in the mud, accounting for the low 19-8 victory. Six-foot eight-inch center Joe Fortenberry of McPherson, Kansas, matched Canada's total to lead the U.S. scorers.

The Cold War heightened the competitive aspects of Olympic basketball, the political rivalry of the United States and Russia translating in all arenas—from the United Nations to the playing fields—where these two nations faced each other. Since the USSR first fielded an Olympic basketball team in 1952, the two met in four of the next seven gold medal games. The U.S. had won three and had the other one stolen by incompetent scorekeeping and officiating and blatant politics.

That, of course, seemed to be the final terrible chapter in a truly tragic Olympic Games, when in 1972 bitter hatred among nations demolished any sense of athletic neutrality. An Israeli team was taken hostage and murdered. A few days later, the U.S. and Russia played the gold medal basketball game, and while the American team did not play well, it nonetheless stormed back from an eight-point deficit with six minutes to play with some smothering defense that held the Russians without a legitimate field goal for the remainder of the game.

With six seconds to play, Doug Collins, the future coach of the Chicago Bulls of the NBA, picked up a loose ball at midcourt. With his team trailing 49-48, he drove for the basket. On the way he was fouled, awarded two shots and made both of them, a horn sounding just as he released his second shot. Three seconds remained to be played, and under international rules, which govern the Olympic Games, no time outs were allowed at that point of the game, so the Russians quickly put the ball in play.

Steve Alford fakes a shot and passes the ball off around Spain's Fernando Romay (9) during Olympic contest in 1984 at Los Angeles Forum.

*North Carolina's Phil Ford
passes off in finals vs.
Yugoslavia.*

Basketball has been described as a non-contact sport, but that is not the case in Olympic competition.

In 1948 a British referee was knocked unconscious during a game between Chile and Iraq, but that was nothing compared to working the games played by Uruguay in 1952.

Uruguay's team had been reduced to three players in a game against France because of excessive fouling, but with one minute to play they tied the score, whereupon the American referee, Vincent Farrell, whistled a foul.

The Uruguayan team rushed off the bench and abused Farrell for five minutes before he could communicate to them through an interpreter that the tie-making field goal counted because the foul occurred after the basket. But France's Jacques Dessemme scored an easy layup to win the game, and once again the Uruguayans attacked Farrell. This time he was kicked in the groin and had to be carried from the court.

Three days later, Uruguay played the Russians, and in the second half, three Soviet players had to receive first aid. And when the Uruguayans played their bitterest rivals, the Argentinians, with third place at stake, so many fouls were called that only four Uruguayan players finished the game—but Argentina was left with just three, all of whom took part in a giant brawl involving 25 persons at the end of the game. Uruguay won the game, but no one knows who won the fight.

Americans weren't immune, either.

In the 1976 gold medal game against Yugoslavia, Adrian Dantley of the American team played most of the

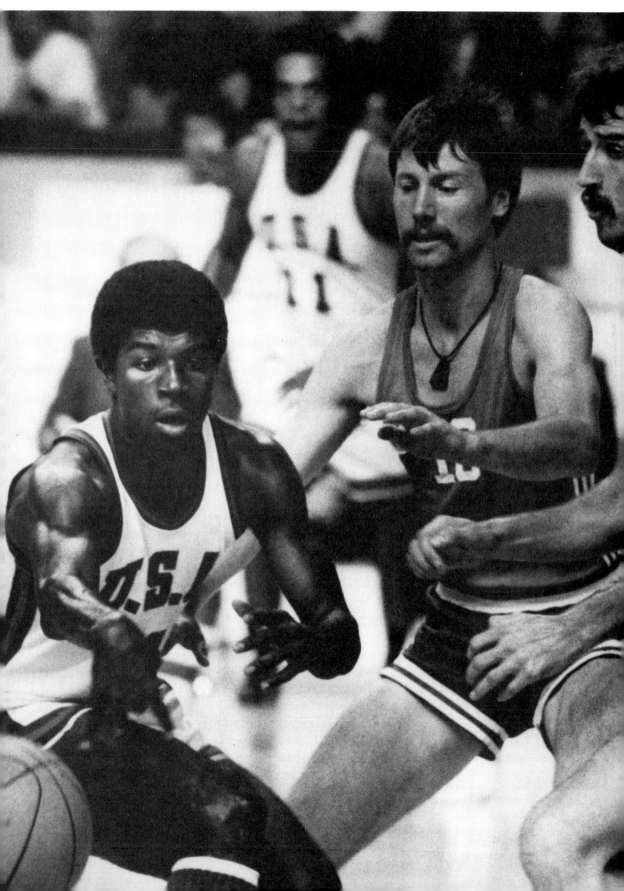

second half with a bandage over his right eye after being whacked with an elbow. Stitches were required to close the wound, but Dantley still led all scorers with 30 points, and held Yugoslavia's top scorer, six-foot ten-inch Kresimir Cosic, to just 15 points.

Some non-contact sport . . . or, as Bill Russell once said, "Dancing is a contact sport, and basketball is a collision sport. But non-contact it ain't."

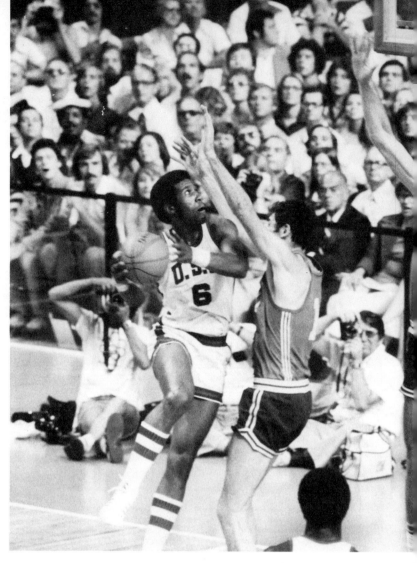

Two seconds later, head referee Renado Righetto of Brazil noticed a disturbance at the scorer's table and called an administrative time out. It seems the Russian coach, Vladimir Kondrashkin, was arguing he had called a legitimate time out after Collins's first foul shot, accounting for the horn sounding. There was no record of it in the official scorebook, so timekeeper Andre Chopard waved him off, and Righetto directed that the last second be played, which ended without a Russian score and an apparent 50-49 U.S. victory.

But Kondrashkin kept up his protest, and R. William Jones of Great Britain, the Secretary-General of the ruling International Basketball Federation, improperly intervened and ordered the clock reset to three seconds. Onto the scene roared Henry Iba, the 69-year-old U.S coach. Matters quickly got so heated that he had to be physically restrained by his players from going after the ruling officials, particularly Jones, who had no technical right to intervene.

So for the second time after the U.S. thought it had wrapped up a victory, the Russians had a chance. Kondrashkin brought in Ivan Yedeshko, who then threw a court-long pass to Sasha Belov, with U.S. players Kevin Joyce and James Forbes guarding him. Belov knocked down both American players, without a foul call from either referee, caught the ball and scored the winning basket.

The whole scene erupted in a mass of shouting, shoving and near-blows as the U.S. and those who were rooting against the Russians stormed after the officials. The American officials filed a formal protest, and it took 12 hours before the Russian victory became official—in strictly Cold War style, with three of the five-man Jury of Appeals members from Russian bloc nations voting to uphold the win, and two from Western bloc countries saying the U.S. really won the game.

In the years before and after that travesty, the U.S. has dominated, particularly the 1960 and 1984 teams, which are considered the most purely talented to ever represent this country. In fact, despite the 1956 team's 8-0 record with an average score of 99-46, and with players such as Bill Russell and K. C. Jones, the 1960 team had been considered America's crown jewel until coach Bobby Knight of Indiana put together his 1984 squad.

Coached by Pete Newell of California, the 1960 team had such players as Jerry West, Jerry Lucas, Oscar Robertson, Terry Dischinger, Walt Bellamy, Bob Boozer and Adrian Smith. It was so good that John Havlicek, Lucas's teammate at Ohio State and later a great NBA player, qualified only as an alternate. This unit averaged 102 points a game, and in its final three games to decide the gold medal, it defeated Russia 81-57, Italy 112-81, and Brazil 90-63.

"This was the most explosive team I have ever seen," said Newell. "It could run off a 20-point burst before the opposition knew what hit them."

It also was a tribute to Newell's coaching acumen that, with little time to put the team together, he abandoned his preferred ball control and deliberate style of play that had worked so well for his college teams at San Francisco and California. Instead, he allowed his players to play fast-break, freelance basketball. Only twice did the U.S. team fail to score 100 points in the eight games, and in the gold medal game against Brazil, it led 33-11 after 10 minutes of the first half. Lucas, a six-eight forward, scored 23 points in just 25 minutes, and he got 12 straight on tip-ins. Of the 12 players on that team, eight went on to distinguished NBA careers.

The most courageous U.S. team probably was formed for

Opposite bottom: *Phil Hubbard and Kenny Carr pick themselves up after collision.* Opposite top: *Adrian Dantley leads U.S. to gold medal with 30 points against Yugoslavia in 1976.* Above: *Steve Alford salutes crowd after taking gold medal in 1984.*

Above left and right: *On-court and off-court players celebrate victory over Yugoslavia. The U.S. had lost only once in Olympic competition, a disputed game against the U.S.S.R.*

the 1968 Olympics in Mexico City. Iba's tallest player was a six-nine reserve, Ken Spain, because the team was snubbed by some of the nation's best collegians, such as Elvin Hayes of Houston (who turned pro) and seven-one Lew Alcindor of UCLA (now Kareem Abdul-Jabbar), who staged his own personal protest of the racial climate in this country. Further, only one player, James King, was accustomed to Iba's no-nonsense defense-oriented style because he played for Iba at Oklahoma State.

Thus the American team, for the first time ever, was picked no better than third. But it rallied around collegians Jo-Jo White of Kansas and Spencer Haywood of Seattle University, who at 19 was the youngest player ever to make a U.S squad, and won seven games by an average of 28 points.

The Americans met Yugoslavia in the gold medal game and gave up an 11-6 early lead, but with White shooting from the outside, tied the score. Iba, one of the game's greatest coaches, then went to his bench and used all 12 players in the first half so his team would have enough left for a finishing burst. The U.S. held a 10-point halftime lead; in the second half the team played a furious stretch of near-perfect basketball, running off 17 straight points. White and Haywood each got eight, and the Americans led 49-29. The U.S won the game, 65-50.

After the debacle at Munich, the Olympic basketball program was revamped and the coaching and selection process turned over to a group of college coaches. In the past, the U.S. team had been comprised of collegians, players from AAU industrial teams and the armed services. Now the teams were comprised solely of America's best collegians, and the first to benefit from this was Dean Smith of North Carolina.

Though he was criticized because 7 of the 12 players on his team were from the Tar Heels' Atlantic Coast Conference—and 4 played for him—the team regained a gold medal for this country with a nifty 95-74 victory over Yugoslavia in Montreal. Before the team went onto the court for the final game, John Thompson, an assistant U.S. coach just beginning his career at Georgetown, gave a fiery pep talk, harkening back to his brief career with the Celtics in the mid-sixties.

"I told them with the Celtics the idea was not letting opportunity get away from you," said Thompson, who became coach of the 1988 U.S. Olympic team.

The team didn't. Adrian Dantley of Notre Dame, later an NBA star, hit 13 of 19 shots in a 30-point performance, helped out by North Carolina guard Phil Ford, who dished out a dozen assists, and Phil Hubbard of Michigan, who contributed 10 second-half points while filling in for an injured Scott May of Indiana.

The game was intensely physical as Yugoslavia went with a front line that averaged six-ten, but they never got the lead, coming to within 10 points midway through the second half. The quick, aggressive Americans simply harassed the Yugoslavs into continued ball-handling mistakes and missed shots, many from close to the basket.

Bobby Knight became the U.S coach in 1984 and got a massive response from his emotional appeal for all the nation's top collegians to come to his spring tryout sessions. Knight was able to put together a squad that had his personal stamp of aggressive, mistake-free execution. His team rivaled the 1960 group that had been the best. Knight had Michael Jordan, who average 17 points a game, center Patrick Ewing, the tournament's best shot blocker, and Alvin Robertson's 65 percent shooting average. The team, all around, was as good as could be hoped for from the college ranks.

Together, Knight's team won all eight of its games by an average of 32 points, being pushed only by West Germany, which lost 78-67. In the title game against Spain, the Americans had a 23-point halftime lead. With Knight in command, they played as if the score were tied throughout the game. They made 12 of their first 14 shots for an early 25-17 lead, and when that cooled off, they locked the Spaniards into a vise-like defense that forced repeated errors in the last ten minutes of the first half, at one point allowing just 4 points in 16 scoring opportunities.

Like seven of the other eight postwar gold medal performances, it was awesome, almost too easy. Somehow you got the feeling that yes, the U.S. *could* make up eight teams and go out and win an Olympic gold medal with any one of them.

The 1948 Olympic tournament—the first since World War II and only the second in the history of the Games—had some unusual highlights:

A Chinese player dribbled through the legs of the seven-foot American center, Bob Kurland, and scored a basket.

Iraq lost by 100 points two times—to Korea and China—and gave up an average of 104 points a game. Ireland's offense was even less effective, averaging 17 points per game.

Alfredo de Motta of Brazil was so consumed in his team's game for third place that he lost his pants and had to retire to the dressing room.

One of the Cuban players, J. Llanusa Gobel, went on to become Minister of Education under Fidel Castro.

14

LONGEST GAME, SHORTEST SCORE

March 25, 1961

Utah
vs.
St. Joseph's

There has never been a game like it, a game requiring four overtimes simply to decide the consolation winner. The game remains in the record books as the longest basketball game ever played in NCAA championship competition. The official score: 1-0. The winner: Utah. The loser: the team from St. Joseph's of Philadelphia.

Waiting while St. Joe's took favored Utah into the four overtimes were the NCAA finalists, Ohio State and blue-collar University of Cincinnati. In the press area, a national TV crew sat waiting to film the championship and at their typewriters and telephones sat the press corps, their editors holding Sunday morning editions on the press, hoping to cry the results of the final following the consolation game.

This is how it all happened:

Although the St. Joseph's-Utah game is in the official stats as the longest game and the official score is 1-0, the game's actual score was St. Joe's 127, Utah 120. No other team ever scored so many points in the tournament, and no game score had ever reached the grand total of 247 points.

St. Joseph's was the underdog with a vengeance. Most looked down at the St. Joe's roughneck, scrambling five as interlopers who didn't belong in the final four. The new full-court zone press devised by coach Jack Ramsay was causing turnovers and ruining the best-laid offensive schemes. Such play was not appreciated by their staid opponents.

"We were a bunch of kids who played the Philly street game," says Paul Westhead, a senior guard on that team and later head coach of St. Joseph's, the Los Angeles Lakers, and Loyola Marymount University in Los Angeles. "We went out and played hard all the time. We were always trying to make a steal, we dove on the floor after loose balls and probably did all the things that talented teams never bothered about. We considered scraped knees part of our uniform. All of that effort and scrappiness really bothered teams that had never seen it before."

All of this helped St. Joe's win 21 games and lose just four during the regular season.

"We looked at this game as a great opportunity to vindicate ourselves after getting beaten so soundly by Ohio State in the semifinals," Ramsay recalled. "We were a scrappy team and we loved challenges, and our challenge was to try to take some of the sting out of that loss."

Challenging a team to play well in a tournament's consolation game is never easy, since the big prize has fled and third place becomes something of a hollow achievement. But Ramsay's team had a different idea, and from the outset it went

after Utah and soon dragged that team—whatever its mindset going into the game—into a dogged contest that was always fiercely contested.

The underdog team often surprises the opponent with its stubborn refusal to be beaten. St. Joe's had this incentive and more when it faced off against Utah. Early in the season, Jack Egan and two teammates had been approached by professional gamblers to shave points and the players had agreed.

As the stupidity of their action became clear, Egan and teammates refused any further requests of the gamblers, who cajoled, pleaded and then threatened.

St. Joe's entered the NCAA tourney knowing that an investigative arm of the NCAA had heard Egan's story of being approached, of the points shaved, and of the players' refusal to deal any longer with the gamblers. No final NCAA decision had been reached, and Egan and the two were allowed to play in the championship round.

It was Egan's moment to make amends. There is no

Left: *Jim Lynam, junior co-captain, who ignited fourth-overtime rally.* Right: *Paul Westhead, who went on to coach St. Joe's, the Los Angeles Lakers and Loyola Marymount.*

Although they had to forfeit their victory over Utah in the NCAA tournament, St. Joseph accepted the trophy for winning the Quaker City.

question that he succeeded. When he fouled out in the fourth overtime, Egan had accumulated 42 points, the individual high score on either team. During the game he had waged a duel with Utah's junior center, six-foot-nine-inch Billy (The Hill) McGill.

As Egan returned to the bench, the sellout crowd at Kansas City Municipal Auditorium gave him a standing ovation.

All of which explains how it came about that St. Joseph's fought to a 48-41 halftime lead and, early in the second half, jumped up by 12 points, 56-44. McGill and Jim Rhead took charge for coach Jack Gardner's Utes, who finally tied the score at 74 on McGill's field goal with seven minutes to play. A half minute later, Vince Kempton, who had been guarding McGill, fouled out. A minute after that, Utah took its first lead, 78-77. The game was tied three more times before Utah went ahead, 88-87. The lead was offset by Frank Majewski's field goal with 27 seconds to play for an 89-88 St. Joe's lead. But Joe Morton sent the game into overtime, tied at 89, with a foul shot with 18 seconds to play.

When the overtime began, Utah took a quick lead on an

outlandish play by Billy Hoy of St. Joe. McGill had controlled the tip-off but Hoy had grabbed the ball, dribbled to the wrong basket and scored—for Utah!

"It was strictly a dumb play," an embarrassed Hoy said afterward. "For a moment after it happened, I felt like a grade-school kid, then it simply seemed absurd. The funny thing was that I had once seen a similar play happen when I played in high school, and thought, 'How could someone do that? It will never happen to me.'"

McGill got due credit for his wrong-way basket, then Majewski tapped in a rebound to force a second session.

In that first OT, the teams each scored eight points; each added another four in the second, St. Joseph's saved by Egan's field goal that also helped to foul out McGill with 53 seconds to play. Now the score stood at 101-101.

Scheduled for air time at 9:00, national television began coverage of the St. Joe-Utah contest, coming on the air as the third overtime commenced. Suddenly, an entire nation was wrapped up in this consolation game.

The third overtime saw four ties and three St. Joseph's leads as the two teams became more and more aggressive instead of following an expected "play-it-safe" approach. Hoy lined up a shot in the final couple of seconds for the Hawks,

Late in the fourth overtime period of St. Joseph's NCAA consolation game against Utah, coach Jack Ramsay ordered senior guard Paul Westhead to kill some time with his fine dribbling talents. Utah's Rich Ruffell, trying to steal the ball, knocked Westhead to the floor, spraining Westhead's ankle.

The referee immediately signalled two foul shots, but foul shooting was not one of Westhead's strengths. As he lay there, Ramsay leaned over him, grabbed his sore ankle and said, "How's your ankle?"

"It should be okay," the valiant Westhead told his coach.

Ramsay grabbed it harder, and in a more determined voice asked, "How's your ankle? It really must hurt too badly for you to shoot, doesn't it?"

Westhead got the idea.

"Yeah, yeah, it sure does," he told his coach. "I may not be able to stand on it."

Ramsay immediately told the officials, who allowed Ramsay to substitute Harry Booth, a 73 percent foul shooter. Booth made both. St. Joseph's went on to win the game, and Paul Westhead laughs about his "major" contribution to the win.

Coach Jack Ramsay directs the full-court press that drove St. Joe opponents crazy. Ramsay later had a successful career in the NBA.

but Bo Crain flicked the ball away. It was Crain's second big play, because he sank two foul shots to get a 112-112 tie.

In their respective locker rooms, the finalists were ready to climb the walls. They had expected to go through a normal warmup session and get into their game at the assigned time. Here it was nearly half an hour later, and they remained behind closed doors, worrying more about what was happening on the court than about their tasks. The ultimate effect would be disastrous for the Buckeyes.

In the fourth overtime period, St. Joe's took charge be-

Paul Westhead (right) *although not a superstar, nevertheless brought considerable skill to his position as head coach in the National Basketball Association.*

hind Egan and Jim Lynam, who would coach the Philadelphia 76ers. Egan quickly scored the first four points for St. Joe's, while Bob Cozby got two for Utah. Then Lynam stepped forward.

"Jim just ignited that fourth overtime," Ramsay said. "I've never coached a player who took the ball to the hoop any better than he did. He was a great penetrator, and he made things happen to a defense, which is exactly what happened in that overtime period."

Lynam keyed a 7-point run by sinking a foul shot, and after a Majewski field goal, he hit two more fouls and a field goal; after a Cozby field goal., he got two more fouls. St. Joe's scored 15 points in that fourth overtime and Utah scored 8— that 7-point difference was Lynam's burst, creating St. Joe's 127-120 victory.

Considering the circumstances, the NCAA decision was inevitable. Any gambling contact—if for a single game, a single moment in a lifetime—is one moment too many. The NCAA official verdict was to strip St. Joseph's of its win and to award the consolation to Utah. The St. Joe's team had to accept the loss. They had played the Utah game totally within the rules, had made an effort no one ever could fault. In losing, they had won.

March 25, 1961, at Kansas City					
Utah	FG-FGA	FT-FTA	Reb	PF	Pts
Rhead	12-20	4-10	11	4	28
Ruffell	7-14	0-0	16	3	14
McGill	14-23	6-9	10	5	34
Morton	3-11	5-9	2	3	11
Rowe	3-8	0-0	3	4	6
Crain	5-13	3-3	10	5	13
Thomas	3-7	0-0	1	0	6
Aufderheide	1-4	0-1	1	3	2
Cozby	2-3	2-2	0	1	6
Jensen	0-0	0-0	2	0	0
Totals	50-103	20-34	56	28	120
St. Joseph's					
Majewski	5-9	1-2	12	3	11
Egan	17-33	8-8	11	5	42
Kempton	7-12	2-3	5	5	16
Lynam	9-18	13-14	14	5	31
Hoy	3-14	4-4	6	3	10
Wynne	4-12	7-9	3	4	15
Gormley	0-2	0-0	0	5	0
Booth	0-0	2-2	3	0	2
Westhead	0-0	0-0	3	3	0
Dickey	0-1	0-0	0	1	0
Totals	45-101	37-42	57	24	127

Utah	41	48	8	4	11	8 -- 120
St. Joseph's	48	41	8	4	11	15 -- 127

Officials: Wertz & Glennon

15

DAVID VERSUS GOLIATH

March 15, 1950

Cincinnati
vs.
Ohio State

I f ever in NCAA basketball a David was matched against a Goliath in size, reputation, and recorded skills, it was the night the University of Cincinnati went head to head with the reigning champion, Ohio State University, for the NCAA title.

No one who came to the Kansas City Municipal Auditorium on a late March Saturday night in 1961 could have anticipated the outcome. To begin with, there had been four overtimes, 60 minutes of play, before the consolation game had a winner. Now it would be long after midnight and one more overtime before the champion, and a most improbable one at that, was crowned.

Never before had two schools from the same state played each other for the national basketball championship. Ohio State and Cincinnati, ranked 1-2 in polls, hadn't played against each other since 1922. This evening, the two would square off for bragging rights in the Buckeye State and the NCAA title, in just about that order of importance.

Ohio State was the Goliath of the encounter, already the winner of previous year's NCAA title, with a group of sophomores that included Jerry Lucas, John Havlicek, Mel Nowell, and a scrappy sub named Bobby Knight. During the current season, no one had taken this five. OSU now was riding a 32-game winning streak and looked the most likely kind of candidate to make it two in a row. Some more imaginative observers were already looking ahead to an unprecedented three straight titles.

No less a person than the Baron, Adolph Rupp of Kentucky, called the OSU squad "the greatest team of all time," which was not exactly faint praise coming from someone who never took a back seat in admiring his own coaching. It might be added that Rupp offered this lavish praise after Ohio State defeated his Kentucky team in the playoffs, 87-74.

The ease with which OSU coasted through the 24 games of the regular season had set the team apart and made it easy for the odds makers in selecting OSU as the heavy favorite.

The David in this match-up was the University of Cincinnati. OSU was the university of renown, the glamour campus, the producer of championship football, baseball, and golf teams. The University of Cincinnati was a hometown affair, a blue-collar campus filled with day students who rushed off after classes to their jobs and who lived at home to save the extra dollars for tuition, a city school without the ivy-covered walls and flower-edged pathways.

Mix in the facts that the Cincinnati Bearcats were without their great Oscar Robertson, who had graduated after leading

*Ohio State's strategy against Cincinnati was for Jerry
Lucas (11) to get Paul Hogue into foul trouble. Hogue
got three—but no more.*

Those who believed that the University of Cincinnati's upset of Ohio State in the 1961 NCA basketball finals was a fluke had only to wait until the following season when the two teams, with basically the same players met again.

Final score: Cincinnati 71, Ohio State 59 . . . in another upset.

The scenario was the same, with the nation's 1-2 teams facing each other— Ohio State with a 22-game winning streak and the bearcats with a 22-3 record. Cincinnati had to beat Bradley to determine the Missouri Valley conference champion and gain a berth in the tournament, and they had a close call (72-70) over UCLA in the semifinals.

The Buckeyes cruised through the tournament, but Lucas suffered a badly wrenched knee in the semifinals, and Ohio State paid the price for his immobility as Hogue led the Bearcats with 22 points in a relatively easy victory. Lucas had just 11 points.

Coach Ed Jucker's game plan was to neutralize John Havlicek, and he did it by stationing his man, Ron Bonham, on the outside and effectively taking John out of the close-in play, allowing Hogue and George Wilson to overpower Lucas.

"Everyone said our victory in 1961 was a fluke," guard Tony Yates said. "Well, you don't repeat a fluke."

Oh yes, in 1963 the Bearcats tried to make it three straight NCAA titles and this time the "fluke" went the other way as Loyola of Chicago defeated them in another memorable upset.

In overtime, naturally.

his squad to third place in the NCAA finals, and the Bearcat coach, George Smith, had moved upstairs and his assistant, Ed Jucker, was at the helm.

"None of you is an Oscar Robertson," the new coach observed, "but if we all play together and follow our game plan, maybe collectively we can be a winner." Jucker was all business. Paul Hogue and guard Paul Bouldin were the only returning starters. When Sandy Pomerantz, "the next Oscar Robertson," rebelled at Jucker's deliberate offense— preferring the run-and-shoot of the Robertson era—the new coach sent the player packing. Jucker moved Tom Thacker to forward and installed Tony Yates, a sophomore, at guard. His other forward was Bob Wiesenhahn, a strapping six-four, 215-pounder who became the team's leading scorer. Together the group was a lunchpail team that, after a rough start, hacked out 24 victories—21 in a row—to get its No. 2 national ranking behind the glamorous Buckeyes.

Fred Taylor, Ohio State's coach, decided that the Bearcats' rebounding, particularly the work of Hogue and Wiesenhahn, was his chief concern. Noting Cincinnati's weak bench, he wanted Lucas to work on Hogue and foul him out. Jerry was a great player near the basket with a variety of moves; it seemed like a logical tactic. On the other side, Jucker told his team, "If we can stay in the game for the first half, we can win."

That's what Cincinnati did, and no more than 7 points separated the two teams in the first 20 minutes until Cincinnati tied it at 20 and then fought to three more ties before leaving the floor trailing at halftime by 1 point, 39-38.

The Bearcats had done a masterful job on defense, and the rebounding strength of Hogue and Wiesenhahn had denied Ohio State its fast break offense. Hogue had managed to move Lucas away from the basket, where he was not quite so effective a scorer. In doing this, Hogue also accumulated three fouls. Jucker considered sitting him down at the start of the second half, but decided he'd give Hogue one more foul. Hogue never got another.

Ohio State obviously had been affected by the long wait when the consolation game ground into overtime after overtime. There was no flow for OSU when the game began, and they seemed to be a beat off in running their offense. The Bucks had their scoring opportunities, despite the Bearcats' defense, but there was a glitch here, another there, and Cincinnati was able to gather momentum during the first half. The Buckeyes also had problems handling UC's offense at times, particularly Thacker who, though a guard by trade, was simply too tenacious to be muscled away from the basket. Thacker also did a fine job helping Hogue work on Lucas, constantly sagging off and helping to double-team the Buckeyes' star.

Ohio State also used a sagging defense to work on Hogue, with Siegfried dropping down to work with Lucas. They paid for it early in the second half when Bouldin, left alone, hit five consecutive long-range jumpers, giving the Bearcats a 52-46 lead. Ohio State then found its offense, and with a 12-1 spurt, took a 58-53 lead. A few minutes later Wiesenhahn tapped in a rebound to tie the score at 59 with 4:04 to play, and a couple of minutes after that, Thacker's jumper gave Cincinnati a 61-59 lead.

Twenty seconds later Knight tied the score at 61 with a driving layup with 1:41 to play, so Cincinnati decided to hold the ball for the final shot. Thacker took it with six seconds left, missed and the rebound came to Lucas, who immediately called time out. The Buckeyes then inbounded the ball to Cincinnati's end of the court and called time out again, with four seconds to play, to set up a special alleyoop pass from Havlicek to Lucas under the basket. But the Bearcats deflected the pass, and the two teams went into overtime tied 61-61.

In any overtime, the immediate edge goes to the team that scores first, and Cincinnati carefully worked the ball until Yates flicked a pass to Hogue, who faked another to Wiesenhahn, and then whirled toward the hoop. Lucas, with no help from Siegfried, was caught short and fouled Hogue. In most cases this wasn't too bad because the Cincinnati center was not a good foul shooter, but on this night he sank two for a 61-59 lead.

Opposite: *Although Jerry Lucas pulled down a game-high 12 rebounds, his team lost on the boards by a 30-24 margin.* Top: *Paul Hogue crowns coach Ed Jucker with the net.*

Basketball and politics don't always mix . . . particularly in Ohio.

In 1962 Ohio Governor Michael DiSalle proclaimed Ohio State the No. 1 team in the country, either forgetting, or preferring to ignore, that the University of Cincinnati was the defending national champion, and at the time ranked a close second in the polls.

The good people of Cincinnati—voters all—didn't appreciate the snub, nad the following fall, DiSalle lost his bid for reelection.

There are those who still contend his one-sided pronouncement may have contributed to the loss.

In reality, he also was dead wrong, because while Ohio State did finish first—and Cincinnati second—in the 1962 wire service polls, the Bearcats defeated the Buckeyes and again won the NCAA championship.

Just as serious for the Buckeyes was the fact that Lucas had committed his fourth foul, and he had to back off the boards, leaving this most important area wide open for Hogue and Wiesenhahn. Jucker later said it was the deciding factor in the overtime because it allowed Cincinnati to control the ball and set its own tempo. Nowhere was this more evident than when, with 3:49 to play, Wiesenhahn shoved the careful Lucas from a rebounding position and tapped in a missed shot for a 65-62 lead.

Lucas came back with a jumper to close to within 1 point, his 27th point of the game, but Yates's foul shot pushed Cin-

For two years the nos. 1 and 2 spots in the national rankings were kept in Ohio—but it was Cincinnati who won on the court.

cinnati's lead to 66-64 with 1:06 to play.

Nineteen seconds later, Ohio State blew a golden chance to tie when Siegfried, the team captain, sank only one of two foul shots. The Buckeyes now turned to desperation measures to get the ball as Havlicek fouled Yates, but the gritty sophomore made both free throws, and Cincinnati led 68-65 with 28 seconds to play.

Ohio State still had a chance—in fact, they had defeated Louisville 56-55 after finding themselves needing 3 points with just he same amount of time to play a week prior in the regional playoffs. This time, the Buckeyes worked the ball quickly to Lucas, hoping he could force a 3-point play but uncharacteristically, Jerry rushed a shot and the ball didn't even hit the backboard.

That was it, and the Bearcats leaped up the court in the final seconds, and in an exclamation of victory, Thacker threw in the final basket from the side. Final score: Cincinnati 70, Ohio State 65.

Time on the town clock: nine minutes past midnight in Kansas City . . . six hours after St. Joseph's and Utah had begun a memorable evening of basketball that ended with a new NCAA champion and a renewed meaning to the term "bragging rights."

The University of Cincinnati was the best team in the state of Ohio.

NIT Championship, March 15, 1950, at New York City					
Cincinnati	FG-FGA	FT-FTA	Reb	PF	Pts
Wiesenhahn	8-15	1-1	9	3	17
Thacker	7-21	1-4	7	0	15
Hogue	3-8	3-6	7	3	9
Yates	4-8	5-5	2	3	13
Bouldin	7-12	2-3	4	4	16
Sizer	0-0	0-0	1	0	0
Totals	29-64	12-19	30	13	70
Ohio State					
Havlicek	1-5	2-2	4	2	4
Hoyt	3-5	1-1	1	3	7
Lucas	10-17	7-7	12	4	27
Nowell	3-9	3-3	3	1	9
Siegfried	6-10	2-3	3	2	14
Knight	1-3	0-0	1	1	2
Gearhart	1-1	0-0	0	1	2
Totals	25-50	15-16	24	14	65

Halftime: Ohio State 39, Cincinnati 38

Regulation: 61-61

Officials: Fox & Filberti   Attendance: 10,500

16

ONE MAN'S 100 POINTS

March 2, 1962

Philadelphia
vs.
New York

Wilt Chamberlain, arguably the most talented and, without a doubt, the most enigmatic player in pro basketball history, scorched his name into the sports record book when he scored 100 points against the New York Knicks playing in the relative anonymity of the state fairgrounds of Hershey, Pennsylvania, on the first Friday night of March, 1962.

One hundred points in anonymity?

Consider that this significant of all of pro basketball's scoring records was set not with the glitter of a big-city arena and its media to record every moment, but in an out-of-the-way stop which the NBA's then-Philadelphia Warriors used occasionally to bring the pro game to fans in central Pennsylvania. Thus there are no videotapes, no movies—only a very few truly first-hand accounts of that epic performance, written or broadcast.

It figures. Nothing Chamberlain ever did was clear-cut and simple. For the greatest physical specimen ever to play the game, that would have been too easy. Wilt seemingly relished the complex and unfathomable rather than concentrating on becoming the game's greatest player.

For one night back in 1962, though, he was just that, and it is not unreasonable to wonder or even to suggest what might have been his place in the game if this seven-foot-two-inch, 265-pound athlete had worked as hard during his entire 18-year NBA career as he did that one evening. True, he had plenty of help, but he also created enough energy to lift everyone's game notches above their normal levels, in stark comparison with other times when he appeared bored just playing the game.

Not that Chamberlain ever established that he had a game plan to score 100 points then or any time, whether he was playing with the San Francisco Warriors, the Philadelphia 76ers or the Los Angeles Lakers.

"If you believe in omens," said Harvey Pollack, the Warriors' chief statistician that night, "then perhaps there were a couple. On the bus ride from Philadelphia, there was a card game, and Wilt won every hand. When the team arrived in Hershey and was heading to its locker room, the players passed a shooting gallery that had moving ducks, and Wilt tried his skill. He didn't miss one."

Chamberlain also was having the best scoring season of his career, with a 50-points-per-game average. In just three seasons, he already had scored 60 or more points 14 times. It was apparent that, at that stage of his career, a staggering single game total was not improbable.

Although many have claimed to have been at Madison Square Garden the night Wilt scored 100, the game was played at less-than-full Hershey fairgrounds.

The Knicks of that year were a lackluster outfit, and that night their regular center Phil Jordan, was sidelined with an injury. His sub, Darrell Imhoff, never was a match for Chamberlain, and in this game, he fouled out early trying to guard the big man. Those who followed—Willie Naulls, Johnny Green and Cleveland Buckner—were just as ineffective.

At the start, there was an indication that this would not be just another average Chamberlain effort. Wilt scored 23 points in the first quarter, hitting half of his 14 field goals. There also was another revealing statistic—he made all 9 of his foul shots, and that in itself was a phenomenon because, for all of his talent, Chamberlain was a dreadful foul shooter.

Wilt had 41 points at halftime, and when he added another 28 in the third quarter to raise his total to 69, his teammates dedicated their entire efforts to help him reach an unheard-of 100. Opening the last quarter, Wilt hit with three quick field goals; he now had 75 points with 10:10 to play, topping his 1962 season high of 73.

At this point, public address announcer Dave Zinkoff was

While Wilt Chamberlain scored 100 points against the Knicks in 1962, he might have scored more. It seems the game never officially ended. To this day 46 seconds remain to be played.

Hundreds of fans had rushed onto the floor at the Hershey Arena and showed no inclination of leaving. At that point, no one—players, coaches or officials—had any interest in continuing the game, certainly not the Knicks, who trailed 169-147.

Under NBA rules, a game must be played until there is no time on the clock, and those 46 seconds are still out there. Who knows, Chamberlain someday just might want to return and demand to finish what he started.

Right: *Wilt holds up his point total in Hershey dressing room after setting record that should never be broken.*
Opposite: *The Stilt scores his 100th point over Johnny Green.*

114

keeping the 4,124 fans in the Arena abreast of Wilt's scoring, and the chants began to ring through the building. "Give it to Wilt! Give it to Wilt!"

At the same time, the Knicks were equally determined that they would not be the victim, and New York began to run the clock down on every possession. Chamberlain's sudden flair for foul shooting had rendered useless the usual tactic of deliberately fouling him.

On the flip side, Philly coach Frank McGuire, who had helped to defeat Chamberlain and his Kansas team in the 1957 NCAA finals when he coached the University of North Carolina, had his own idea of how to get the ball into Wilt's hands for more points. He sent players York Larese, Joe Ruklick and Ted Luckenbill into the game to foul the Knicks players quickly. He reasoned this would prevent the Knicks from running down the clock. After the foul shots, he hoped the Phillies would pass off to Wilt for more points.

At the 7:51 mark, Chamberlain broke his high scoring record of 78 points on one of Guy Rodgers's 20 assists for the game. Now his teammates really began to feed him the ball. With 5:14 to play, Al Attles gave up an easy try to give Wilt the ball for his 89th point. Minutes later, Chamberlain banked in a 12-footer to hit 94 points. He headed back down the floor laughing, it was that easy.

On the next possession, Rodgers again lobbed him the ball, but Wilt dropped it, then picked it up and scored his 96th point on his famed fadeaway shot. With 1:19 to play, Larese gave him a high pass and he slammed home his 98th

point. He could have had the 100th in bang-bang fashion if he had controlled the inbounds pass that bounced off his hands a few seconds later.

Richie Guerin of the Knicks then made a pair of fouls (the two teams shot 93 free throws and made 76), and when Philadelphia came back down to the Knicks' end, the ball immediately went to Chamberlain with one minute to play. Wilt shot and missed; Luckenbill rebounded the loose ball and got it to Wilt for a second try. Another miss. Again Luckenbill got the ball and passed it out to Rucklick. He in turn hit Wilt underneath the basket.

Chamberlain dunked it and the 100-point game was his, an all-time game exclamation mark on a night in which the Warriors rolled up a 169-147 victory.

Fans poured onto the court and mobbed Wilt. Chamberlain loved it, his exuberance plain to see. Quickly he paid tribute to his teammates, noting quite correctly that they really had made that mark possible by passing up their own shots to get him the ball.

Someone asked Wilt if he thought the record ever would be broken.

"I'd hate to have to try and do it," he said, adding,

"I hope no one ever asks me when I'll score more because I never will."

And he never did. But then, he never tried.

While the New York Knicks were the patsies in Wilt Chamberlain's 100-point game, they also came out on the plus side in scoring 147 points, the most ever by a losing team.

The 316 total points were the most in NBA history.

The teams combined for 233 shots, and Wilt took 63 of them, making 36 and never in any quarter shooting under 50 percent.

His 28 (of 32) foul shots were the most in an NBA game. He never came close to matching that 87.5 percent foul shooting accuracy.

Three Knicks players—Naulls, Buckner and Guerin—each scored more than 30 points.

Chamberlain led all rebounders that night with 25.

March 2, 1962, at Hersey, Pennsylvania						
Philadelphia	FG-FGA	FT-FTA	Reb	Ast	PF	Pts
Arizin	7-18	2-2	5	4	0	16
Conlin	0-4	0-0	4	1	1	0
Ruklick	0-1	0-2	2	1	2	0
Meschery	7-12	2-2	7	3	4	16
Luckenbill	0-0	0-0	1	0	2	0
Chamberlain	36-63	28-32	25	2	2	100
Rodgers	1-4	9-12	7	20	5	11
Attles	8-8	1-1	5	6	4	17
Larese	4-5	1-1	1	2	5	9
Totals	63-115	43-52	57	39	25	171
New York						
Naulls	9-22	13-15	7	2	5	31
Green	3-7	0-0	7	1	5	6
Buckner	16-26	1-1	8	0	4	33
Imhoff	3-7	1-1	6	0	6	7
Budd	6-8	1-1	10	1	1	13
Guerin	13-29	13-17	8	6	5	39
Butler	4-13	0-0	7	3	1	8
Butcher	3-6	4-6	3	4	5	10
Totals	57-118	33-41	56	17	32	147

Philadelphia	42	37	46	44 --	169
New York	26	42	38	41 --	147

Officials: Smith & D'Ambrosio   Attendance: 4,124

17

"HAVLI- CEK STOLE THE BALL"

April 15, 1965

Boston
vs.
Philadelphia

April 5, 1962

Boston
vs.
Philadelphia

April 19, 1968

Boston
vs.
Philadelphia

May 3, 1981

Boston
vs.
Philadelphia

The voice of Celtics broadcaster Johnny Most rasped through thousands of radio speakers on that April night in 1965, proclaiming the most famous rallying cry in pro basketball:

"Johnny Havlicek stole the ball!"

While it has become legend in Celtics history, more than anything it is the clarion call for one of the NBA's most storied rivalries, Boston versus Philadelphia—for many years shorthand for Bill Russell versus Wilt Chamberlain. Who doubts that the Russell-Chamberlain matchup was the best ever in the NBA? It matched the two best players at the game's preeminent position, center, and became the backdrop for some of the sport's most exciting and physical games.

The Boston-Philadelphia rivalry didn't begin the night that Havlicek stole Hal Greer's inbound pass in the last five seconds of the seventh game of the NBA's Eastern Division championship series. It began in Boston Garden the night in November, 1959, when Russell and Chamberlain first played against each other. Long after those two left pro basketball, the rivalry grew to produce memorable moments for Julius Erving and Larry Bird and, after Russell retired, some victories for Philadelphia.

Whether Russell-Chamberlain or Bird-Erving, the matchups established standards of excellence that may never be equalled in head-to-head confrontations. It has been said time and again that Chamberlain won many of the statistical battles against Russell, but Bill took home the championships; it was almost the same with the Bird-Erving duels.

For the Russell-Chamberlain era, the rivalry was portrayed as good vs. evil—Russell the good guy and Wilt, the seven-foot one-inch giant, the overpowering bully. Never mind that Russell was six-ten and no pushover. What really mattered was that Russell always seemed devoted to team spirit while Chamberlain rolled up individual stats.

Many thought Wilt would simply overwhelm the game when he came into the NBA, and while that didn't happen, the rivalry between the two teams—and the two players— took off right away. In Chamberlain's first season, the Celtics beat his team, the Philadelphia Warriors, in a six-game playoff, winning the final game at the buzzer when Tom Heinsohn topped in a desperate heave by Bill Sharman. Heinsohn still calls it "my greatest moment. The game was played in Philly and you never heard 11,000 people go silent so fast."

Two years later, in 1962's Eastern Division finals, Sam Jones hit a jump shot with two seconds to play, and the Celtics beat the Warriors 109-107 for the title. Sam then intercepted a

Warriors Tom Gola, Vern Hatton and Joe Graboski all go for ball lost by Bob Cousy (14) in a drive for basket.

last-ditch pass by the Warriors as they tried to get off one last shot. The Warriors had appeared to be the stronger team throughout the game. Twice in the third quarter they had 9-point leads, and two of the Celtics' best defensive players, Jim Loscutoff and Tom Sanders, had fouled out.

Then the Celtics took over, as they always seemed to do in these meetings. Frank Ramsey came off the bench and helped the Celtics take the lead for good at 84-80 with a 4-point burst; Russell dominated the middle, blocking shots and firing outlet passes that kept Bob Cousy and Jones on the run to good shooting opportunities.

In the final minutes, a goal-tending call against Chamberlain and Heinsohn's foul shot gave Boston a 107-102 lead. Wilt came back with 5 straight points, the last 3 with nearly half a minute to play, to get the tie. But Jones fought free at his favorite spot, 16 feet from the left side of the key, and swished a jumper for the game.

The Warriors almost spoiled this rivalry by moving to San

Above: *GM Red Auerbach congratulates exhausted Bill Russell after Boston defeated Philadelphia for the 1968 championship.* Below: *Russell is unstoppable as he goes for the basket in earlier game.*

Francisco after that season, but midway through 1965 they traded Chamberlain back to the new Philadelphia team that had moved from Syracuse—just in time to produce two classic confrontations as well as Chamberlain's only shining moment against Russell and Boston, the NBA championship in 1967.

Wrapped around Wilt's golden moment was Havlicek's electrifying game in 1965, and an amazing comeback by player-coach Russell and the Celtics in 1968 that set the standard for all playoff competition.

In 1968 the defending world champion Sixers, with a team dubbed the best ever in one poll, led the Celtics 3-1 in the Eastern Division finals as Chamberlain, now concentrating more on defense than scoring, was magnificent. After the fourth game, Russell, also the Celtics coach, called a team meeting and said, "Let's take things one step at a time. Not even one game at a time. Let's try to win each quarter."

They didn't win every quarter, but in the next two games, they beat the 76ers by 18 and 8 points, respectively, and played game No. 7 on Philly's home court in the brand-new Spectrum. It all came down to the final minute of play—though Chamberlain's willingness to take only two shots and

score only two points during the entire second half remains a sticking point to this day. Again Russell was the difference. First, he put himself on forward Luke Jackson and allowed 265-pound reserve center Wayne Embry to play Chamberlain and effectively muscle him away from the basket. Meanwhile, Russell neutralized Jackson's shooting.

With the Celtics leading 97-95 with 34 seconds to play, Russell made one of two foul shots. Wally Jones of the Sixers missed a jumper, and Chamberlain and Don Nelson battled evenly for the rebound. Wilt tapped the ensuing jump ball to Walker, who drove too close to the basket. Russell switched off Jackson and blocked the shot. Greer got the ball and tossed up a jumper that bounced off the rim. Russell grabbed that ball, too. Moments later, two foul shots nailed down Boston's 100-96 victory, and the Celtics thus became the first team ever to come back from a 3-1 deficit in the playoffs and emerge the winner.

That same scenario was acted out again in 1981, without Russell or Chamberlain. This time Larry Bird was the hero, and inexplicably, the 76ers hit another scoring slump in which they got just one foul shot in the final 5:24 of the game. Their inability to bury the Celtics for good in game No. 5, when they were on top of a 109-103 score with 1:51 to play, led to a loss of the game, 111-109.

In game six, Boston trailed 89-82 after Erving's reverse layup with 5:34 to play, after which Bird stole the ball three times (among five 76ers turnovers). Finally, he grabbed a rebound and dribbled the length of the court before pulling up on the left side and hitting a perfectly arched 17-foot jump shot with 63 seconds to play, to give Boston a 91-89 lead.

"I don't really know what happened under our basket [Robert Parrish and Cedric Maxwell stuffed Darryl Dawkins's layup attempt], but I wanted the ball in my hands," Bird said later. "That's the only place in the world I wanted it, and when I got it, I knew that I was going to take the shot. No one else was going to get the ball at that moment."

The game wasn't over. Philly forced a Celtics turnover with 29 seconds to play, but Gerald Henderson saved a tie-making basket when he fouled Maurice Cheeks. Cheeks made only one of two shots, and the Celtics controlled the ball until, with 5 seconds left, M. L. Carr had to shoot. The 76ers eventually got the rebound and called time out with 1 second to play.

Philly coach Billy Cunningham diagrammed what he wanted—a lob pass from Bobby Jones at midcourt to Erving leaping to stuff the ball Alley-Oop style, a play that Jones

"Anytime Russ took Wilt to dinner, he had an ulterior motive," one Celtics insider from that time declares. "He used to play with Wilt's mind like a master psychologist, never doing anything to get him really riled up. If we were up by 20 points, Russ would lay off and let Wilt score 17, and then come back and shut him off.

"Or if we had the game really locked up by the fourth quarter, he'd let Wilt score a bunch of meaningless points and grab some rebounds, and Chamberlain would go away feeling satisfied—his statistics looked good. Russell didn't want to give Wilt any extra motivation the next time he played us."

never had tried before. As the team broke its huddle a network microphone picked up one final plea from Cunningham: "Ya gotta do it, Bobby, ya gotta do it."

He and the 76ers didn't. The ball ricocheted off the backboard, and Erving never got his hands on it.

It was in 1965, though, that the series produced "the steal." The Celtics took early command of the seventh game of

Auerbach is swept away by fans after his team beat the 76er's in 1965 Eastern Division Championship. Title was the ninth straight for Celtics.

April 5, 1962, at Boston Garden					
Boston	FG-FGA	FT-FTA	Ast	PF	Pts
Cousy	8-21	5-8	8	4	21
Heinsohn	9-22	7-7	2	5	25
K. C. Jones	1-4	2-3	10	4	4
S. Jones	12-29	4-4	2	2	28
Loscutoff	1-5	0-1	1	6	2
Ramsey	1-2	2-2	0	0	4
Russell	7-14	5-5	3	3	19
Sanders	2-8	2-3	1	6	6
Totals	41-105	27-33	27	30	109
Philadelphia					
Attles	0-4	0-0	1	4	0
Arizin	4-22	11-11	1	4	19
Chamberlain	7-15	8-9	3	3	22
Conlin	0-0	0-0	0	1	0
Meschery	10-19	12-13	2	3	32
Rodgers	6-15	6-8	6	6	18
Gola	7-14	2-2	2	2	16
Totals	34-89	39-43	15	23	107

Boston	34	18	28	29 -- 109
Philadelphia	23	33	25	26 -- 107

Officials: Borgia & Rudolph

April 15, 1965, at Boston Garden						
Boston	FG-FGA	FT-FTA	Reb	Ast	PF	Pts
Havlicek	10-30	6-7	11	1	5	26
Heinsohn	1-5	0-0	7	2	5	2
K. C. Jones	2-9	2-3	4	10	5	6
S. Jones	15-31	7-9	2	1	3	37
Naulls	0-0	0-0	0	0	1	0
Russell	7-16	1-2	29	8	3	15
Sanders	8-17	2-2	10	2	5	18
Siegfried	2-4	2-3	3	0	1	6
Totals	45-112	20-26	66	24	28	110
Philadelphia						
Bianchi	3-11	1-1	0	0	4	7
Chamberlain	12-15	6-13	32	2	1	30
Costello	7-7	1-1	3	0	5	3
Gambee	6-15	13-14	6	0	6	25
Greer	5-12	2-2	8	9	4	12
Jackson	3-10	2-4	2	0	2	8
Kerr	0-1	0-2	0	0	0	0
Walker	10-19	4-5	5	1	4	24
Totals	46-90	29-42	56	12	26	109

Boston	35	26	29	20 -- 110
Philadelphia	26	36	20	27 -- 109

Officials: Powers & Strom

their Eastern Division final against Philadelphia. Chamberlain led the 76ers back into the game before Havlicek led a scoring charge in the third period that gave Boston the lead for good. With the score 110-107 and only a few seconds to play, the Celtics allowed Chamberlain an uncontested layup, reducing their lead to 1 point.

Only five seconds remained as Russell stepped out of bounds to toss in the ball for the final time. He arched it high downcourt and away from the 76ers basket, but he had to get it over Chamberlain's mighty arms. Bill was really inexperienced in such long throws, so his toss hit one of the guy wires securing the basket, and the ball bounced out of bounds. Thus, the 76ers had the ball with five seconds left, and they called a time out before putting it into play from midcourt.

Coach Dolph Schayes of Philadelphia wanted Greer to inbound the ball to Chet Walker, who would come around a pick and take the final shot. Havlicek stationed himself just off line between Greer and Walker, but with his back to Greer, who was about 30 feet away from Walker. It would be a long toss, so Havlicek took one last look at Greer, and then sensing when the ball was coming into play, stepped between the two Philadelphia players. At just the precise moment, he leaped and deflected the ball into his hands, controlling it for a couple of seconds before flipping it over to Sam Jones, who dribbled out the clock.

High above courtside at Boston Garden, true Garden fans were mimicking the Celtics announcer's "Havlicek stole the ball" routine, carving out a gallery bit of glory. At that moment the 76ers and Chamberlain trudged off the court with nothing to show for their truly gallant comeback effort. Havlicek, in the meantime, was swept up by the 14,000 delirious fans and carried off the court. When he finally was deposited in the Celtics locker room, all he had on were his supporter, his socks and sneakers, his basketball shorts barely clinging to his ankles. Years later, he attended a party and saw a woman wearing a ragged piece of green cloth. "It's part of your jersey from the night you stole the ball," she told Havlicek. "I've worn it ever since."

How intense was the Bill Russell-Wilt Chamberlain rivalry?

On the court, there has never been a more personal battle. Off the court—well, that might have been something else.

Russell often claimed he and Wilt were fast friends away from the game, frequently going to dinner together, and they weren't always alone.

"When we were in Philly," K. C. Jones recalls, "we would have dinner at Wilt's mother's house and then drive to the game together."

"In fact," says Sam Jones, "I picked up a stool to defend myself when Wilt came after me during a game in Boston. Thankfully, someone broke up the fight. The next time we were in Philly, Wilt came to the hotel and took me over to his mom's for dinner. His mother asked me if I really intended to hit her boy with that stool, and I said, 'Yes, ma'am, I did.'"

Of course, among those who know Russell well, some believe the off-the-court socializing was part of Bill's effective scheming to psych out Chamberlain.

Larry Bird in action against Sixers Tim McCormick in 1987 game. In 1981 championship series against Philly, Bird was the star.

April 19, 1968, at Philadelphia			
Boston	FG	FT	Pts
Embry	1	0	2
Havlicek	7	7	21
Howell	8	1	17
Jones	9	4	22
Nelson	5	0	10
Russell	4	4	12
Siegfried	7	4	18
Thacker	0	0	0
Totals	41	20	102
Philadelphia			
Green	1	2	4
Greer	8	6	22
Goukas	2	0	4
Jackson	7	1	15
W. Jones	8	2	18
Chamberlain	4	6	14
Melchionni	0	0	0
Walker	8	3	19
Totals	38	20	96

Boston	26	20	27	27	--	100
Philadelphia	21	19	29	27	--	96

Bill Russell was mightily impressed the first time he ever played against Wilt Chamberlain.

"Both of us grabbed a loose ball at the same time, and I tried to yank it away from him," Russell recalled. "Did you ever try to bend a lamppost with your bare hands? That's how strong Wilt's arms were.

"Then he began to pull on me. I actually felt my feet leaving the floor, and I thought, 'I'm going to look awful silly if he stuffs the ball and me through the hoop.'

"Fortunately, the referee blew the whistle for a jump ball."

May 3, 1981, at Boston Garden						
Boston	FG-FGA	FT-FTA	Reb	Ast	PF	Pts
Maxwell	9-12	1-5	6	2	1	19
Bird	8-17	6-7	11	5	1	23
Parrish	7-17	2-2	8	0	5	16
Archibald	3-14	7-11	1	0	1	13
Ford	3-10	1-2	4	3	2	7
Robey	1-5	2-4	7	1	1	4
Carr	1-6	0-0	3	2	2	2
McHale	0-4	1-2	2	2	3	1
Henderson	2-4	2-2	4	1	1	6
Fernsten	0-0	0-0	0	0	1	0
Totals	34-89	22-35	46	16	18	91
Philadelphia						
Erving	11-21	1-2	8	5	5	23
C. Jones	6-7	0-0	15	2	1	12
Dawkins	7-12	2-3	4	0	5	16
Hollins	1-9	0-0	3	5	3	2
Cheeks	3-8	6-7	5	7	4	12
B. Jones	5-10	3-3	6	2	5	13
Toney	4-9	0-0	1	2	3	8
Mix	2-4	0-0	3	0	1	4
Totals	39-80	12-15	45	23	27	90

Three-point field goal: Bird.

Boston	26	22	23	20	--	91
Philadelphia	31	22	22	15	--	90

Officials: Garretson & O'Donnell

18

WHEN MINERS STRUCK GOLD

March 19, 1966

Kentucky
vs.
Texas Western

Upset.

The word itself is stimulating. When an upset in sports occurs it brings instant joy to the fan who loves to see the forlorn underdog rise to smite the top-heavy favorite.

Why, in NCAA championship tournaments, with every team boasting a splendid winning record, should there be those select few who are tagged sure winners?

Mystique is a likely answer. For instance, when Texas Western found itself in the finals against mighty Kentucky, coached by the legendary Adolph Rupp, the Miners had to overcome more than the Wildcat five: It had to conquer an inferiority complex.

Many times this reflected glory blinded the opponent, regardless of its record, personnel and style of play. In the 1966 NCAA championship game it was assumed that Rupp would celebrate his last hurrah with a win.

Someone apparently forgot to tell Don Haskins, a chunky former player for Hank Iba of Oklahoma State, just how great his opponent was, and how little chance his Texas Western team had to win.

Texas Western was not one of the college game's elite, but a school once known as Texas Mines (now the University of Texas-El Paso) which played as an independent and had not beaten a single top-ten team all season. Yet somehow, the Miners also won 23 of 24 games, losing the final game of the regular season to Seattle by just 2 points.

This was no prairie dog team but rather a collection of quick, talented kids from the inner city playgrounds of New York, Detroit, Houston, and Gary, Indiana, who played a run-and-gun game. Opinion was that once they got into the NCAA tournament, their game would disintegrate in the face of more disciplined coaching of chalkboard Xs and Os.

In fact, the Miners were a very disciplined team indeed, dedicated to the defensive game by the demands of their coach, who had it drilled into him during four years of playing for Iba. Haskins hounded his players repeatedly in practice, often to the point of near-rebellion, but the players stayed together, they listened, and they worked—oh, how they worked. What many took as the run-and-gun approach really was the result of a quick ball-hawking defense that forced turnover after turnover and worked to build a dynamic fast-break offense.

Kentucky? Well, Kentucky was still Kentucky, though this team had been nicknamed "Rupp's Runts" because no starter was over six-feet five-inches. Like every Wildcats

Texas Western brings the ball downcourt against Kentucky. The Miners were a disciplined team that could fastbreak.

Preceding pages: *Thad Jaracz (55) tries to stop Miner drive.* Below: *Future pro David Lattin snares rebound.* Opposite: *Cliff Berger (45) stops shot from Bobby Joe Hill.*

team, this one, with Pat Riley and Louis Dampier, was quick, shot well, and displayed the exceptional teamwork that Rupp made his trademark. The old Baron of the Bluegrass seemed to have mellowed at age 64, and these were his pets, favorites of all the teams he ever coached; they were playing a big man's game without big men, with flawless execution, desire, and often a bit of guile.

It was the public perception as the championship game neared that this could be Rupp's last try for a fifth collegiate title. (Kentucky had a mandatory age 70 retirement rule.) No actual part of any NCAA contest, sentiment existed to allow the old man "to get one more."

Certainly there was no sentiment in Texas coach Haskins's heart. He noted, "Mr. Rupp is 64 and he made it a lot of times. I'm 36 and it may be a once-in-a-lifetime for me."

Kentucky opened with a zone defense, as expected, and Haskins immediately sprang his first surprise, five-foot six-

inch Willie Worsley at forward instead of six-eight Nevil Shed, in effect using a three-guard offense to counteract Kentucky's speed. Haskins depended on six-seven David Lattin and six-five Harry Flournoy to handle the rebounding, the overall combination allowing his team to control the pace of the game. Texas Western never had to alter the original strategy; the three guards played the entire game.

The contest really turned on a two-play sequence midway through the first half, Texas Western ahead, 10-9. Wildcats guard Tommy Kron dribbled up the court, Hill flashed in, stole the ball and scored easily. Next, Dampier, Kentucky's star, brought the ball to the midcourt line, tried to maneuver around Hill and also got picked. Suddenly the Miners were ahead, 14-9.

Haskins then set his defense to cut off Kentucky center Thad Jaracz, upsetting the timing of the Wildcats' offense to the point where Kentucky became almost impotent. Shots were forced and badly selected. All of this made it shockingly clear to those who had pooh-poohed Texas Western that those guys were quicker and fresher than the Wildcats. Kentucky had struggled to beat number three-ranked Duke in the semifinal game that was supposed to nail down Kentucky's fifth NCAA title, since the Miners weren't to present any problem.

Actual play made it clear that Kentucky couldn't handle the Haskins concept of attacking defense. The Wildcats trailed

34-31 at halftime, having shot a miserable 37 percent. It was no different in the second half, though after seven and a half minutes, Kentucky had managed to scramble to within 47-45 when Texas Western's offense went cold and the squad committed 10 of their total of 12 turnovers.

Kentucky had a golden opportunity—its only real chance—to take control of the game, but it missed on three consecutive trips down the floor, and the Miners finally steadied themselves and began denying Kentucky good shots again.

At this point, the Wildcats, frustration mounting, began

Hard driving coach Don Haskins may have felt privileged to play against Rupp, but was happy to let his co-captains accept the trophy.

to foul to try and gain possession of the ball. But the Miners made 28 of 34 free throws, offsetting a 5-field-goal edge by Kentucky. Rupp's team shot only 13 free throws and sank 11— a great percentage, but so overwhelmed by the Miners' totals as to be of little consequence.

Willie Worsley, Orsten Artis and Bobby Joe Hill built a Miners lead back to 60-51 with 6:54 to play, and Kentucky made another run, behind Larry Conley, and closed the score to 62-56 with 4:27 to play. But that was as close as the Wildcats ever got as the Miners continued to play their controlled game and finally put the game on ice when Lattin scored on a 3-point play for a 71-61 lead with 2:06 to play.

As great as the game was considering the enormity of the upset, it was almost awesome to watch the reactions of Kentucky's followers as Texas Western played their team to an absolute standstill in the 72-65 victory. The mystique that bound them to their team turned to awe as the discipline and athletic skills of their opponents became so overwhelming. Many remarked what a great job Haskins had done "with a bunch of undisciplined kids."

But Haskins was not so inclined because he never considered his players undisciplined. Yet he certainly felt a certain humility at what he achieved that day . . . and against the man who was the target of that achievement.

"I'm just a young punk," Haskins said. "It was a thrill playing against Mr. Rupp, let alone beating him."

One other huge ramification touched the sport of college basketball following Texas Western's upset of Kentucky in the 1966 NCAA finals.

Coach Don Haskins fielded the first all-black starting five in the history of the tournament finals and played against an all-white Kentucky team. The climate of the country at that time underscored the difference, and it soon became an issue.

"I never thought there was anything special starting five black players," said coach Haskins, who is white. "It wasn't the first black team we played with, and it wasn't the first black team in the country. There were others. But after we won the title with five black guys, everybody made a big deal out of it. My philosophy always was to play my best guys."

Haskins said he received thousands of pieces of hate mail, most of it from the South and not all from whites. The blacks who wrote accused him of exploitation.

"There was a time," he said, "when I almost wished we hadn't won."

But there also was a positive effect because Rupp began recruiting black players at Kentucky, and big-time college basketball programs throughout the South soon followed suit.

March 19, 1966, at College Park, Maryland					
Kentucky	FG-FGA	FT-FTA	Reb	PF	Pts
Dampier	7-18	5-5	9	4	19
Kron	3-6	0-0	7	2	6
Conley	4-9	2-2	8	5	10
Riley	8-22	3-4	4	4	19
Jaracz	3-8	1-2	5	5	7
Berger	2-3	0-0	0	0	4
Gamble	0-0	0-0	0	1	0
LeMaster	0-1	0-0	0	1	0
Tallent	0-3	0-0	0	1	0
Totals	27-70	11-13	33	23	65
Texas Western					
Hill	7-17	6-9	3	3	20
Artis	5-13	5-5	8	1	15
Shed	1-1	1-1	3	1	3
Lattin	5-10	6-6	9	4	16
Cager	1-3	6-7	6	3	8
Flournoy	1-1	0-0	2	0	2
Worsley	2-4	4-6	4	0	8
Totals	22-49	28-34	35	12	72

Halftime: Texas Western, 34-31

Officials: Honzo & Jenkins

March 23, 1967

UCLA
vs.
Houston

March 21, 1968

Houston
vs.
UCLA

Houston vs. UCLA

Subtitle: Elvin Hayes vs. Lew Alcindor
  A three-act drama that takes place in Freedom Hall, Louisville, Kentucky, in the spring of 1967; in Houston's Astrodome in January 1968; and in the Los Angeles Sports Arena in the spring of 1968.

Cast of Characters

The Big A—most sought-after high school player in the country.....................................Lew Alcindor
The Big E—All American player and Player of the Year, 1967 ....Elvin Hayes
Coach of UCLA Bruins and Alcindor's coach.....................................John Wooden
Coach of Houston Cougars and Hayes's coach ....Guy V. Lewis
UCLA Supporting Cast ....Mike Warren
Lynn Shackleford
Ken Heitz
Lucius Allen
Jim Nielsen
Mike Lynn
Houston Supporting Cast ....Don Kruse
Don Chaney
Melvin Bell

Act I

Time: March 23, 1967.
Place: Freedom Hall, Louisville, Kentucky.
Setting: Semifinal round of Final Four NCAA Championships, matching UCLA, 28-0, against the University of Houston, 26-3.
Footnotes: UCLA star is Lew Alcindor, the most sought-after high school prospect in history, seven-feet one-inch and still growing, a quick, lithe, graceful athlete who makes basketball seem easy. More than 200 colleges had sought his talents for their basketball program. On May 4, 1965, he decided he would attend UCLA and play for John Wooden.
  Houston has never been to a Final Four until 1967, when junior Elvin Hayes, known as the Big E, has carried the team with his all-around play, abetted by his teammates' superb skills.
Action: The plot of Act I is built around the game plan of

*In the matchup of the '60s, two teams and two men
vied for bragging rights—Houston and UCLA and
Elvin Hayes and Lew Alcindor.*

Houston coach Guy Lewis to take the ball directly at Alcindor, trying to muscle him out of the picture and get him into foul trouble.

For the first eight minutes of the game, the Cougars handle UCLA's defense very tidily, passing over its press and limiting Alcindor to just one basket in taking a 19-18 lead. At that point, Lynn Shackleford (who later would gain national fame as a TV soap opera star) hits a jump shot, and Alcindor gets a slam dunk after the Bruins force a Houston turnover. In a matter of moments, UCLA leads 28-19, and the Cougars never get any closer. UCLA comes away with a relatively easy 73-58 victory. They also go on to win the NCAA title with another easy victory, 79-64 over Dayton.

(As Act One ends, we hear Elvin Hayes talking about his antagonist: "Alcindor's not aggressive enough on the boards, particularly on offense. Defensively he just stands around. He's not, you know, all they really put him up to be." Alcindor finishes with 20 rebounds and 19 points. Hayes has 25 points and 24 rebounds.)

March 23, 1967, at Louisville, Kentucky					
UCLA	FG-FGA	FT-FTA	Reb	PF	Pts
Heitz	0-0	1-1	0	1	1
Shackleford	11-19	0-1	8	1	22
Alcindor	6-11	7-13	20	1	19
Allen	6-15	5-5	9	2	17
Warren	4-10	6-7	9	0	14
Nielsen	0-3	0-0	3	5	0
Sweek	0-4	0-0	1	2	0
Saffer	0-0	0-0	0	0	0
Totals	27-62	19-27	50	12	73
Houston					
Hayes	12-31	1-2	24	4	25
Bell	3-11	4-7	11	4	10
Kruse	2-5	1-1	0	2	5
Grider	2-7	0-0	2	2	4
Chaney	3-11	0-2	4	4	6
Lentz	1-2	0-3	4	1	2
Spain	1-5	0-0	4	2	2
Lewis	0-0	0-1	0	1	0
Lee	2-3	0-0	1	0	4
Totals	26-75	6-16	50	20	58

Halftime: UCLA, 39-28

Act II

Time: January, 1968.

Place: The Astrodome, Houston, Texas.

Background: A regular season game between UCLA and Houston, their first meeting since the NCAA playoffs the previous spring. UCLA has won 47 straight games and is ranked first in the country. Houston has not lost since playing UCLA, a 17-game streak, and Elvin Hayes is the third leading scorer in the nation. Again, he will battle Lew Alcindor, but this time, the UCLA center will play with a scratched left eyeball from a game the previous Friday night that forced him to sit out two games, and he will wear an eyepatch.

The game is set in a carnival atmosphere inside the Astrodome, where 52,693 persons—the most ever to see a basketball game in the United States—have jammed every inch of space; and into the living rooms of 49 states, with 150 television stations carrying the contest to the largest basketball audience in history.

To add intrigue to this plot, Houston coach Guy Lewis panders to superstition. He won't wear his favorite pink-and-white checked sport coat that was part of his wardrobe during the NCAA loss to UCLA; he moves the Cougars bench from the left side of the scorer's table, where it had been all season, to the right side because it had been on the left when the teams met before; and he sees to it that UCLA is brought into the Astrodome through Gate 13!

Action: Lewis, on the more practical side, uses a zone defense against the Uclans throughout the game, but allows the middle man to play man-for-man with Alcindor. It works—aided by Alcindor's still foggy vision. Lew scores on only 4 of 18 shots and is badly outplayed by Hayes, though UCLA's supporting cast is strong enough to keep the game close throughout and set up a rip-roaring finish. It boils down to the fact that UCLA can't handle Hayes, who scores 39 points on a 69 percent shooting night and also takes down 15 rebounds and blocks some key shots.

After Houston leads 46-43 at halftime, the Big E gets the Cougars off in the second half by blocking two shots—one by Alcindor—hitting a jumper and then forcing UCLA to double cover him. But UCLA rallies to tie the game at 54-54 and, at 65-65 with 3:02 to play, Lucius Allen gets a 69-69 tie. With 28 seconds left and the roof about ready to blow off the Astro-

No one had ever played basketball in the Astrodome before UCLA came to Houston to play the University of Houston in America's first indoor sports palace. That meant there had to be some barrier-crashing . . . a lot of it.

For one thing, Judge Roy Hofheinz, the major domo of the Dome who also owned Ringling Bros.-Barnum & Bailey Circus at the time, envisioned not one but three games going on simultaneously on the huge arena floor, not unlike a three-ring circus. Fortunately, those who knew more about the game cooled him down a bit.

Jack O'Connell, vice-president in charge of special events at the Dome, had the task of putting the place in shape for a basketball game. The first thing he needed was a floor, because basketballs don't bounce too well on Astroturf and red clay.

He settled on the floor at the Sports Arena in Los Angeles, which was at no charge. The 225-panel court weighed nearly 18 tons and cost about $10,000 to transport, round trip, by truck. It was jigsaw-puzzled together three nights before the game and tested by Houston coach Guy Lewis, who dribbled a ball over its surface and found no dead spots.

Below: *Alcindor out-rebounds Hayes.* Bottom: *52,693 people—the most ever to see a basketball game—jam the Astrodome.*

dome, Jim Nielsen fouls Hayes—a good-news/bad-news deal in the minds of many Cougars fans because Hayes is not a good foul shooter.

But this is his night, in his town, and before his fans, so he makes both shots for a 71-69 lead. UCLA, hurrying its offense in the last seconds, has a pass picked off. The Cougars immediately give the ball back on a traveling violation, only to get it a second time when UCLA again loses the ball out of bounds.

Coach Lewis orders his team, directing that the in-bounds pass be lobbed high to Hayes, who is to hold it for as long as possible and then dispose of it without making a turnover. Elvin does just that, and when pressed by UCLA, the Big E astounds even his own coach with a marvelous dribbling display that leaves the Bruins grabbing at air, and Houston a 71-69 winner.

Afterward, everyone is unanimous in praise of Hayes, who has totally outplayed Alcindor. Lucius Allen tries for the last line:

"I hope they get into the NCAA, and come to LA unde-feated. That would be nice."

UCLA	FG	FT-FTA	Pts
Allen	10	5-9	25
Warren	5	3-3	13
Shackelford	4	2-2	10
Alcindor	4	7-8	15
Lacey	0	0-0	0
Lynn	2	0-0	4
Nielsen	1	0-0	2
Totals	26	17-22	69
Houston			
Reynolds	5	3-3	13
Chaney	5	1-2	11
Hayes	17	5-9	39
Spain	1	0-0	2
Lee	1	2-4	4
Gribben	1	0-0	2
Lewis	0	0-0	0
Totals	30	11-18	71

Halftime: Houston 46-43.

Act III

Time: March 21, 1968.

Place: The Sports Arena, Los Angeles, California.

Action: Semifinal round of the NCAA Final Four, matching Houston (31-0) against UCLA (28-1).

Scene 1: The workers have just finished laying the basketball court that had been returned to the Sports Arena from the Astrodome after the earlier meeting between the two teams—the same floor on which Houston defeated UCLA 61-59. For all of its opulence, the Dome does not have a basketball court, and the closest portable one is in the LA Sports Arena.

Elvin Hayes already has been chosen Player of the Year in college basketball; in three previous NCAA tourney games, he had averaged 41 points per game. UCLA has not lost since the Houston game.

(Enter stage left, Elvin Hayes.)

Hayes: "This is the rubber match, the game that will decide which team is best. I don't want to hear another word about how Lew Alcindor's eye injury affected his play and cost UCLA the victory. Last year when they beat us in the tournament, I didn't make any excuses. All I said was that he had beaten me, but I wasn't going to believe he was better than me until I had one more look. Well, I had one more look and I won. We won. I guess this will definitely settle it."

During their 71-69 victory at the Astrodome, Houston effectively kept Alcindor from making the big plays.

Scene 2: The UCLA coaches are gathered around a table; the talk is about how to stop the potent Houston offense, Hayes in particular.

Assistant coach Jerry Norman: "Let Lynn Shackleford take Hayes while our other four players play a diamond-shaped zone defense. We'll put guard Mike Warren at the top of the key, Lucius Allen and forward Mike Lynn on the wings and Alcindor under the basket. At the same time, we'll pick up the zone press defense as the game goes on and see if we can create turnovers for easy baskets."

Coach John Wooden: "I like it."

Scene 3: Hayes cannot ditch Shackleford and soon disappears from Houston's offensive schemes. Houston is unable to match some early hot outside shooting by the Bruins, and UCLA bolts to a 21-5 run midway through the first half, finishing the first 20 minutes with a 41-24 lead.

Scene 4: In the second half, the Uclans continue to pour it on, and at one time hold a 44-point lead. At that point, Wooden pulls out his regulars, and the final score becomes 101-69.

Scene 5: (In the Houston dressing room)

Coach Guy Lewis: "That was the greatest exhibition of basketball I've ever seen."

Alcindor has won the bragging rights with a 19-point, 18-rebound performance, while Hayes had only 10 points and 5 rebounds; and UCLA's defense limited Houston to a 28 percent shooting average.

As Scene 5 fades, a solitary UCLA player, Mike Warren, is seen standing by his locker, talking to a writer.

Warren: "We haven't said anything publicly, but we're a vindictive team. We've been looking forward to this game for a long time."

Curtain.

March 21, 1968, at Los Angeles					
Houston	FG-FGA	FT-FTA	Reb	PF	Pts
Lee	2-15	0-0	4	4	4
Hayes	3-10	4-7	5	4	10
Spain	4-12	7-10	13	1	15
Chaney	5-13	5-7	7	2	15
Lewis	2-8	2-2	5	0	6
Hamood	3-5	4-6	0	2	10
Gribben	0-5	0-1	5	1	0
Bell	3-8	3-4	5	0	9
Taylor	0-0	0-0	0	0	0
Cooper	0-2	0-0	1	0	0
Totals	22-78	25-37	45	14	69
UCLA					
Shackleford	6-10	5-5	3	4	17
Lynn	8-10	3-3	8	4	19
Alcindor	7-14	5-6	18	3	19
Warren	7-18	0-0	5	3	14
Allen	9-18	1-2	9	1	19
Nielsen	2-3	0-0	1	4	4
Heitz	3-6	1-1	1	1	7
Sweek	1-1	0-1	0	0	2
Sutherland	0-1	0-0	0	1	0
Saner	0-2	0-0	1	2	0
Totals	43-83	15-18	46	23	101

Halftime: UCLA 53-31

Officials: Honzo & Fouty

20

FRUST-RATION'S END

May 8, 1970

New York
vs.
Los Angeles

May 7, 1972

New York
vs.
Los Angeles

Two teams with brilliant centers and all-star guards began the 1970 season hell-bent on taking the NBA championship.

The New York Knicks had not won an NBA title in the 24 years of their existence. The Los Angeles Lakers had not won an NBA title since moving from Minneapolis after the 1960 season.

Jerry West had been a rookie the first Lakers year in Los Angeles. A decade later he was the Los Angeles shooting star and frustrated. The Lakers had been on the losing side in seven championship games.

West's teammate, Wilt Chamberlain, pro basketball's most dominant player, was almost as frustrated. For all his talent, he had just once won it all, in 1967, when he led Philadelphia to the top. His crown over these long years was more of thorns than of victory jewels, a star who couldn't "win the big one."

Willis Reed was center, captain, and the spiritual leader of the New York Knickerbockers. The team's acknowledged star was guard Walt Frazier. Like West, Frazier was a great shooting guard, a total player who scored, assisted, and played defense. Frazier and West supplied most of the offensive power in the most significant games in their teams' history. Reed and Chamberlain fueled the engine, driving their teams to end years of frustration.

The Knicks gained satisfaction first, winning their championship series against the Lakers. West and Chamberlain waited until 1972. Ironically, when Los Angeles won their championship, the New York Knicks were the victims.

The 1970 finals pitting the Knicks against the Lakers reached its first dramatic turn in game No. 5, the series tied at two games each. Reed drove the lane for a layup, injuring a muscle in his right leg and crashing to the floor, writhing in agony.

"Oh, my God," Knicks forward Dave DeBusschere cried when he saw Reed hit the floor.

His reaction cut two ways—seeing his teammate in pain, and knowing that Reed's injury could doom the Knicks' chances. Reed was carried to the Knicks dressing room, where he listened to the rest of the game on the radio while stretched on a rubbing table. At halftime, it was definite that he couldn't play—not then, probably not in game 6. Game 7, if there was one, was up for grabs. Who could guess whether Reed would make it?

Before going back for the second half of the fifth game, Knicks coach Red Holtzman told his team, "Let's win this for

Jerry Lucas and Dave DeBusschere fight Wilt Chamberlain and Happy Hairston for ball in Laker's overtime victory over Knicks.

Top: *Wilt uses Lucas for support as he scores and is fouled.* Above: *Chamberlain grabs rebound from DeBusschere during fourth game at Garden.*

Willis. He's won plenty for us." And the Knicks did, with as much inspiration as muscle, helped by 19 Lakers turnovers to a gambling New York defense. Los Angeles was held to just 26 shots—from a team with such offensive stars as Chamberlain, West, and Elgin Baylor.

That bought time; Reed accompanied the team to the West Coast for the sixth game and spent nearly all of his waking hours tended to by trainer Danny Whelan. He could only watch from the bench as Chamberlain dominated the Knicks in a 135-113 victory during which Wilt scored 45 points and grabbed 27 rebounds. The script clearly was written for the seventh game with no one able to handle the Lakers with Wilt.

But someone forgot to tell Reed.

He hustled back to New York for more treatments, and three hours before the game, took additional heat therapy and a cortisone shot. His teammates held out little, if any, hope that he could help them in this decisive game.

Shortly after six o'clock, before 19,500 empty seats at Madison Square Garden, Reed walked onto the court, in uniform. He moved deliberately around the court, pumping up some one-handed shots, without jumping or putting undue stress on his injured leg. A solitary figure appeared out of the runway by courtside after Reed had been working for a while—Wilt Chamberlain. He watched without any show of emotion, until Reed passed him and said, "I can't go to my right that well."

A tipoff? Not really. Wilt laughed, because he—and everyone else in the NBA—knew that Reed never had gone to his right very well.

Reed returned to the locker room with the word every Knicks player expected—he would be on the court with them.

"It was like getting your right arm sewed back on," teammate Cazzie Russell said.

When it was time for pregame warmups, every Knick except Reed left the locker room. Willis stayed for a final pain-killing shot. ("The needle was *that* long," teammate Phil Jackson told courtside observers, holding his hands a foot apart.) Ironically, in the Lakers dressing room West already had gotten his shots in each hand, which had been injured during the playoffs.

The Garden was packed with fans unaware of the events of the past 90 minutes. None expected Reed to play; when he walked down the runway and onto the court, a burst of energy sent cheering thousands to their feet in a deafening roar.

"We got a tremendous boost in the locker room knowing Willis would play, but after our warmup period that had pretty much worn off," Bill Bradley, one of the Knicks forwards, recalled. "But when he loped out of the tunnel, and that whole arena just blew up with noise, it energized us all over again."

Reed did some energizing of his own at the start of the game. On the Knicks' first play, about a minute into the game, Reed fired a jump shot from the top of the key. Thirty seconds later, he took another for a second goal. "He ain't hurt," Frazier said to himself, but Reed's physical condition was of less consequence than the confidence he fed his team. Reed didn't score another basket for the rest of the game, but he had lit a fire in the bellies of his teammates and then fanned it on defense as he fought Chamberlain and denied Wilt his usual array of good shooting positions.

Reed did it for 27 of the game's 48 minutes and the Knicks crushed the Lakers with a 113-99 victory for that long-sought title. Reed was named series MVP, but more than anything, it was his gutsy, inspirational play for just those few minutes—and the inspiration that he fired into his teammates in game No. 5—that were his chief contributions.

Such inspirational heroics are not the property of any one player. In 1972 a groundswell of feeling built for West as he neared the end of his career without once knowing the heady feeling of being a member of a world championship team.

Above: *Jerry West takes it in for an easy score. West led his team in scoring during seventh game of 1970 Playoffs. Below: Hairston gets rebound from Barnett, Monroe and Dave DeBusschere.*

Although Coach Bill Sharman had remade the Lakers, West and Chamberlain remained his key players. When the Lakers played the Knicks again for the 1972 championship, it first appeared that New York might repeat its 1970 triumph when game 1 went to the Knicks. Once more injuries played a role, specifically with the Knicks. DeBusschere was so hampered by a pulled muscle in his right side that he put himself on the bench, feeling he was hurting his team. Without their great power forward, the Knicks defense was ineffective and the Lakers quickly ran off three straight victories, returning in high spirits to Los Angeles for game No. 5—and, they hoped, the clincher.

Suddenly, a thunderbolt: Chamberlain sprained his right wrist. When the team reached the West Coast, Dr. Robert Kerlan, the team's physician, announced the sprain was so severe that it was "very, very doubtful" Wilt could play. And there was the spectre of past frustrations against the Celtics

Below left: *Walt "Clyde" Frazier takes behind-the-back dribble against lakers.* Below right: *Jerry West gets ball past Reed to a startled Chamberlain.*

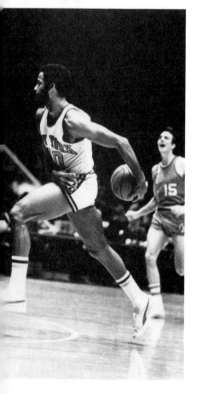

146

West drives the sideline successfully, but is about to run into "The Captain," Willis Reed, who led the Knicks to their first NBA championship in 1970.

and Knicks haunting the team. In 1969 they had loaded thousands of balloons into nets beneath the Forum ceiling to be released the moment the team beat the Celtics in the seventh game, but that never happened. There had been an in-and-out shot for the championship and a final loss. And of course, they had experienced the miracle of Willis Reed just two years ago.

Perhaps the only unconcerned player was West. He had assured his friends early in the series that the Lakers would win in five games. In fact, he admitted losing sleep only over trying to figure out how he should act when he finally won.

Chamberlain got a shot of cortisone in his wrist before the game after a night of hot and cold whirlpool treatments, and had only to prove to Dr. Kerlan that his wrist could handle the pressure of the ball.

"We brought one into the locker room, and as soon as I

saw him palm it, catch it, and throw it, I knew there was enough flexibility that he could play," Dr. Kerlan said.

And how he played!

Wearing a padded handwrap, Wilt scored 24 points and took down 29 rebounds. On defense, he harassed Knicks shooters far outside and still scrambled back inside to block shots near the basket. He forced the Knicks from their driving, pot-shooting inside game to long shots, and New York wasn't up to it.

In fact, no one was up to Wilt Chamberlain in this game. The Lakers led by only 2 points going into the fourth quarter, then Wilt and West triggered a 10-point run that eventually keyed the 114-100 victory.

You could almost see, in the joy and exultation of victory, the years and years of frustration simply float away from the Lakers, even those who had just joined the team as rookies but who, nevertheless, were part of that agonizing losing mystique.

And Jerry West? He smiled an awful lot that night, 12 years worth, in fact.

Top: *Chamberlain and Leroy Ellis sandwich Frazier.* Above: *Frazier, DeBusschere and Hairston watch as ball eludes them.*

New York	FG-FGA	FT-FTA	Reb	Ast	PF	Pts
		May 8, 1970, at New York				
Barnett	9-20	3-3	0	2	4	21
Bowman	3-5	0-1	5	0	5	6
Bradley	8-18	1-1	4	5	3	17
DeBusschere	8-15	2-2	17	1	1	18
Frazier	12-17	12-12	7	19	3	36
Reed	2-5	0-0	3	1	4	4
Riordan	2-3	1-2	2	1	2	5
Russell	1-4	0-0	3	0	0	2
Stallworth	1-5	2-2	2	1	3	4
Totals	46-92	21-23	43	30	25	113
Los Angeles						
Baylor	9-17	1-2	5	1	2	19
Chamberlain	10-16	1-11	24	4	1	21
Egan	0-2	0-0	0	0	2	0
Erickson	5-10	4-6	6	6	3	14
Garrett	3-10	2-2	4	1	4	8
Hairston	2-5	2-2	2	0	1	6
Tresvant	0-4	3-3	2	0	2	3
West	9-19	10-12	6	5	4	28
Totals	38-83	23-38	49	17	19	99

New York	38	31	25	19 -- 113
Los Angeles	24	18	27	30 -- 99

Officials: Rudolph & Powers

Reed had played little since leading the New York Knicks to their 1970 NBA title; his knees were wracked with tendinitis. But he wouldn't quit and battled back not only against the crippling effects of the tendinitis but also against a legion of doubters who had decided he had become a liability to his team.

His coach, Red Holtzman, felt otherwise and patiently—oh, so patiently—he allowed his captain to come back at his own pace, to win a second MVP trophy in the 1973 NBA playoffs.

He could take only one more season of the pain before he retired, the Knicks paying him their ultimate tribute—they retired his jersey, the first so honored in more than a quarter century.

New York	FG-FGA	FT-FTA	Reb	Ast	PF	Pts
		May 7, 1972, at Los Angeles				
Barnett	0-0	0-0	1	1	0	0
Bradley	4-16	4-4	1	2	3	12
DeBusschere	6-15	1-3	14	2	6	13
Frazier	14-24	3-6	6	10	3	31
Jackson	4-6	2-2	3	1	3	10
Lucas	5-14	4-4	9	5	4	14
Mast	0-0	0-0	0	0	0	0
Meminger	2-3	0-0	2	1	3	4
Miles	0-0	0-0	0	0	0	0
Monroe	4-15	8-8	2	3	1	16
Paulk	0-0	0-0	0	0	1	0
Rackley	0-1	0-0	0	0	0	0
Totals	39-94	22-27	38	25	24	100
Los Angeles						
Chamberlain	10-14	4-9	29	4	2	24
Cleamons	1-2	0-0	1	0	0	2
Ellis	0-0	0-0	8	1	1	0
Goodrich	6-18	13-14	4	3	4	25
Hairston	4-8	5-5	14	3	2	13
McMillian	8-15	4-5	3	0	4	20
Riley	2-8	3-4	3	0	3	7
Robinson	0-1	0-0	0	0	0	0
Trapp	0-0	0-0	0	1	0	0
West	10-28	3-5	5	9	3	23
Totals	41-94	32-42	67	21	19	114

New York	24	29	25	22 -- 100
Los Angeles	26	27	30	31 -- 114

21

STREAK MAKERS AND BREAK- ERS

January 26, 1971

Notre Dame
vs.
UCLA

January 28, 1973

UCLA
vs.
Notre Dame

January 19, 1974

Notre Dame
vs.
UCLA

I n 1971 UCLA's basketball team had won 48 consecutive games outside the Pacific-8 Conference and was ranked first in the nation, establishing a new winning streak.

In 1973 UCLA needed one more win to set a collegiate winning streak record of 61 games.

On January 19, 1974, UCLA was establishing a new winning streak that had reached 88 games. By day's end, it was over.

UCLA, the streak team always running up a new consecutive win total, found itself pitted these three times against Notre Dame. The Irish responded by playing at heights normally reserved for the Bruins. The resulting games became moments of very special basketball.

What was it with these two teams, which always seemed to wind up playing each other with national rankings on the line? What was it with Notre Dame, which played the spoiler role so well and against John Wooden, one of basketball's greatest coaches? (Wooden had made his early reputation in nine seasons as the head man at Central High School in South Bend.)

In their six previous games, Notre Dame had won just once, in 1953. When a 208-station television network was strung together for this 1971 Saturday afternoon game, and more than 11,000 persons jammed Notre Dame's Athletic and Convocation Center to watch the Bruins against an Irish team that had won 8 of 12 games and had lost to Duquesne in its last outing, it seemed as though a world championship was on the line.

Anyone watching was justified in considering the Irish the top-ranked team in the nation. Notre Dame never trailed, and the score was tied just once, at 47-47, with nearly 17 minutes to play. In fact, coach Johnny Dee's team once led by 13 points with 5 1/2 minutes to play in the first half.

Now this was no ordinary UCLA team, though the Lew Alcindor era had ended a few years earlier. The Bruins had hardly skipped a beat with the likes of Sidney Wicks, Curtis Rowe, Steve Patterson and Henry Bibby. Notre Dame's best player was Austin Carr. It was Carr, along with the defensive work of Collis Jones, John Pleick and Sid Catlett, that did in this talented UCLA team.

Jones held Wicks without a field goal for the first eight minutes of the game, enabling the Irish to get off flying, sending Wicks to the bench for a few minutes to get his head screwed back on straight. He did, too, returning to lead the Bruins' scorers with 23 points.

That couldn't offset the combined efforts of Notre Dame's

Dwight Clay sinks 1 of his 10 points from long range as Notre Dame upsets UCLA in 1974 at South Bend.

lesser lights. Pleick, for instance, scored 9 points in the first half, 4 over his average, and added 7 rebounds to help Notre Dame control the boards. Catlett played almost the entire second half with 4 fouls, and then took over the boards when Pleick fouled out with 14:20 to play. In all, this tough defensive squad forced UCLA to commit 20 ball-control errors.

But it was Carr who emerged the hero, scoring 46 points, on 17-of-30 field goal attempts and 12-of-16 foul shots. Wooden tried Kenny Booker on him, but that didn't work; UCLA's defense time and again failed to help out. In the second half, it was Carr who helped the Irish break out of the tie. In one 6 1/2-minute stretch, he scored 15 points, and the

Digger Phelps was the thorn in John Wooden's side. Twice his teams stopped a long UCLA winning streak.

Bruins got so frustrated with his drives to the basket, they began to foul him on nearly every play. Result? He wound up scoring his team's final 17 points, single-handedly holding off UCLA's attempts to get back into the game.

Even Wooden gave up. With seven seconds to play, he walked over to the Notre Dame bench and congratulated Dee on his team's 89-82 victory, and then was almost run over as thousands poured from the stands and hoisted Carr to their shoulders and paraded him around like the all-conquering hero. On this day, he was.

On January 28, 1973, two years later, there was a different hero—a grizzly-haired sophomore wearing Bruin blue. In this game, Bill Walton, six-feet eleven-inches, dominated inside play, scored 16 points and set the fempo for a rough-and-tumble 82-63 victory that at one point became so heated that Wooden walked over to the Notre Dame bench and scolded Irish coach Digger Phelps. Wooden was incensed at what he considered overly aggressive play by John Shumate, who was trying to take on the entire UCLA team.

"If it happens again," said Wooden, like a teacher scolding his pupil, "I'll put in someone to take care of Shumate."

He didn't say who, but shortly thereafter Shumate dropped by the UCLA bench and apologized to Wooden. None of this really took away from the fact that the UCLA Bruins had established themselves in the record book with a 61-game winning streak, breaking the mark of 60 set by the University of San Francisco during Bill Russell's era (and 5 games after he left).

UCLA led from the beginning, with the combination of Walton's board play and Keith Wilkes's shooting. Walton and Larry Farmer set the early pace for UCLA with 12 points apiece, and the Bruins led 38-25 at halftime. Wilkes got 6 baskets in the second half to push his team's lead at one point to 61-39.

When the game ended, Wooden admitted that his team had been under extreme pressure as it moved closer and closer to the record. "But," Wooden added, "this really doesn't compare with winning my first national title."

The UCLA record continued to grow through another NCAA championship and on into the 1974 season when, lo and behold, UCLA again found itself at Notre Dame, ranked first and playing an Irish team that was ranked second. Naturally, the Bruins were starkly reminded that it was at this very site three years earlier that they had last been beaten—and that it was here just a year ago that they had established their new winning streak.

Austin Carr is unstoppable as he scores 46 points in 1971 streak-stopper against UCLA at home.

For this game, Phelps took a page from Johnny Dee's book and assigned three of his players—Adrian Dantley, John Shumate, and Gary Brokaw—some heavy defensive responsibility on UCLA's top scorers. Shumate had the biggest job, working on Walton, and when the game came to the showdown late in the second half, Shumate stopped Walton's famed turnaround drop shot by fronting him at the basket and sticking his arms in Walton's face whenever he turned to shoot the ball. Shumate also outrebounded Walton, 11-9.

Dantley, a freshman forward, grabbed 3 rebounds and at one point, so frustrated UCLA's Dave Meyers that the Bruins player growled, "Get off me, fat boy."

All of this was part of a game that swung in mighty surges. Notre Dame got tantalizingly close many times, only to see UCLA rip off a 6- or 8-point surge. Brokaw, who led all scorers with 25 points, including 15 in the second half, and Shumate combined to bring Notre Dame to within 45-43 in the first five minutes of the second half. UCLA then got nine in a row. When the Bruins padded their lead to 70-59, Wooden decided it was time to sit on the ball.

It was a bad decision.

Notre Dame owned the game in the final three and a half minutes, shutting out UCLA and stunning not only the Bruins but also millions around the nation who had tuned in expecting just this kind of theater from the team that had ended UCLA's first winning streak.

Phelps made the first move, pulling forward Bill Paterno and inserting guard Ray Martin, and then ordered his team into a full court press—a weapon that UCLA had used so effectively. But this time, the Bruins got rattled badly, commiting one turnover after another, with baskets by Shumate, Dantley and Brokaw. Shumate got the first two to close the deficit to 7 points, and after Dantley's field goal, Brokaw recovered a Bruins turnover and scored, making it 70-67. A few seconds later, he did it again, and with 1:11 to play, Notre Dame trailed by 1 point.

UCLA turned the ball over with 45 seconds to play on Wilkes's charging foul, but Notre Dame saved its biggest surprise for last in the person of Dwight Clay, a 36 percent shooter, whose last-second shot the previous season had stunned Marquette and ended its streak.

"I wasn't the number one guy on the play," Clay said. "We wanted Shumate and Brokaw to set up a two-on-one situation on one side because they had been so effective. Curtis Rowe began to cheat and help Wilkes stop their action.

"That left me alone in the corner and I waved my hands. Brokaw read it and got me the ball. Rowe tried to recover but couldn't and I just let the ball go.

"I knew it was good as soon as it left my hands. It was just like our practice all over again. We had worked against zones and I had become deadly from that spot."

The ball swished through the net with 29 seconds to play, giving Notre Dame a 71-70 lead. Now it was up to its defense to hold on, withstanding furious action under the basket. Pete Trgovich and Meyers both missed tip-ins before the ball bounced to Walton. Though there still were six seconds to play, Bill rushed his shot and missed—only his second miss of the game—and Shumate snagged the rebound. He dribbled momentarily, then threw the ball toward the ceiling as thousands of Irish fans rushed onto the court, recreating their madcap jubilation of 1971.

January 26, 1971, at South Bend, Indiana

Notre Dame	FG-FGA	FT-FTA	Reb	PF	Pts
Jones	6-19	7-9	14	4	19
Catlett	2-9	0-0	5	4	4
Pleick	3-8	3-3	7	5	9
Carr	17-30	12-16	5	1	46
Meehan	1-3	1-2	1	4	3
Gemmell	3-3	0-1	5	2	6
Regelsen	0-0	0-0	1	0	0
Sinnott	1-1	0-1	0	0	2
Totals	33-73	23-32	38	20	89

UCLA	FG-FGA	FT-FTA	Reb	PF	Pts
Rowe	6-13	4-6	9	4	16
Wicks	8-19	7-10	11	5	23
Patterson	7-11	1-2	10	3	15
Bibby	6-12	4-5	4	4	16
Booker	3-4	0-1	3	3	6
Schofield	0-1	0-0	1	0	0
Ecker	0-0	0-0	0	1	0
Farmer	0-0	0-0	0	0	0
Hollyfield	3-5	0-0	0	1	6
Betchley	0-0	0-0	0	0	0
Hill	0-0	0-0	1	1	0
Totals	33-65	16-24	39	22	82

Halftime: Notre Dame, 43-38

January 28, 1973, at South Bend, Indiana

UCLA	FG-FGA	FT-FTA	Reb	PF	Pts
Wilkes	10-16	0-0	9	1	20
Farmer	8-19	0-1	7	0	16
Walton	8-12	0-0	15	2	16
Lee	2-7	3-3	1	0	7
Hollyfield	4-10	0-0	4	2	8
Trgovich	1-4	1-2	3	0	3
Meyers	3-3	0-0	3	2	6
Webb	0-1	0-0	0	0	0
Nater	1-3	0-0	3	0	2
Carson	1-1	0-0	0	1	2
Franklin	0-0	2-2	0	0	2
Totals	38-76	6-8	45	8	82

Notre Dame	FG-FGA	FT-FTA	Reb	PF	Pts
Shumate	8-20	5-5	12	3	21
Novak	0-4	0-0	1	1	0
Crotty	3-6	1-4	5	1	7
Brokaw	8-18	0-0	6	3	16
Clay	5-17	0-0	3	2	10
Silinksi	2-3	1-1	0	0	5
W. Townsend	1-2	0-0	1	1	2
Stevens	0-2	0-0	0	1	0
Hansen	0-0	0-0	0	1	0
M. Townsend	0-0	0-0	1	0	0
Wolbeck	1-2	0-0	2	0	2
Totals	28-74	7-10	31	13	63

Halftime: UCLA, 38-25

Does John Wooden, now retired, take greater pride in his 10 NCAA championships or in the fact that his teams amassed an astounding winning streak of 88 games?

"I take pride in the 88 straight because it's equivalent to 4 straight undefeated seasons," Wooden said. "But it doesn't rank with 10 national championships, 7 in a row."

January 19, 1974, at South Bend, Indiana

Notre Dame	FG-FGA	FT-FTA	Reb	Ast	PF	Pts
Brokaw	10-16	5-7	3	3	4	25
Clay	2-5	3-4	6	2	3	7
Shumate	11-22	2-4	11	1	1	24
Dantley	4-7	1-1	3	2	3	9
Novak	0-3	0-0	0	2	0	0
Paterno	2-6	0-0	6	1	4	4
Martin	1-3	0-0	2	0	2	2
Totals	30-62	11-16	31	11	17	71
UCLA						
Curtis	3-11	3-4	1	0	3	9
Trgovich	3-5	1-1	0	1	4	7
Walton	12-14	0-0	9	0	3	24
Drollinger	0-0	0-0	0	0	0	0
Meyers	5-10	0-2	7	3	2	10
Wilkes	6-16	6-7	5	7	2	18
Lee	0-0	2-2	0	0	1	2
Johnson	0-0	0-0	0	0	0	0
Totals	29-56	12-16	22	11	15	70

Halftime: UCLA, 43-34

UCLA'S RECORD STREAK

1. UCLA 74, Calif.-Santa Barbara 61
2. UCLA 64, S. California 60
3. UCLA 69, Oregon 68
4. UCLA 67, Oregon St. 65
5. UCLA 94, Oregon St. 64
6. UCLA 74, Oregon 67
7. UCLA 57, Washington St. 53
8. UCLA 71, Washington 69
9. UCLA 103, California 69
10. UCLA 107, Stanford 72
11. UCLA 73, S. California 62
12. UCLA 91, Brigham Young 73
13. UCLA 57, Long Beach St. 55
14. UCLA 68, Kansas 60
15. UCLA 68, Villanova 62
16. UCLA 105, The Citadel 49
17. UCLA 106, Iowa 72
18. UCLA 110, Iowa St. 81
19. UCLA 117, Texas A&M 53
20. UCLA 114, Notre Dame 56
21. UCLA 119, Texas Christian 81
22. UCLA 115, Texas 65
23. UCLA 79, Ohio St. 53
24. UCLA 78, Oregon St. 72
25. UCLA 93, Oregon 68
26. UCLA 111, Stanford 79
27. UCLA 82, California 43
28. UCLA 92, Santa Clara 57
29. UCLA 108, Denver 61
30. UCLA 92, Chicago Loyola 64
31. UCLA 57, Notre Dame 32
32. UCLA 81, S. California 56
33. UCLA 89, Washington St. 58
34. UCLA 109, Washington 70
35. UCLA 100, Washington 83
36. UCLA 85, Washington St. 55
37. UCLA 92, Oregon 70
38. UCLA 91, Oregon St. 72
39. UCLA 85, California 71
40. UCLA 102, Stanford 73
41. UCLA 79, S. California 66
42. UCLA 90, Weber St. 58
43. UCLA 73, Long Beach St. 57
44. UCLA 96, Louisville 77
45. UCLA 81, Florida St. 76
46. UCLA 94, Wisconsin 53

47. UCLA 73, Bradley 38
48. UCLA 81, Pacific 48
49. UCLA 98, Calif.-Santa Barbara 67
50. UCLA 89, Pittsburgh 73
51. UCLA 82, Notre Dame 56
52. UCLA 85, Drake 72
53. UCLA 71, Illinois 64
54. UCLA 64, Oregon 38
55. UCLA 87, Oregon St. 61
56. UCLA 82, Stanford 67
57. UCLA 69, California 50
58. UCLA 92, San Francisco 64
59. UCLA 101, Providence 77
60. UCLA 87, Chicago Loyola 73
61. UCLA 82, Notre Dame 63
62. UCLA 79, S. California 56
63. UCLA 84, Washington St. 50
64. UCLA 76, Washington 67
65. UCLA 93, Washington 62
66. UCLA 96, Washington St. 64
67. UCLA 72, Oregon 61
68. UCLA 73, Oregon St. 67
69. UCLA 90, California 65
70. UCLA 51, Stanford 45
71. UCLA 76, S. California 56
72. UCLA 98, Arizona St. 81
73. UCLA 54, San Francisco 39
74. UCLA 70, Indiana 55
75. UCLA 87, Memphis St. 66
76. UCLA 101, Arkansas 79
77. UCLA 65, Maryland 64
78. UCLA 77, SMU 60
79. UCLA 84, No. Carolina St. 66
80. UCLA 110, Ohio U. 63
81. UCLA 111, St. Bonaventure 59
82. UCLA 86, Wyoming 58
83. UCLA 90, Michigan 70
84. UCLA 100, Washington 48
85. UCLA 55, Washington St. 45
86. UCLA 92, California 56
87. UCLA 66, Stanford 52
88. UCLA 68, Iowa 44

22

THE WIZARD OF WEST- WOOD

March 21, 1964

UCLA
vs.
Duke

March 26, 1973

UCLA
vs.
Memphis State

March 31, 1975

UCLA
vs.
Kentucky

I t is unique in college basketball history, the John Wooden era: 10 national championships in 12 years, 7 in a row with 16 NCAA tournament appearances; 885 victories in 40 years of coaching, 26 of them at UCLA with 620 wins, and 4 perfect seasons.

The "Wizard of Westwood"'s great seasons with the Bruins glittered with talented players like Walt Hazzard, Gail Goodrich, Kareem Abdul-Jabbar (then known as Lew Alcindor), Keith Wilkes, Sidney Wicks, Curtis Rowe, Bill Walton, Henry Bibby, Lynn Shackelford, Dave Meyers, Richard Washington, and Andre McCarter. Talented, say many of Wooden's players, thanks a great deal to his coaching.

"He was such an inspirational person to me and the other players that we loved being around him every day," said Walton, Wooden's three-time All-American center of the seventies, who led the Bruins to a pair of NCAA titles. "One of his key tenets was always making the game fun. Playing for him, basketball never was drudgery."

Wooden may be best remembered during that time for attracting two great centers like Alcindor and Walton and putting a strong supporting cast around them. But the first time he won an NCAA championship, in 1964, he did so with a team that did not lose a game, and did so with the smallest team in the NCAA tournament's history. No player stood over six-feet five-inches.

"That title is much like a first child," Wooden said. "It is very, very special."

Wooden helped make it so by running the zone press defense that he had used to such excellence as a high school coach in South Bend, Indiana. Though John had coached at UCLA since 1949 he didn't even experiment with this beloved concept until the 1964 season when he had a center who was only six-five, and needed something to keep opponents away from the basket.

However he had two superb guards in Walt Hazzard, a creative passer, and Gail Goodrich, a six-one "runt" who, though a marvelous shooter, got his only major college offer from UCLA. Wooden also had a great volleyball player named Keith Erickson, an astonishing leaper and graceful runner who was adept at picking off the long court passes that the trap defense's point men forced opponents, out of desperation, to throw.

"When we do it properly," Wooden said, "our press sets a tempo for the whole game, and when we get the other team falling into our tempo, we have gained a big advantage."

That's how it worked for UCLA in 1964, and for nearly

The ball breaks free from Mike Warren (44) and Don May (21), and heads for Rudy Waterman (22) during 1967 NCAA championship.

every season thereafter. In 1964 Goodrich and Hazzard did the scoring and kept the Bruins in game after game until that point when the press finally ensnared a victim, and then crested an explosion of points that sewed up the victory. That is precisely what happened in the 1964 NCAA title game against Duke. The Blue Devils led 30-27 with 7:14 to play in the first half, but over the next 2 minutes and 14 seconds, Wooden's team ran off 16 straight points for a 43-30 margin as the press forced Duke into 29 turnovers and an eventual 98-83 UCLA victory.

There were some who considered UCLA's 30-0 record in 1964, and its use of the zone press defense to compensate for having an undersized team, to be a one-season phenomenon. But the greatness of Wooden's coaching was his ability to adapt to the conditions at hand and to tailor his talent to deliver the most. He did that the following season, in 1965, and wound up with a second straight NCAA title, beating top-ranked Michigan 91-80, with much the same script as in 1964.

The Wolverines led 20-13 in the first seven minutes, but they too were caught by the press and found it almost impossible to get the ball into UCLA's end of the court as the Bruins took command. UCLA then blew open the game with a 12-1 run in the final four minutes of the half.

In 1969, the final year that Alcindor played for them, Wooden and the Bruins became the first team ever to win three consecutive NCAA titles. The two previous years, UCLA had defeated Dayton and North Carolina, and in 1969 faced a fine Purdue team that featured forward Rick Mount, who averaged more than 30 points a game. Wooden put Ken Heitz on Mount—he had smothered another 30-point scorer, Don May of Dayton, two years earlier, and that had worked fine. Mount scored 28 points but made only 12 of 36 field goal tries, and most of them came in the second half when UCLA had the game in hand. Alcindor, meanwhile, scored 37 points in 36 minutes and added 20 rebounds in an easy 92-72 victory.

Two years—and two NCAA titles—later, the Walton era began. This was primarily a homegrown California team that featured a six-eleven center who had huge hands, a take-charge attitude, and an intrinsic knack to play the game as if it had been invented for him. In 1972 Keith Wilkes, another sophomore, moved in as a forward and classmate Gregg Lee directed the offense, freeing the only returning starter, Henry Bibby, to concentrate on his jump shot.

Again, Wooden did a fine tailoring job, mainly by allow-

Opposite top: *After beating Dayton, UCLA players head for the net*. Opposite bottom: *Alcindor stops Carolina's Larry Miller*. Above: *Alcindor controls ball after Miller's miss. UCLA defeated North Carolina, 78-55.*

Earlier in the 1967 season, Elvin Hayes, the star of the University of Houston's basketball team, was asked by a teammate to be best man at his wedding.

"That doesn't surprise me one bit," said Houston coach Guy Lewis. "He's been my best man for three years."

Coach Wooden plots last-minute strategy against Duke. His teams won 10 national championships. Opposite: *Walt Hazzard.*

What were John Wooden's feelings after he had coached and won his final game at UCLA, a 92-85 victory over Kentucky for the NCAA championship in 1975?

"I suppose anyone would like to go out with a victory," he said matter-of-factly. "The fact that the win was for the national championship doesn't lessen the pleasure."

Nearly an hour after the game, when all of the postgame meetings and interviews were concluded, Wooden walked out of UCLA's locker room for the last time and met his wife Nell.

The two of them looked at each other for a moment, and then embraced.

It was over.

ing Walton to be Walton within guidelines, and when UCLA reached the NCAA finals it had not lost a game. In the first seven minutes against Florida State, UCLA found itself behind by 7 points, its biggest deficit of that season. Minutes later Lawrence McCray, the Seminoles' six-eleven center who was caught in a vise trying to control Walton, went to the bench with three fouls. UCLA broke out and by halftime the Bruins led 50-39, with Walton, Bibby, and Wilkes combining for 43 of the points. The Bruins easily turned back a couple of runs by Florida State in the second half and won the game, 81-76.

There were few around the country in 1973 who believed that UCLA could be stopped, and they were correct as the Bruins ran off their second straight perfect season, including an 87-66 victory over Memphis State for their seventh straight NCAA championship. Wooden proclaimed this team his best ever from a pure production standpoint and moved another coach, Norm Ellenberger of New Mexico, to note, "There are two leagues in college basketball, and one contains only UCLA."

This was when the Bruins were in the midst of setting a record 88-game winning streak, Walton being the dominant force in nearly every victory. And never did he dominate so as during the NCAA title game, making 21 of his 22 field goals and adding 2 free throws for 44 points (in his spare time snapping up 13 rebounds). Memphis State was competitive only when Walton sat down with three fouls in the first half. To that point, his first 22 points had helped UCLA to a 37-30 lead. Walton's bench time helped Memphis State to a misleading 39-39 halftime tie.

The Tigers even went ahead 41-39 in the first minute of the second half, but Walton whipped in three straight baskets and UCLA moved to a 57-47 lead. When Walton sat down with his fourth foul, Memphis State got to within 6 points, but there was too much other firepower on the Bruins to jeopardize the game.

A slight tremor was felt in the basketball world in 1974 when the Bruins and Walton, playing his final NCAA series after having their winning streak ended by Notre Dame earlier that season, were dumped in the semifinals by North Carolina State in double overtime. The next tremor from Westwood was even bigger at the close of the 1975 NCAA semifinal round when, after UCLA had defeated Louisville 75-74 in overtime, Wooden told his team that the championship game two days later would be his last as head coach.

"I'm bowing out," he told his team in the hushed silence

Above: *Bill Walton takes to the air for a layup. His three years at UCLA were called the "Walton Era," in which the Bruins won three titles:* Right: *Walt Hazzard draws a foul.*

of the locker room. "I don't want to, but I have to."

No one really knew what he meant by that, though he had suffered a mild heart attack a couple of years before. He admitted later that the strain of the game had been affecting him. "But," he told everyone who asked, "I don't want to use this to hype up my ballplayers. I don't believe in that."

That season had not been easy for Wooden. He had no overpowering star, but he had a group that he later said "were

a delight because they gave me no problems on or off the court, and I think that, as a team, they came closer to their level of competency than any other team I ever had."

Competency was one thing, but playing against Kentucky, who most felt was the best physical team in the country, was something else. The Wildcats had great depth and had rolled through the playoffs in easy fashion, including a 92-90 upset of previously unbeaten Indiana. "We have great momentum at the present time," said Wildcat Joe B. Hall, who had succeeded Adolph Rupp as head coach. "I don't think Wooden's resignation will have any negative effect on our team psychologically, but what it does to his team, I can't say."

"Good luck, fellows" is all that Wooden said to his team when he sent it out on the court.

UCLA overcame an early Kentucky lead and after eight minutes of the second half had pushed its lead to 66-56 before Kevin Grevey of Kentucky found his scoring touch en route to a game-high 34 points. He scored two 3-point plays and, bit by bit, Kentucky began to chip away until, with seven minutes to play, the Bruins led 76-75.

UCLA's Dave Meyers then went up for a shot with Grevey in his face, and both men hit the floor; referee Hank Nichols charged the UCLA player with an offensive foul—two shots on a one-and-one situation for Grevey. At that moment, Meyers slammed the ball on the floor in frustration, and Nichols tagged him with a technical foul, to be shot after the one-and-one, and automatic possession—all of which added up the opportunity to score at least five points and take a four-point lead.

Kentucky didn't score a point.

Grevey missed the front end of the one-and-one, and then the technical; and Kentucky turned over the ball on the subsequent possession and never got closer than one point for the rest of the game. McCarter's drive put UCLA ahead 90-85 with 40 seconds to play, and Richard Washington, the game's MVP, added a pair of fouls that cemented the 92-85 victory. Wooden had used only six players in that game, and at the end, they bounded off the court, fists thrust victoriously into the air.

Quietly, walking behind them holding the game ball, came John Wooden. His career, and UCLA's basketball dynasty, had ended just as it had begun . . . with a group of overachievers doing all that their bespectacled coach commanded . . . and doing it his way—with excellence.

Alcindor reaps the fruits of his effort against North Carolina—34 points and nine blocked shots.

How hard is it to replace John Wooden and match the championship results that he brought to UCLA?

Between the 1975-76 and 1987-88 seasons, five different coaches led the Bruins basketball team and only one—Larry Brown in 1980—reached the NCAA finals, losing to the University of Louisville.

Each of the five coaches—Gene Bartow, Gary Cunningham, Brown, Larry Farmer, and Walt Hazzard—had winning records in every season, but none of them could withstand the pressure cast from the giant shadow of Wooden.

"Coaches told me it's the toughest job in the country because of the expectations," said Farmer, in agreement.

23

THE
FABU-
LOUS
FIFTH

June 4, 1976

Boston
vs.
Phoenix

The Boston Celtics, on a sultry June night in Boston Garden, defeated the Phoenix Suns 128-126 in three overtimes in the fifth game of the 1976 NBA championships, in a game of action and chills—as well as the bizarre, ridiculous, and unbelievable.

There were game-saving shots and game-tieing shots. There were near winning shots and enough heroes, expected and improbable, to give nearly every participant, including the officials, a piece of the action of what is now dubbed "The Fabulous Fifth."

By now, probably ten times the 15,320 persons who actually attended the game claim to have been at the Garden when everything and anything that could happen during a basketball game actually happened.

The teams had each won the first two games in their own buildings, surprising many who couldn't believe that the Suns had come from last place on February 15 and made it to the NBA finals. The games were rugged, revealing the differences between the free-wheeling style of the blue-collar Celtics and the environment from which they came and the deliberate, often laid-back smoothness of the Sun Belt which Phoenix represented. The media had picked up on the complaints by some Phoenix players about the rugged play of the Celtics and by the Celtics that the officials were over-protecting Phoenix. It became an issue. CBS, which televised the finals, took the controversy a bit further and constructed a story line that had the "poor, underdog" Suns being bullied and harrassed by the mighty Celtics, a David without slingshot facing Goliath.

All of which failed to sit well in Boston, creating a smoldering resentment, fanned by more than a little impatience since the Celtics were having so much trouble dispatching the pesky Suns. Certainly the tension was there at Boston Garden that night. The fans were expecting, indeed demanding, a full-scale blowout in classic Celtics style, and when the game went from that expectation to the spectre of an impending Phoenix upset, patience and tempers, to say nothing of law and order, were in short supply.

Boston roared off to a 22-point lead in the first quarter and slipped slightly to hold a 16-point halftime lead at 61-45. Everything turned around in the second half. Phoenix hit the Celtics with a 19-7 burst that cut the lead to 68-64 late in the third quarter. Boston righted itself, and although the Suns had forced the Celts to give up their devastating fast-break game and work from the outside, Boston never seemed to be in any real danger, particularly when John Havlicek gave his team a 9-point lead with 3:49 left to play.

After the Celtics had beaten the Phoenix Suns in the third overtime of their NBA championship fifth game, Boston forward Paul Silas, who played 44 of the 63 minutes, looked wearily at his tattered sneakers and wondered aloud:

"Can these go one more game?

"Better yet, can I?"

Lewis's team worked out the next night and found that some 300 lights shining down on either end of the court blinded players looking up at the basket to grab a rebound, so they were turned off. Nonetheless, 1,400 lights supplied more than enough illumination—and even more heat—for television and spectator viewing.

Then there was the matter of seats. The nearest ones, plush red and priced at five dollars each, were more than 100 feet from courtside, and none were placed on the stadium's dirt floor. To avoid blocking the spectators' view, seats for press, players, and officials were placed in an 18-inch-deep trench on either side of the court.

Then, of course, there was the trip to the dressing room—a long, long one . . . but when all was in place, the entire event was good old-fashioned American hoopla complete with three bands, two sets of pompon girls, and sundry other mascots and people dressed like mascots to fulfill all of Judge Hofheinz's grandiose carnival ideas.

And certainly the two basketball teams played a game worthy of the fanfare.

Enter Paul Westphal, a Suns guard who had been a No. 1 Celtics draft pick until he was traded for Charlie Scott. In three minutes Westphal zapped 9 of the Suns' next 11 points. Phoenix silenced the raucous Garden crowd when it knotted the score at 94-94 with 39 seconds to play. The silence turned sullen 17 seconds later when Curtis Perry of Phoenix made a free throw to put the Suns ahead 95-94.

Matters, as they often did, fell on Havlicek's shoulders. John had played the series with a broken bone in his foot, and he certainly was no longer the Havlicek of old who barrelled up and down the court, dragging others along with him. No longer so spry, he took the ball with 16 seconds to play and drove toward the basket, forcing Phoenix center Alvin Adams to foul him and foul out of the game. Havlicek, with a chance to win the game, made only one of the two shots for a 95-95 tie. With three seconds to play, he got the ball back, and his shot from the corner bounced off the rim and into the hands of a Phoenix player. The Suns called time out to plot a last shot, which Garfield Heard missed. The stage for the first overtime was set.

Boston had a 4-point lead with 1:58 to play in the first overtime, but Perry sent the game into a second overtime with 4 straight points, and the fans in the Garden grew more restless, with some zealots surrounding TV analyst Rick Barry and beginning a chant of "Barry is a bum! Barry is a bum!" One even threw a soda on Barry, as if Rick were to blame for the quicksand in which the Celtics found themselves.

In the second overtime, the Celtics controlled the action, and had a 109-106 lead with 19 seconds to play before Dick Van Arsdale of the Suns hit his only basket of the game, and Westphal stole the ensuing in-bounds pass and fed it to Perry, giving Phoenix a 110-109 lead with just 5 seconds to play.

Then came Havlicek—again. He had already played 50 minutes on that bad foot, but he took a pass and headed up the court, dogged by Ricky Sobers. Near the sideline, he received a good pick from Don Nelson and banked in a running shot for a 1-point lead . . . and a seeming 1-point victory.

Boston headed for its dressing room, hooting and hollering, and an unruly mob surged onto the court, enveloping everyone, including referee Richie Powers, who was holding two fingers aloft indicating that there were two more seconds in the game. At that point, the ugly side of Boston's fans came to the fore; they assaulted Powers, and any Phoenix players in sight. It took security people nearly ten minutes to clear the floor and get the Celtics back on the court to finish those elusive two seconds.

The Suns, particularly Westphal, were anything but beaten. Coach John MacLeod called a time out, though his team had none and thus incurred a technical foul. It gave him time to plot a final shot, and despite Jo-Jo White making the foul, the Suns were within a tie, or even a win.

The time out allowed Phoenix to put the ball in play at midcourt, and it meant all the difference in the world. "One second is a lot of time," Garfield Heard said later. "I knew I could get a shot off. Don Nelson was overplaying me because he was afraid I was going to the basket."

After taking an in-bounds pass, Heard hit a 20-foot jumper to tie the score again and force a third overtime.

Where the first two overtimes had featured incredible clutch shooting by White and Havlicek of the Celtics, and Sobers, Heard and Westphal of Phoenix, the third overtime featured the lesser-knowns. The toll of this game had been so great that Celtics coach Tom Heinsohn, already afflicted by a stomach virus, required medication from the team doctor to overcome dehydration and was almost useless on the Celtics bench. Assistant John Killelea and GM Red Auerbach assumed some of his duties.

Help also arrived from an unexpected source—litle-used sub Glen McDonald, a No. 1 pick, and reserve center Jim Ard, who had to come into the game when the Celtics lost Paul Silas and Dave Cowans on fouls. McDonald played a superb 64 seconds, scoring two baskets and getting a pair of fouls to give Boston a 126-120 lead with just 36 seconds to play.

As one last gasp to this incredible night, the Suns made a final run—Westphal banking a fallaway jumper from 20 feet and a spinning right-hander in the lane. Perhaps the two most underrated points of the night were a pair of foul shots Ard made between Westphal's two baskets, which represented the final difference in the Celtics' 128-126 victory.

It was left for White, who led all scorers with 35 points, to seal the game by dribbling away the last 12 seconds following Westphal's basket . . . not exactly a thrilling way to end this game considering all the last-second scoring heroics.

At that point, the Celtics would take a win any way they could get it. It was quite a victory. Two days later in Phoenix, the Celtics won the NBA title.

John Havlicek was peppered with questions following the overtime victory, particularly about what it took to make the two clutch baskets that kept Boston from losing in regulation and in the second overtime.

Finally, a bit weary of all the explanations, Havlicek encapsuled what the victory was about, particularly in terms of little-used players Glen McDonald and Jim Ard.

"The rookies, the young players, learn through osmosis," he said. "They look and they absorb. They see what it is like to be part of this team. It's the long, green line, and there is always someone to step in, to take over when necessary."

June 4, 1976, at Boston Garden						
Boston	FG-FGA	FT-FTA	Reb	Ast	PF	Pts
Havlicek	8-19	6-7	5	8	2	22
Silas	8-11	1-1	4	4	6	17
Cowens	9-23	8-11	5	4	6	26
White	15-29	3-4	0	9	2	33
Scott	3-14	0-0	2	3	6	6
McDonald	3-5	2-2	0	3	2	8
Ard	3-6	2-2	1	1	1	8
Kuberski	2-5	0-0	3	0	1	4
Stacom	0-0	0-0	0	0	0	0
Nelson	1-4	2-2	0	1	1	4
Totals	52-116	24-29	20	33	27	128
Phoenix						
Perry	10-20	3-4	15	6	5	23
Heard	8-19	1-2	12	4	1	17
Adams	9-16	2-2	9	5	6	20
Sobers	11-22	3-4	2	6	2	25
Westphal	11-20	3-3	2	2	4	25
Van Arsdale	1-5	3-4	4	1	1	5
Erickson	0-2	0-0	0	1	0	0
Awtrey	2-3	3-3	4	0	6	7
Lumpkin	0-2	0-0	1	4	0	0
Hawthorne	1-3	2-2	4	0	3	4
Totals	53-112	20-24	53	29	28	•126

Boston:	36	25	16	18	6	11	16 -- 128
Phoenix	18	27	27	23	6	11	14 -- 126

Officials: Powers & Murphy

24

A KNIGHT IN HOOSIER-LAND

March 29, 1976

Indiana
vs.
Michigan

March 30, 1981

Indiana
vs.
North Carolina

March 30, 1987

Indiana
vs.
Syracuse

Bobby Knight.

An NCAA basketball championship victory over the University of Michigan that capped an unbeaten season in 1976 . . . a second NCAA title by defeating North Carolina in 1981 . . . and a third national crown with a last-second victory over Syracuse in 1987.

Bobby Knight.

A folding chair hurled across the court in a fit of anger and frustration . . . a smashed telephone on the scorer's table . . . a finger wagged, and red-hot language in the face of one of his players.

Bobby Knight . . . an enigma . . . a superb basketball coach . . . a firm believer in education for his players . . . a hot-tempered perfectionist who drives his players to produce their best, and sometimes even more . . . an occasionally insensitive and immature man whose sporadic outbursts or ill-conceived utterances feed ammunition to his critics and, for a time, dim his achievements as one of the game's greatest coaches.

Take the 1976 NCAA championship game in Philadelphia. The Hoosiers had just missed in 1975 when their unbeaten team was upset 92-90 by Kentucky in the finals of the Midwest Regionals, and in 1976 they came into the final game against Michigan again unbeaten. When top playmaking guard Bobby Wilkerson went out with a concussion in the third minute of the game, the Hoosiers easily could have folded their tent.

Not a Bobby Knight team. He experimented with three different guards in that spot until Jimmy Wisman, who had never played in a tournament game, solved the problem. Wisman was quick and a good ball handler, and his style in the second half forced Michigan coach Johnny Orr to junk his game of switching between zone to man-to-man defense and concentrate solely on man coverage.

Knight's team had plenty of talent in Scott May, Quinn Buckner, and Kent Benson to take advantage of man coverage. Benson worked over freshman center Phil Hubbard and fouled him out, en route to his own 25-point, 9-rebound game, and an MVP award. May did the same with Wayman Britt, and he started the Hoosiers on a victory-clinching point run in the final ten minutes with a tie-breaking jump shot. In quick succession came another field goal, two free throws by Buckner, and another pair by Tom Abernethy. Indiana had a 10-point lead and the game, an eventual 86-68 victory.

"We were a true role-playing team," said May. "When Bobby went out, I had to take up the slack on the boards, and

Junior college transfer Dean Garrett blocks a shot by Syracuse big man Rony Seikaly, as Indiana took their third NCAA championship.

Bobby Knight isn't afraid to call on other athletes and friends to help give his team some psychological boosting.

Take the NCAA title game in New Orleans in 1987.

Knight had a couple of volunteer assistants—former Cincinnati Reds catcher Johnny Bench and Bobby's Ohio State basketball teammate, John Havlicek.

Bench talked to the Hoosiers before their semifinal victory over the University of Nevada-Las Vegas. Havlicek spoke to the Indiana team before its victory over Syracuse, the fourth time he had that job. He's 3-1, but his message is always the same.

"When you come into the locker room after the game," he told the young Hoosier players, "each of you should be able to look in the mirror and not have to say, 'There's something that I could have, or should have, or would have done to better the performance.'"

Bobby Knight couldn't have said it better.

Above: *Keith Smart.* Right: *Bobby Knight with stars of his 1976 team, Scott May and Quinn Buckner.*

Quinn had to take over the floor leadership. Kent had to dominate the boards and give us more chances and give them less. All of us did our jobs because that's how we were coached."

And their feelings for Knight?

"When I hugged him at the end of the game," said Buckner, "I was thinking that after four years of hard work it was coming through for us. All the hard work coming through, and nobody worked harder than he did."

The scene was repeated in Philadelphia five years later, against North Carolina. Indiana never had the lead in the first half until Randy Wittman hit a corner shot as the clock was ticking off the last second, to give Indiana a 27-26 lead. For a time, Knight feared his team would get blown out by a Tar Heels team that included James Worthy and Sam Perkins, but Wittman hit four long-range shots and Landon Turner got three inside to close the gap.

But this also was the Indiana team of Isiah Thomas, the talented sophomore who would turn professional a few days later and in 1988 score an NBA playoff-record 25 points in one quarter for the Detroit Pistons. He flashed into view in such dramatic fashion in the second half that even the Tar Heels were stunned. First, he snapped up a muffed North Carolina

pass and broke away for a layup that gave Indiana a three-point lead. A couple of minutes later, he picked off a pass in the middle of North Carolina's key, put a nifty move on Al Wood and upped the Hoosiers' lead to five points.

"That was the turning point in the game," North Carolina coach Dean Smith said later.

But Thomas wasn't finished. In the first half, he had been almost lethargic, holding the ball at the end of the half until Wittman had to yell for the pass for his last-second shot. But Isiah was wide awake in the second half, and after the two steals, he hit a baseline field goal and then a layup for a 39-30 lead.

That was the game, even with 15 minutes still to play, because North Carolina never got closer than 7 points, and Isiah skipped off with a 23-point game and became the third Hoosier to win the MVP award in the NCAA title game as Indiana romped to a 63-50 victory. It was also the mark of a Knight-coached team that it got better as the season got later and the "money" games came on line, because that Hoosier team defeated five tournament opponents by a combined margin of 113 points, or 23 points per game.

But it was in 1987, when the Hoosiers won their third national championship—second only to Kentucky and

Bobby Knight was not happy when the NCAA Basketball Rules Committee instituted the three-point shot and drew the line on the court to mark the area from which the shot could be taken.

"I got on Ed Steitz [spokesman for the Rules Committee and the colleges' expert on the subject] about the three-point shot the first time I saw him after it was in," Knight said. "He came right back at me.

"'Let me tell you why we did it: So you could use it with [Steve] Alford and win the national title,' he told me long before we ever played Syracuse for the NCAA title.

"So after the game, I looked at the box score. The thing I like least in basketball is the three-point shot. We made three more of them than Syracuse and that was the difference in the game.

"Now when I see him, all I say is, 'Thanks a lot, Ed.'"

Knight and his ubquitous sport coat, celebrate Indiana's 1976 victory. The coach's teams have won three championships.

Nothing is ever simple where Bobby Knight's basketball team is concerned:

• When the Hoosiers defeated Michigan in 1976 for their first NCAA crown, the finalists became the first team ever from the same conference to play each other in the championship game.

• When the Hoosiers defeated North Carolina in 1981 for the NCAA title, their nine losses during the season were the most ever at that time by any champion.

• And in his first-ever NCAA championship game, Knight's team lost to UCLA, which capped a perfect season for coach John Wooden. When Knight won his first title, he too polished off a perfect season.

UCLA—that Knight's real coaching genius came to the fore. In a five-year period the game had changed, both in susbtance and style, and Bobby confounded his critics who called him a moss-bound troglodyte by using those changes to his own advantage.

First, he realized that Indiana's recruiting base, which had been limited to the Midwest, was not producing enough talent to keep his team competitive, so he set aside a personal prejudice and recruited junior college players. Thus, Keith Smart transferred from Garden City (Kansas) Junior College and Dean Garrett from San Franciso City College and blended into Knight's squad of hand-picked recruits.

Secondly, the adoption of the shot clock and three-point field goal forced Knight to abandon his prejudice against zone defense. Those two new elements also worked against his deliberate offense, and he upped his team's on-court tempo. The result was a play for the national championship, coming from 14 down to beat Auburn, from 12 to beat LSU and, finally, from 8 down in the second half to win the championship game.

In the first half against Syracuse, Indiana's brilliant guard, Steve Alford, had kept his team in the game with four 3-point baskets, the last just a second before the end of the half to put Indiana ahead, 34-33. With almost half of the second half gone, Syracuse had gained an 8-point lead, 52-44, when Knight decided to go with a three-guard offense, which had a dual effect.

First, it plugged Smart into the offense, and secondly, it caused Syracuse coach Jim Boeheim to use his best defensive player, Howard Triche, on Alford, a smaller man. Triche helped shut down Alford, but in the meantime, there wasn't anyone able to cope with Smart once he got rolling with about five and a half minutes to play. He scored 12 of Indiana's final 15 points, including the last 6.

The entire game boiled down to the final minute. Triche

put Syracuse ahead 73-70 with 53 seconds to play, but Smart grabbed the rebound of a missed foul shot and drove the length of the court for a layup, closing Indiana's deficit to 1 point. Indiana then fouled Syracuse freshman star Derrick Coleman, and he missed the shot. Incredibly, no Syracuse players contested the rebound, so the Hoosiers had a free ball and quickly called time out with 28 seconds to play.

Smart had so plagued Boeheim that the coach then moved Triche to guard him, but in the other huddle, Knight had plotted for the deciding shot to go to Alford, his proven clutch player. He would be guarded by Sherman Douglas. Knight told his team to work the ball until there were 15 seconds to play because "I wanted a shot, and a crack at it on the backboards if we missed. But I certainly didn't mean for them to take as long as they did to get off the shot."

Stymied trying to get Alford open on the right side of the court, the Hoosiers swung the ball around to the left side, and into Smart's hands. He started a drive that pulled the defense toward him, then dropped a pass in to Daryl Thomas in the low post. Coleman immediately came over to shut down Thomas. Thomas hesitated, then made a head fake to get Coleman off his feet. The freshman didn't bite, so Thomas looked for Smart again.

At this point, more than 60,000 fans in the New Orleans Superdome were on their feet and screaming—and so was Knight and the Indian bench—as the clock hit :09 . . . :08 . . . :07. At the same time, Smart cut toward Thomas, then flared sharply left. Thomas threw him the ball and turned to screen Coleman out of the play, and as the clock turned from :06 to :05, Smart let fly with a soaring jump shot.

It went up and up . . . and then down and cleanly through the net for the game's winning points. It was Thomas's only assist of the game, and when Syracuse, which had just one second to get off the final shot after diddling away time following Smart's basket, tried a court-long pass, it was intercepted—by Smart—and the Hoosiers romped off the floor with a 74-73 victory.

Perhaps Alford, who had played four seasons for Knight plus one with the 1984 U.S. Olympic gold medal winners (Bobby got that one, too), put everything into perspective:

"Coach Knight wants to play that perfect basketball game. He would love to win 100-0. But one of his greatest traits is that he tries to perfect each player's ability and then the team's ability to perform on the basketball court.

"When we beat Syracuse, it was the end result of all that teaching, and of all that perfection."

25

A DOSE OR TWO OF MAGIC

May 16, 1980

Los Angeles
vs.
Philadelphia

*"God and all of His
Apostles could not have
stopped that move."
—Lakers play-by-play
announcer Chick Hearn
after seeing Magic Johnson
sweep in, pirouette 360
degrees and score.*

Magic. Most think of a tall silk hat and a rabbit, but
for basketball fans, say the word and you're talking
about Earvin Johnson, Jr.

Magic fits. When Earvin Johnson, Jr. gets the
ball, there is no telling what he will do with it, or
where it will wind up. Since 1980, he has run the Los Angeles
Lakers offense with a flair and a talent that defies all but the
one description. He is six-feet nine-inches tall, outsized for a
guard in any level of basketball, yet plays in a dimension the
game has never known. He can zoom up the court and fly to
the basket in a straight line, or he can get there via any
number of geometric deviations, such as the one that left
Chick Hearn agape. At other times, he whips passes like
major league pitchers whip fastballs. In game after game, be it
regular season, All-Star or playoff, he performs his magic.

Away from the court, confronted by the public and the
media, he is engaging and charming. He was born to smile,
his face ready to light up a room or sparkle for an interview.
He is always himself, bringing creativity and joy to the game
and to those around him.

Rarely has a basketball player been ticketed for stardom
so long before he ever stepped onto an NBA court. From the
moment Earvin Johnson came out of high school to play at
Michigan State, it was obvious a new quality had entered the
game of basketball. As sophomore, he led the Spartans to the
1979 NCAA title. In his first season in the NBA he helped
lead the Lakers to the world championship.

It was that season—and the final game of the playoff
finals against the Philadelphia 76ers—that enshrined Johnson's persona into the sport for all time.

In 1980, Magic's rookie year, Kareem Abdul-Jabbar, main
man for the Lakers, ruled pro basketball. Johnson easily eased
his talents into that team as he went about learning the
nuances of the pro sport. He'd had only two years of collegiate
experience to give him guidance.

"I think Magic rejuvenated Kareem," Denver coach
Doug Moe said. "It appeared to me that Kareem loafed a lot,

*Magic Johnson (32) tries to drive by Michael Jordan as
the pair of MVP candidates battle during the 1987 All-
Star game at the Kingdome.*

had just about had it with the game. After Magic got there, he started playing a lot harder. I'm sure part of it was the basketball skills Magic brought. Then too, he made the game fun with his personality."

Kareem says, "All he wanted to do was get the ball to somebody else for the score. If you're a big man, it's not hard to like somebody like that."

It also wasn't hard to like a rookie who could step in when Jabbar went down with a serious ankle injury in the fifth game of the final series and carry his team to the championship.

Jabbar had been having a spectacular series, averaging more than 33 points and nearly 14 rebounds a game before he suffered a seriously sprained ankle in the Lakers' 108-103 victory at The Forum. Doctors ruled him out of Game No. 6 in Philadelphia and made no promises about Game No. 7, if that had to be played in Los Angeles.

Lakers coach Paul Westhead decided to put Johnson at the center position, at least for the tip-off, and then use what

Jabbar gets off pass while guarded by Dawkins and Julius Erving. The Laker center was rejuvenated when Magic joined the team.

Seldom has any athlete achieved the heights that Magic Johnson has.

In 1977 he led his high school team in Lansing, Michigan, to the state championship. In 1979 he led Michigan State to the NCAA championship. In 1980 he led the Los Angeles Lakers to the clinching victory in the NBA championship series.

"When you're young, you dream of getting all the championships, high school, college and pro. But when they become reality, that's something else.

"You think, 'You gotta wake up tomorrow.' I dreamed it, and it came true."

Jabbar and Magic form a bridge trying to cover Caldwell Jones during the 1980 NBA Championship Game.

amounted to three forwards in lieu of the dominant big man.

"We made the decision, and then we wanted Philadelphia to get the message," Westhead said. "We told the Spectrum's PA announcer, Dave Zinkoff, to be sure to introduce Magic as the center. But just before we went out there, Jim Chones came up to me and said, 'Coach, let me jump center. I can get the tap.' I said, 'Jim, I guess you just don't get it.'"

Everyone thought that Westhead and the Lakers were crazy to use a rookie—even a six-nine rookie—at center against seven-one Caldwell Jones, and even Magic was a bit mystified. He hadn't played the position since his senior year in high school.

"I didn't know whether to stand with my right foot forward, or with my left one forward," he recalled. "I looked at Caldwell and thought, 'He's got arms that make him around nine-five,' so I just decided to jump up and down quick."

Above left: *Jabbar takes rare jump shot as Bucks center.* Above right: *Magic looks for an outlet against Dawkins and Erving. Johnson scored 42 points in deciding game against Sixers in the finals.*

Earvin Johnson Jr. got his nickname, Magic, while he was playing at Everett High School in Lansing, Michigan.

When his mother, Christine Johnson, a devout Seventh Day Adventist, first heard her son referred to as Magic, she considered it blasphemy. She was also the first to consider the practical consequences.

"When you say 'Magic,' people expect so much," she said. "I was afraid that it would give him a lot to live up to."

Even Mrs. Johnson has to admit her son has done a pretty good job of it.

May 16, 1980, at Philadelphia					
Los Angeles	FG-FGA	FT-FTA	Reb	Ast	Pts
Chones	5-9	1-1	10	3	11
Wilkes	16-30	5-5	10	2	37
Johnson	14-23	14-14	15	7	42
Nixon	1-10	2-2	3	9	4
Cooper	4-9	8-9	4	6	16
Landsberger	2-7	1-2	10	0	5
Holland	3-4	2-2	0	0	8
Byrnes	0-0	0-0	0	0	0
Totals	45-92	33-35	52	27	123
Philadelphia					
Erving	13-23	1-4	7	3	27
C. Jones	2-3	2-2	6	2	6
Dawkins	6-9	2-5	4	1	14
Hollins	5-13	3-4	1	6	13
Cheeks	5-11	3-3	2	8	13
B. Jones	4-8	0-0	9	1	8
Bibby	4-10	0-2	3	3	8
Mix	8-11	2-2	4	2	18
Sparnakle	0-0	0-0	0	1	0
Toone	0-0	0-0	0	0	0
Richardson	0-1	0-0	0	0	0
Totals	47-89	13-22	36	27	107

Los Angeles:	32	28	33	30 -- 123	
Philadelphia:	29	31	23	24 -- 107	

He did just that. The Lakers sped to a 7-0 lead, Johnson taking command. First, he fed Michael Cooper from the high post for a field goal. On defense, he snapped off a rebound playing down low and dribbled the length of the court for another field goal and an 11-4 lead. Next, he drove by another famous moniker—Dr. J, Julius Erving—and banked home 2 more points. On the Lakers' next possession, he started a power move to the hoop, only to be confronted by another giant, Daryl Dawkins.

"That time, I wanted to dunk it, like Kareem," he recalled, "but I saw Dawkins coming and I thought, 'Better change to something a little more . . . uh . . . magical.'"

So he bought some hang time, double pumped, made the shot and was fouled. On completion of the 3-point play, the Lakers were ahead 16-4, and Johnson had stamped himself firmly into the game. He scored 13 points in those first 12 minutes. It just got better after that as he responded to the challenge, mesmerizing everyone.

"With no Kareem, I had the green light, and without having to think first about feeding him, I was a little more free to do my thing," he said.

That included, before the game was over, playing every position—center, strong forward, small forward and both guard spots, the latter made a necessity because Norm Nixon badly smashed his hand and could not shoot. Magic had 7 assists and sealed the Sixers' doom in the final two-and-a-half minutes by stealing the ball and setting up a 3-point play.

After the Sixers had closed to within 103-101, it was Magic Johnson who did the heavy preliminary work before Nixon's final nail driver, and he did it in the final five minutes. The Lakers took down a missed rebound by Philly's Bobby Jones and lit out on their patented fast break. Steve Mix blocked the shot with a fine defensive play but Magic was there to put in the rebound, and that sent LA on a 10-point run. Six were successive 3-point plays by Jamaal Wilkes, who teamed with Johnson to score between them 79 points, grab 25 rebounds and add 9 assists for a 111-103 lead with 2:27 to play.

In the Lakers 123-107 victory, Magic scored a then career-high 42 points and had 15 rebounds and 7 assists, after which he noted, "Everybody thought we were going to come in here and fold without Kareem. But I love being the underdog, and I thrive on pressure. We fooled all of you.

"And," he added, flashing that magical smile, "I loved every minute of it."

When the chartered Greyhound bus carrying the Los Angeles Lakers pulled away from Philadelphia's Spectrum after they had won the NBA title in the sixth game of the 1980 playoff finals, their irrepressible star, Magic Johnson, slipped back into the ongoing disc jockey role that had helped keep his team loose that season.

"This is E.J. the D.J. coming to you over Greyhound Radio and telling you that playing with the Los Angeles Lakers has been a tremendous thrill for this 20-year-old veteran."

Veteran, indeed!

26

THE UPSET

December 23, 1982

Chaminade
vs.
Virginia

While everyone knows an upset when they see it, not everyone will agree on what constitutes "the biggest" upset. Some will argue, for example, that for a truly great upset a championship must be at stake, or a gold medal. But our choice involves a "meaningless" regular-season game when nothing more was at stake than pride and reputation.

The game was supposed to have been more of a toning-up exercise during a vacation swing for the Virginia Cavaliers, ranked number one in the nation, en route home from a tournament in Japan. Virginia was not scheduled to play again until early in the following month, so why not schedule a tune-up against a local team during a four-day layover in Hawaii? How about Chaminade, a 1,000-student NAIA school with a good local following? Stay sharp and impress prospective collegians with the benefits of enrolling at the famous East Coast institution. And so, on December 23, 1982, the mighty Cavaliers of Virginia agreed to play the Silver Swords of Chaminade in Honolulu.

Certainly the ingredients for an upset were present. Virginia was still basking from their defeat of Georgetown, 68-63, earlier in December, in one of those "games of the century," when center Ralph Sampson outdueled Patrick Ewing. The players had traversed the Pacific twice in a week and were looking forward to reuniting with their families for the holidays. Two previous games against Chaminade had produced solid Virginia victories. And a touch of the flu sapped some of Sampson's strength. The signs were there all right—overconfidence, lack of concentration, a tiring schedule, and a touch of illness. Still . . .

Chaminade, of course, was delighted to be playing the nation's top-ranked basketball team. It harbored no serious illusions about an upset, and the team's coach, Merv Lopes, admitted afterward that on the morning of the game he would have been reasonably satisfied if his team stayed within 20 points.

However, Lopes's team was by no means a sacrificial lamb for improving statistics and solidifying rankings. The Silver Swords were ranked fourth in the NAIA poll with a 9-2 record and the week before had upset the University of Hawaii—that by itself made the season a success—and Seattle University, both Division I schools. They did, however, lose to Wayland Baptist two days before playing Virginia, apparently caught in their own little snare of too much celebrating for the first-ever win against the Rainbows and looking ahead to the top-ranked Cavaliers.

Chaminade's Tony Randolph, a high school rival of Ralph Sampson, held the All-American center to 12 points to help the Silverswords to the upset.

The Christmas season is supposed to be a time of good will toward all . . . and well it may be in Hawaii, except when opposing college basketball teams come in to play a holiday game against Chaminade University.

The Swords defeated top-ranked Virginia in 1962.

In 1983 Louisville's top-ten-ranked Cardinals came over for some fun in the sun and were upset.

In 1985 as the host team in its Chaminade Classic Tournament, the Swords upset Louisville again in the first round and then knocked off unbeaten Southern Methodist in the championship game, on Christmas Day. Each win came on last-second baskets.

How's that for a lump of coal in your stocking?

Sampson, slowed a bit by flu, tries to keep pace with Chaminade guard Mark Wells.

The Chaminade basketball program was only seven years old. The team even was second choice in its own gym, St. Louis High School using the facility in the afternoon and the collegians having to practice at night. Lopes was a full-time counseler at Kalakaua Intermediate School and coached Chaminade as much for the love of the game as for any other rewards, but he did well enough to have a 118-37 record at that time.

Lopes's style of coaching may have seemed antithetical to the laid-back atmosphere of Hawaii, but it was successful. He demanded a tenacious approach to the game and put great stress on defense. He loudly upbraided his charges during practice, and his players were not above screaming back when they had had enough. But the end result was a bond of mental toughness that could carry the team through an intense game.

Before this contest Lopes went out of his way to convince his players of their parity with Virginia's depth, size and skill. "What's the difference between 10 [Chaminade's Mark Wells] and 11 [Virginia's Odell Wilson], or 44 [Tony Randolph] and 50 [Sampson]?" he asked them. "Who's to say what you can do against them?"

Actually, the difference between Randolph and Sampson was nearly a foot, but Randolph had played against Sampson four times in high school and countless other times on the playgrounds. He even had dated Sampson's sister.

"He's bigger than you are by almost a foot," Lopes told Randolph, "but you can beat him with your brain. You have more speed, and just as much ability. Use it."

Just before his team took the floor, Lopes told them:

"You have nothing to lose, so just go out there and play. It's an honor to be able to play a team like Virginia, but let's be sure we make them believe that we aren't just showing up to be beaten."

Taking their coach's words to heart, Chaminade raced to a 7-0 lead and led the favored Cavaliers for the first ten minutes of the game. Virginia surged ahead by 3 points before Chaminade pulled into a 43-43 halftime tie—a lot of points by such a small team.

Richard Haenisch sits atop the rim as he expressed his feelings after his team played in perhaps the biggest upset of all time.

Lopes walked off the court thinking, "Well, if we lose by just 10 points instead of 20 we'll have played a great game."

His players were almost as unbelieving, and one of them said, "Hey, coach, let's go to the hospital and say we're sick, and we'll call the game a tie."

But Lopes knew his strategy of jamming the middle against Sampson had its desired effect, and Randolph set himself up outside where his quickness worked better—in fact, his variety of long jumpers would net a 19-point game. "He was letting me have that shot, and I was content to stay out there because I knew I couldn't handle him inside," Randolph said.

"Tony wasn't the least bit intimidated by him," said teammate Richard Haenisch. "He stayed with him like a dog."

In the second half, the game was tied eight times before the Cavaliers pulled away to a 56-49 lead with 11 minutes to play. But Chaminade remained unfazed and scored the next 7 points to tie the game.

"A lot of teams might have been happy playing one good half against Virginia," noted Chaminade assistant coach Pete Smith, "but as the game went on and we stayed with them, that didn't mean anything to us. We wanted to take 'em down to the wire, and then beat them if we could."

With 1 minute and 37 seconds to play, Chaminade opened a 70-68 lead, thanks to the free shooting of Wells and Jim Dunham. Still, Virginia had an opportunity to tie or win

the game in the final 10 seconds, but Wilson was called for travelling. Virginia then fouled to try to regain possession, but Chaminade made its last three foul tries to clinch the victory.

Of course, the 3,400 spectators at the Neal Blaisdell Center Arena went bonkers, and Lopes probably wasn't too far wrong when he breathlessly called the victory "the greatest upset in college basketball history. Not too many people get to beat the number one team in the nation. What we did was amazing."

He added, almost as an afterthought, "I was just trying to give these people a good game."

Chaminade University's basketball team is nicknamed the Silver Swords, which is a very rare plant found only in the volcanic craters of Hawaii.

The plant blooms only once every several years . . . and 1982, the year in which the team upset top-ranked Virginia, was one of those years.

How appropriate!

December 23, 1982, at Honolulu			
Chaminade	FG-FGA	FT-FTA	Pts
Wells	2-8	3-8	7
Rodrigues	3-5	1-1	7
Smith	0-0	0-0	0
Dunham	5-15	7-8	17
Strickland	1-3	3-4	5
Pettway	4-7	5-8	13
Haenisch	4-7	1-2	9
Randolph	9-12	1-2	19
Totals	28-57	21-33	77
Virginia			
Miller	3-8	0-0	6
Robinson	4-6	2-3	10
Wilson	6-14	3-8	15
Stokes	2-5	4-4	8
Edelin	1-2	0-0	2
Carlisle	7-21	1-2	15
Mullen	2-8	0-0	4
Sampson	4-9	4-7	12
Totals	29-73	14-24	72
Halftime: Chaminade 43, Virginia 43			

The Silverswords of Chaminade, upset winners over Virginia in 1982. Earlier that season they defeated Hawaii, their bitter cross-state rivals.

27

GIVE THE DOCTOR A RING

May 31, 1983

Philadelphia
vs.
Los Angeles

The ring is the thing.

It certainly was to Julius Erving. He had nearly everything during his career in pro basketball: popularity without compare, a salary to match, adulation and attention for his swooping moves to the basket that made him one of the game's most popular players. He lacked only the one reward he wanted most, the ring.

Yes, he had won a championship ring when he led the New Jersey Nets to an American Basketball Association title before that league merged with the NBA in 1976, but it was the NBA championship ring that players coveted. And when his Philadelphia 76ers, whom he joined in 1977, lost in three NBA finals and in two other Eastern Conference finals in a six-year span, it became almost a crusade for Erving and his team to win one just so he could get "the ring."

When it finally happened in 1983, after the 76ers swept the Los Angeles Lakers in four games, there was a sense of universal joy.

Why would there be such all-out concern for one player who certainly had more than enough opportunity for that one great reward?

As the chancellor of the University of Massachusetts noted when, a few years ago, he draped the hood of honorary doctor of humanities around the shoulders of one of his school's most distinguished alumni, it was the man on and off the court, and what he brought to the game of basketball, that made setting the ring so important.

Years before, the ABA, and then the NBA, had bestowed its own title of "doctor" on Julius Erving by signalling that for all time Julius Erving would be known as Dr. J, as in Dr. J making one of his patented "house calls" with graceful leaping or flying trips to the basket as he performed airborne basketball acrobatics never seen before in the sport.

It was not that the game had never had acrobatic scorers. Elgin Baylor of the Lakers, for example, seemed to move six ways at once when he had the basketball. But no one in sneakers and shorts could fly without wings as Erving did during his 17-season pro career. He was a consummate entertainer, combining ballet and high-wire trapeze with dribbling and shooting, bringing a new dimension to the game that has since been carried on by Michael Jordan of the Chicago Bulls and Dominique Wilkens of the Atlanta Hawks.

While his presence on the court was overpowering, he was not a physically intimidating player at six-feet six-inches and a lean 210 pounds. Even in the ABA, which did not have a great number of physical players, he quickly learned that it

An older Dr. J is just quick enough to get the ball by a younger Magic Johnson during 1983 playoff action.

was better to fly over than try to drive through, and he began developing the creative moves that inspired his notoriety. When he retired in 1987, he was only the third player in pro basketball history to score more than 30,000 points (including 11,662 during his ABA seasons), and he was most valuable player in both leagues four times.

Throughout Erving's career, fans went to see Dr. J to glean that one unforgettable moment, and he always seemed to offer it. But he also offered just as much away from basketball and made his life as multidimensional as his game with a series of corporations, some 200 personal appearances a year and myriad charitable ventures. A day after skying the basketball at the Spectrum and scoring 30 points, he narrated *Peter and the Wolf* with a youth orchestra at the Philadelphia Zoo. He lofted a 20-foot jump shot with the same ease with which he read portions of the Declaration of Independence at Philadelphia's Independence Day celebration. He also filled the lane on fast breaks with the same compatibility with which he

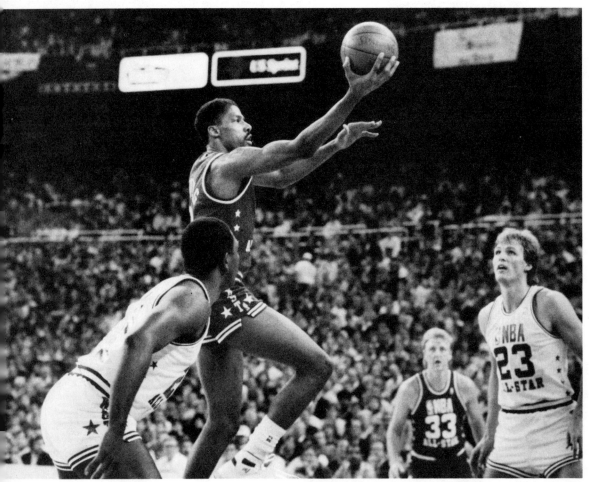

Top and above: *The hair shortened as The Doctor aged.*
Opposite: *The ABA's best player was sold to the 76ers to help pay the New York team's debts.*

During Julius Erving's final NBA season in 1977, he was showered with appreciation by fans throughout the NBA. Ever appreciative, he noted: "It allowed me to spend time with people I might not see again."

It also enabled him to take home some interesting mementos from those stops. Here are a few examples:

Boston: A piece of the Boston Garden's famed parquet basketball floor.

Los Angeles: A rocking chair and a TV set were presented by Kareem Abdul-Jabbar on behalf of his teammates, and Erving made Kareem sit in the chair during his thank-you remarks.

Golden State (San Francisco/Oakland): What else? Six cases of California wine and a silver-plated wine bucket.

Indiana: This original ABA franchise gave him a red, white and blue ABA basketball listing all of his accomplishments.

New York: Two giant aspirins symbolizing all of the headaches Erving caused them.

Erving soars over all players on way to scoring 30 points and winning MVP in the 1977 All-Star game in Milwaukee.

In stints with two leagues, Erving scored over 30,000 points and garnered four MVP awards.

once filled a charity's coffers by waiting on tables at a busy pub.

Perhaps his most enduring quality was that he really became famous with what are popularly considered to be "hot dog plays," somehow never triggering the animosity of rival fans when he did them in their building. He was not brushed off as a fluke or treated as a sideshow freak.

"I never was booed, even in Boston or Los Angeles," he said, leaving one to acknowledge that it is almost inconceivable that he could be so good and be so popular.

Which, in all likelihood, explains why so many were rooting for him to get his ring. Actually, it was Erving himself who helped lay the groundwork for that moment when, during an All-Star summer exhibition tour of Europe, he and Moses Malone, then of the Houston Rockets, struck up a friendship. Erving made it clear to Malone that he certainly would be welcome in Philadelphia if he ever decided to change teams (Moses had just led the Rockets into the NBA finals that spring) and that the two of them would make quite a tandem.

Two years later it happened, and Moses led the 76ers to their Promised Land of the NBA finals with his promise of "Fo-Fo-Fo" (a four-game sweep in each of the playoff rounds, though it was five in the middle set). Philadelphia played the Lakers in the finals, and in the first three games, Erving and Malone led their team to come-from-behind victories.

On the last night of May in 1983, the Sixers were poised

to grab that long-sought title in the series' fourth game at The Forum. As in the other three games, the Lakers took command in the first half, holding a 14-point lead at halftime.

The Sixers got it down to 11 going into the last quarter when Malone and Erving took over, with Dr. J finally putting his team ahead 108-107 with just 59 seconds to play. Erving's free throw made it 109-107, but Kareem Abdul-Jabbar hit a foul shot with 42 seconds to play.

Being this close to that long-sought ring, Erving took matters into his own hands as he seemed to have done throughout the series when it came time to win a game. In fact, Jack Ramsay, then coaching Portland, recalled a play in the LA series where Erving moved along the baseline, took off on one side of the rim, floated underneath and laid the ball in on the other side.

Now with half a minute to play and everything on the line, Erving got the ball 18 feet from the basket and cooly canned a jump shot that soared so majestically it seemed like his personal signature to all that he ever achieved. "That shot found me and I just let it fly," he said after his team's 115-108 victory.

He also found his NBA championship ring. And he's got one more coming— on the day that he is inducted into the Basketball Hall of Fame.

It will be his last "house call."

May 31, 1983, at Los Angeles					
Philadelphia	FG-FGA	FT-FTA	Reb	Ast	Pts
Erving	8-13	5-5	5	6	21
Iavaroni	2-8	0-2	3	2	4
Malone	9-22	6-9	23	1	24
Cheeks	7-10	6-8	1	7	20
Toney	6-10	11-12	2	9	23
O. Johnson	2-3	0-0	2	0	4
Richardson	2-8	2-2	2	2	6
B. Jones	6-7	1-2	3	2	13
Totals	42-81	31-40	41	29	115
Los Angeles					
Rambis	3-9	1-2	5	2	7
Wilkes	9-20	3-5	5	1	21
Abdul-Jabbar	10-15	8-10	7	3	28
Cooper	5-11	2-2	3	4	13
E. Johnson	8-21	11-12	7	13	27
McGee	3-9	0-0	7	1	6
Landesburg	2-2	0-0	7	2	4
D. Jones	1-5	0-0	2	0	2
Totals	41-92	25-31	43	26	108

Three-point field goal: Cooper

Philadelphia:	24	27	31	33 --115
Los Angeles:	26	39	28	15 --108

28

IN YOUR FACE, PHI SLAMA JAMA

April 4, 1983

North Carolina State
vs.
Houston

The entire nation was invited to view a fun-filled party, the Phi Slamma Jammas from the University of Houston entertaining a bunch of kids from North Carolina State in Albuquerque, New Mexico, a romp all the way.

That's how the invitations read. The "frat" guys from Houston were a high-jumping, leaping band of collegians who firmly believed that the team that dunked the basketball the most times in a game came away as the winner. No one in the country dunked the ball more, or better, than the Phi Slamma Jammas did during the 1983 season.

The name, Phi Slamma Jamma, invented by a clever sportswriter looking for a tag, was eagerly accepted by coach Guy Lewis's team as the perfect monicker to describe their high-flying routines.

The party givers, however, had overlooked Jim Valvano and his North Carolina State team, who found their fun living on the edge, known as the Cardiac Pack because so many of their victories and a few of their ten losses had been down-to-the-wire thrillers. Three of these came in the NCAA playoffs—one a double overtime, 2-point victory over Pepperdine, and a pair of 1-point wins over Nevada-Las Vegas and Virginia.

Houston was the top-ranked team in the country, North Carolina State just another team from the Atlantic Coast Conference, which had somehow battled its way into the Final Four. They were expected only to play the foil as either Houston or Louisville romped to the NCAA title. The latter two teams played each other in the first semifinal game—an ideal matchup of the top two teams in the country that were supposed to pay their dues in that game, with one collecting its reward in the finals.

Houston put on a great closing finish to win its semi, 22 of its second half points coming from a vast array of dunk shots. The Cougars certainly were fun to watch. A high vertical spring would block an opposing shot, and a race to the other end would polish off the rejection with, what else, a dunk.

In answer to all this, Valvano, whose team defeated Georgia in the other semifinal round, quietly assessed the game and noted, "We'll try to handle their team by playing, shall I say, a slower tempo. If we get the opening tip, we may not take a shot until Tuesday morning."

Valvano, also known for his sense of humor, signaled Thurl Bailey of N.C. State to score the game's first basket with a dunk.

Valvano had constructed his defense to limit Houston's

Larry Micheaux, left, fights with N.C. State's Cozell McQueen during "in your face" basketball at Albuquerque in 1983.

Houston coach Guy
Lewis was a firm advocate of
his team's Phi Slamma Jamma
routine, and before the Cougars played North Carolina
State for the NCAA title, he
noted:

"The team with the most
dunks wins the game. That's
our slogan."

He was absolutely cor-
rect.

N.C. State had two
dunks—its first and last baskets of the game—and
Houston had only one.

fast-breaking opportunities by falling back quickly, then packing its zone around the basket, forcing Houston's players to zig
and zag when trying to dunk. The strategy worked so well it
wasn't until five minutes remained in the first half that Akeem
Olajuwon, perhaps the most intimidating player in college
ball, got Houston's first—and last—dunk shot. The Cougars
were forced instead to settle for short jump shots that resulted
in a meager 31 percent shooting mark.

Bailey, on the other hand, was the only offensive weapon
working for Valvano. His team had lived by long shots during
the season as part of an ACC experiment with the 3-point
shot, but it wasn't happening for them now. Instead, Bailey
roamed the baseline at will and scored 11 of his 15 first-half
points during a 19-10 stretch that helped the Wolfpack to a
33-25 lead.

That wasn't the only bit of bad news for Houston. Clyde
Drexler, the jamminest of the Phi Slamma crew, had accumulated four fouls in the first twenty minutes, somehow being

Opposite right: *Olajuwon outmuscles McQueen for rebound.* Opposite left: *Whittenburg takes shot that missed, but . . .* Above: *Charles dunked the rebound for State win.*

allowed to stay in the game after getting No. 3 with less than eight minutes played. He was finally pulled five minutes later, then sent back in with less than two minutes left, and got No. 4.

Lewis kept him on the bench, along with Larry Micheaux, the other starting forward, as the second half began, yet such was the team's depth and talent that they went on a 17-2 binge in the first ten minutes and romped to a 42-35 lead.

North Carolina State clearly was dazed and more than a bit disorganized—just primed for the deadly Phi Slamma Jammas' full routine when, unaccountably, Lewis called them off and ordered his team into a delay. He called it his "locomotion" offense, one that he felt would force North Carolina State to come out of its constrictive zone defense to cover his spread-out players. From that, he believed his team could peel off and begin making straight-line runs for easy baskets.

A good theory, but his players on the floor weren't convinced. "I felt that we should have kept playing the way we were," Micheaux said. "Our game is to get up and down the floor and dunk the ball. We were doing that in the second half, and the other team couldn't keep up."

Worse still, the style really handcuffed the Slamma Jammas, who managed just four field goals—and only one layup—the rest of the game.

To all of this, Valvano said, "Thank you very much," and his team methodically clawed its way back. Sidney Lowe, his six-foot guard and long shot specialist, canned two deep shots, Dereck Whittenburg got two more, and the score was tied 52-52 with 1:59 to play. Valvano instructed his players to foul Houston freshman Alvin Franklin with 1:05 to play, and Franklin, who hadn't been to the foul line at all during this intense game, missed. Cozell McQueen grabbed the rebound for the Wolfpack and with 44 seconds to play, Valvano called time out to plot his winning play.

"We wanted Whittenburg to get open for a jump shot, but I told Lorenzo Charles in the huddle that if the ball missed to pretend it was a hubcap, grab it and do something good with it," Valvano said with some of his irrepressible, off-the-wall humor.

When the time came for Whittenburg to get the ball, a pass from Bailey was high and Drexler slapped it away. Whittenburg grabbed it on the first bounce, but his desperation 30-footer was short. Yet Olajuwon, who made no effort to grab it, seemed handcuffed. Instead, Charles, a six-seven sophomore, took the ball.

Left: *Thurl Bailey (41) fights Olajuwon (rear) and Micheaux for rebound.* Below: *Olajuwon manages a tip-in, not a slam dunk, in first half.*

"I knew when Whit let the shot go it was going to fall short," Charles said. "I didn't know where Akeem was, just that he was behind me, and I knew I was the closest one to the basketball. So I slid down the lane, grabbed it and put it in."

More precisely, he dunked it with just one second to play, a dunk in the best tradition of Phi Slamma Jamma. And the Wolfpack had the game, 54-52, in one of the Final Four's most exciting finishes.

Live by the dunk, die by the dunk.

April 4, 1983, at Albuquerque, New Mexico					
North Carolina State	FG-FGA	FT-FTA	Reb	PF	Pts
Bailey	7-16	1-2	5	1	15
Charles	2-7	0-0	7	2	4
McQueen	1-5	2-2	12	4	4
Whittenberg	6-17	2-2	5	3	14
Lowe	4-9	0-1	0	2	8
Battle	0-1	2-2	1	1	2
Gannon	3-4	1-2	1	3	7
Meyers	0-0	0-0	1	0	0
Totals	23-59	8-11	32	16	54
Houston					
Drexler	1-5	2-2	2	4	4
Micheaux	2-6	0-0	6	1	4
Olajuwon	7-15	6-7	18	1	20
Franklin	2-6	0-1	0	0	4
Young	3-10	0-4	8	0	6
Anders	4-9	2-5	2	2	10
Gettys	2-2	0-0	2	3	4
Rose	0-1	0-0	1	2	0
Williams	0-1	0-0	4	3	0
Totals	21-55	10-19	43	16	52

Halftime: N.C. State, 33-25

Officials: Nichols, Housman & Forte

29

APRIL FOOL

April 1, 1985

Villanova
vs.
Georgetown

ere are the Villanova Wildcats playing Georgetown for the 1985 NCAA championship in Lexington, Kentucky, where one columnist, with straight face, suggests that the game be cancelled to prevent an ignominious case of Wildcat embarrassment.

Here is the clock in Rupp Arena showing five mintues to play in a game in which Villanova has tenaciously clung to leads and grudgingly surrendered them. Here is Georgetown coach John Thompson ordering his team to spread itself over the court to begin the slow strangulation of their audacious opponent.

Here, too, is a terrible pass from Horace Broadnax, one of the Hoya stranglers. The ball bounces off the foot of teammate Bill Martin and into the hands of Villanova's Dwain McClain.

Here, then, is evidence that the end is coming for a team that was heralded as the greatest in college basketball history.

Both teams knew each other well, having met twice previously in Big East competition. In each game, Villanova roared out to early leads, eventually to be cut down by narrow margins, with one game ending in overtime. Enter Wildcats coach Rollie Massimino, who sent his players to their rooms for a pregame rest with the message that they should think about playing the game to win, not to lose or just survive. "In a one-shot deal, you can beat anyone in the United States. That includes the team you're playing tonight."

"That" team was being anchored by seven-foot one-inch Patrick Ewing, college basketball's most dominating player during his four years at Georgetown. Patrick was surrounded by a splendid cast that included Dave Wingate, Reggie Williams, Broadnax and Martin, all disciplined players who took their coach's cue and worked as hard to intimidate opponents physically as they did to beat them with their shooting skills. In four seasons with Ewing as their leader, the Hoyas had won 121 times, including an NCAA championship the previous season.

So perhaps deep down the Wildcats did not believe that they had a chance against Georgetown. Anyone listening heard the experts declare that Villanova was no match for the Hoyas' power and skill.

What those experts forgot to mention was that playing Villanova was like wading through a pool of set gelatin. Massimino employed myriad defensive coverages that made it difficult for an opponent to settle into any successful offensive pattern, and enable his team to stay close. On offense, the Wildcats were careful and deliberate; they, too, had their stars

Dwain McClain (right) on defense for Villanova.
McClain led his team with 17 points, but defense
counted as much.

Above: *Gary McLain looks for the open man.* Opposite: *Ed Pinckney's quickness neutralizes the strength and size of Georgetown's Ewing.*

in six-nine center Ed Pinckney, forward Howard Pressley and their three superb guards—McClain, Gary McLain and cool sophomore Harold Jensen.

The experts also overlooked one other factor that favored the Wildcats: there was no 45-second shot clock in this game as there was in Big East competition when the two teams played each other, and that gave Massimino's style of play a decided edge. But what no one could foretell was that Villanova would play such a perfect game, perfect as in scarcely missing a shot.

At the start of the first half, the Wildcats bumbled a bit, the Hoyas grabbing four turnovers for 8 points and a 20-14 lead. Making good an incredible 13 of 18 shots, Villanova climbed right back into the game, and held a 29-28 halftime lead when Pressley scored with four seconds left.

Except for a brief period when Patrick thundered home three monstrous dunks, Villanova had good control of Ewing,

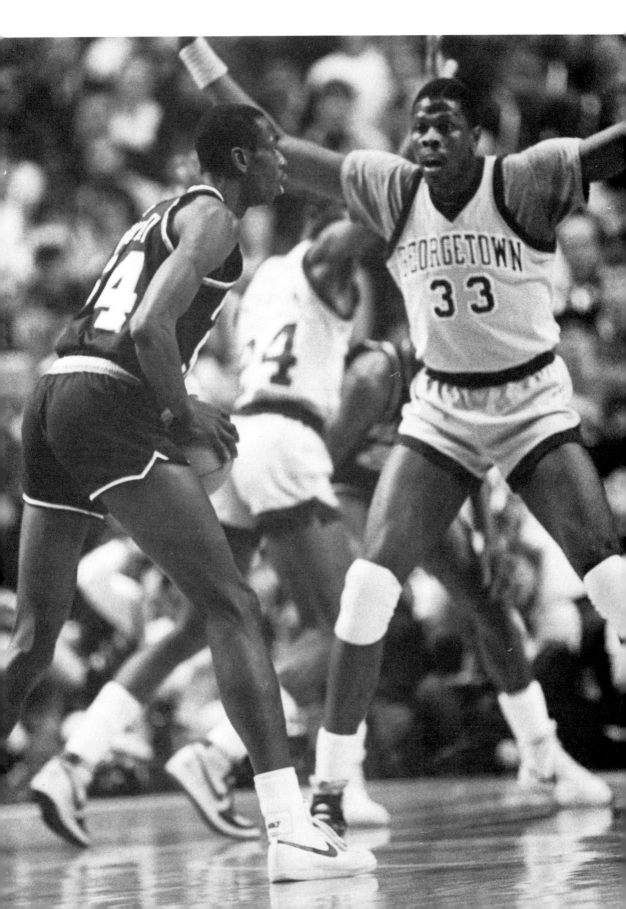

often triple-teaming him as Pinckney hammered at his elbows while Pressley and McClain sandwiched him from the front. Occasionally, for variation, one of the guards would drop down on him.

This grinding, gelatinous play continued into the second half, to the point where Ewing, the All-American center, got only two points in the final 13 minutes and never shot a free throw. Villanova wasn't missing any of its shots where Patrick could get involved in the rebounding action and draw fouls.

Incredibly, Villanova shot only ten times during the entire second half and made nine! The Hoyas got off to a fast 9-2 start in the second half, coming back to regain the lead. Six other times they fell behind until they opened a 5-point lead with about seven minutes to play. Georgetown, which had not ensnared the Wildcats in its tenacious trap defense since early in the game, suddenly had Villanova rattled, helping the team to regain the lead with 4:48 to play before Broadnax spoiled the strangulation plans with his bad pass.

Here, then, is Villanova with 2:37 to play and trailing 55-54. Massimino calls time out and tells his team:

"Settle down. Run a play. Look, this is a great team you're playing. They were bound to make a run, and we're just one point behind. We're going to win this game."

He then instructed his men to return to their carefully conceived offense and look for the open shot. Out they went, with Jensen set up on the right side. Georgetown, suddenly looking tentative and not in control, chased McLain to the left, where he reversed the ball to McClain, who then got it to Jensen.

That was it, a wide-open patch of air to the basket, and the sophomore, cool beyond his years, fired a line-drive jumper that ripped through the net to give Villanova a lead it would not relinquish, though 2 minutes and 11 seconds of very tough basketball remained.

Pinckney, whose quickness had neutralized Ewing's height and strength during the game, batted away a Wingate shot and drew him into a charging foul. The Villanova senior then made the two free throws for a 57-54 lead. At 1:48, Wingate missed a jumper and Pinckney sealed Ewing off from the rebound, allowing Jensen to grab it. Georgetown immediately fouled him. He also made a pair of free throws for a 59-54 lead with 1:24 to play.

Georgetown cut the lead to 3 points with 1:10 to play. Jensen's final two foul shots put the Wildcats back up by 5 points, 61-56. All the Hoyas had left now was the hope that their shots would go in, not unreasonable considering that

Coach Rollie Massimino uses both body English and prayers to lead his team to an April Fool's day NCAA finals upset.

What is a great game? It's in the eye of the beholder.

A couple of days after Villanova had upset Georgetown, someone asked Ed Pinckney of the Wildcats whether that wasn't his greatest game ever. After all, he'd been chosen the game's MVP, had scored 16 points and had held Hoya star Patrick Ewing to just 14 points and only 5 rebounds in the 66-64 upset.

He seemed insulted.

"My greatest game was two years ago, 27 points, 22 rebounds," he said, and added:

"Against Georgetown."

Sophomore Harold Jensen cooly took the fourth quarter shot that gave Villanova the lead for good.

they shot 55 percent from the field. But it wasn't until Ewing stuffed an offensive rebound that any Georgetown offense was generated, and this didn't seem to faze Villanova a bit. The Wildcats, who had missed the front end of two consecutive one-and-ones a few seconds earlier, canned their last four to lead 65-60, and that sealed the final 66-64 victory.

Massimino, who seems to endure the tortures of the damned during a game as he jumps up and down and pours out raw emotion with nearly every shot, exploded with joy. So did his players.

"I'm not excited!" he yelled. "It's April Fool's Day, and the joke's not on us!"

April 1, 1985, at Lexington, Kentucky						
Villanova	FG-FGA	FT-FTA	Reb	Ast	PF	Pts
Pressley	4-6	3-4	4	1	1	11
McClain	5-7	7-8	1	3	3	17
Pinckney	5-7	6-7	6	5	3	16
Wilbur	0-0	0-0	0	1	0	0
McLain	3-3	2-2	2	2	3	8
Jensen	5-5	4-5	1	2	3	14
Plansky	0-0	0-1	0	0	1	0
Everson	0-0	0-0	0	0	0	0
Totals	22-28	22-27	14	14	12	66
Georgetown						
Martin	4-6	2-2	5	1	2	10
Williams	5-9	0-2	4	2	3	10
Ewing	7-13	0-0	5	2	4	14
Jackson	4-7	0-0	0	9	4	8
Wingate	8-14	0-0	2	2	4	16
McDonald	0-1	0-0	0	0	0	0
Broadnax	1-2	2-2	1	2	4	4
Dalton	0-1	2-2	0	0	1	2
Totals	29-53	6-8	17	18	22	64

Halftime: Villanova, 29-28

Officials: Rutledge, Clougherty & Dibler

Dwain McClain receives congratulations from Big East Commissioner Dave Gavitt after win over Georgetown.

McClain goes for rebound with the Hoyas' Martin McClain helped direct a deliberate offense.

30

MICHAEL THE MAGNIFI- CENT

April 20, 1988

Chicago
vs.
Boston

First, there was Elgin Baylor, who once scored a playoff record 61 points against the Boston Celtics with his mind-boggling array of head-faking and body-leaning moves that never seemed to allow a defender an honest try to stop his shooting.

Now, there is Michael Jordan, who broke Baylor's 61-point playoff record by scoring 63 points in a playoff game against the Celtics with the flying, skying, hanging, swooping, gliding, stop-in-the-air and back-to-the-basket shooting gyrations that the six-foot six-inch star of the Chicago Bulls performs in nearly every game; and which make one believe that when the laws of gravity were set, someone granted Jordan an exemption.

And, of course, there is the other Michael Jordan, who once said he would rather be known as a great defensive player than for all of the points he produced; and who in 1988 harnessed all of his skills and made the NBA's All-Defensive team—in the same season that he also was named the NBA Player of the Year.

No one dares to predict just what horizons Jordan will break before his professional career ends, but everyone is eagerly anticipating to what ends he will go as he brings his Barishnikov-type ballet to pro basketball and raises the game's great athleticism to new heights.

His fellow pros are probably more excited about what he can do—and will do—than anyone else. And also more awed.

"Jump with him and he'll outhang you," says former NBA player Fred Carter, "because he has more hang time than [former Raiders punter] Ray Guy."

"I don't know whether his first step is legal," said another NBA guard, "because I never had time to judge it."

There is no "book" on Jordan, who plays point guard for the Bulls but can also swing into the small forward's role at any time. In his rookie season, during a game against the Los Angeles Clippers, he took the ball to the left, then shot it right, in a five-foot hanging banker that mesmerized center Bill Walton; and the next trip down, he tossed a left-handed, back-to-the-basket shot while being sent sprawling to the court by Clippers guard Norm Nixon.

He has scored after being grabbed from behind, yet somehow managing to keep his arms free and floating the ball over the rim. "The amazing thing about him," one NBA coach noted, "is that to survive in this league, you can't do the same thing twice against the intelligent defensive teams, but he always manages to come up with something new every time."

That is why he is creating a litany of games in which he

Michael Jordan pulls out a spinning reverse slam dunk to beat out Dominique Wilkins in the Slam-Dunk of 1988.

has scored more than 60 points, and an ever-increasing array of 50-point efforts. For that reason, everyone probably has a "favorite" Jordan game because, like all true artists, everything this player does seems to be unique.

Yet it is hard to top Jordan's overall performance against the Celtics in the 1986 playoffs when, in the first game of that best-of-five set, he scored 49 points in a losing effort. Three days later, back at Boston Garden, he put on a truly epic performance with his 63 points in a double-overtime, 135-131 Boston victory.

In the minds of many, Jordan's importance to his team—and to the game itself—was firmly established that year when

Opposite: *Michael Jordan puts a move on San Antonio's Alvin Robertson in 1987 All-Star game.* Left: *On his way to the 1988 All-Star MVP award.* Above: *Air Jordan.*

he came off a 64-game absence because of a broken foot, and over the protests of the Bull's management, team doctors and his own agent who wanted him to sit out the rest of the season, literally carried Chicago to a hair-breadth playoff finish. The Celtics, who won 67 of 82 games that season, had too much overall firepower and, despite Jordan's 49 points, gunned down the Bulls 123-104 in the first game of the series.

In the second game, Chicago got a 4-2 lead in the first quarter and clung to it until the opening minutes of the fourth quarter as Jordan's 36 points in the first three periods seemed to come every time the Celtics began a run. In fact, he got his team a 65-55 lead in the third quarter by arching up a soft 20-footer over the flailing arms of 6-11 Kevin McHale. He later said that on the way back down the court, he kept saying to himself, "All day, baby, allllll day."

"Michael was doing so much and so well that I found myself just wanting to stop and watch him . . . and I was playing," said Chicago guard John Paxson.

The Bulls upped their lead to 69-59 before the Celtics' Danny Ainge, who hadn't scored a point till then, slammed home 13, including 11 in the final two and a half minutes of that quarter, and brought Boston to within 1 point at 84-83.

Jordan got his 50th point as part of an 18-point fourth quarter that helped to turn a 108-104 Boston lead into a 111-110 Chicago advantage; and a few minutes later, he turned in the biggest play of the game. Boston led 116-114 with six seconds to play when Jordan got the ball, and five seconds later, he up-faked Boston guard Dennis Johnson and tried a 3-pointer that clanged off the rim.

But referee Ed Middleton signaled that McHale, who came to help on the play, had hit Jordan, and awarded a pair of foul shots with no time left on the clock. McHale then led a hand-waving rally with the crowd, hoping to distract Jordan; and Ainge tried to distract him by reminding him that they had once discussed what it would be like to have to win a game with foul shots and 17 seconds on the clock.

Jordan was unfazed, because he calmly sank both shots, and the game went into overtime. With 1:39 to play in the first OT, Michael put his team ahead 125-121 with a 3-point play. Jerry Sichting and Ainge then hit baskets for Boston to tie the score. Then came one of Jordan's truly disappointing moments in the game, because he had a chance to win it and missed an unmolested jump shot from the left side.

By then, Jordan had 59 points, and midway through the second overtime period he tied Baylor's playoff record of 61 points. But it didn't seem important in the overall scheme of

Michael Jordan has the box-office appeal that certifies him as a bonafide star in the nation's entertainment spectrum.

In 1986 Jordan missed 34 games, but when he played a full season in 1987, the Chicago Bulls' attendance increased by 181,492. On the road, the Bulls increased their drawing power by 39 percent and added more than 276,000 fans to the NBA's attendance roster—or one-third of its overall attendance increase.

In dollar figures, based on an average ticket price of $13.40, that's $3.71 million in revenue.

Now, there's a star!

Michael Jordan of North Carolina shoots the winning basket against Georgetown during the 1982 NCAA championship game.

things. A bit later, with Boston ahead by 2 points, Jordan swooped past Celtics center Robert Parrish and jammed home his 22nd field goal of the game—and his record 63rd point—to tie the game for the 13th time.

"Jordan," Parrish noted, "does anything he wants on a basketball court, and it's not like he does it in a summer league, either."

The gloss came off the record with 57 seconds to play when Jerry Sichting of the Celtics undid Jordan's tie and canned a baseline jumper, though Jordan had one more opportunity when his long baseline jumper missed and Boston converted Parrish's rebound into its final points.

"I didn't think anyone was capable of doing what Michael has done to us the past two games," a weary Bird said afterward. "He is the most exciting, awesome player in the game today. I think it's just God disguised as Michael Jordan."

Amen.

Although Jordan has a bunch of 50- and 60-point games, and an array of mind-bending shots, his best overall performance was probably against the Celtics in 1986 playoffs.

April 20, 1986, at Boston Garden						
Chicago	FG-FGA	FT-FTA	Reb	Ast	PF	Pts
Woolridge	9-27	6-8	9	2	5	24
Oakley	3-5	4-6	14	0	5	10
Corzine	4-9	0-0	7	1	5	8
Jordan	22-41	19-21	5	6	4	63
Macy	3-4	1-1	1	2	4	7
Green	2-6	3-4	5	0	4	7
Banks	3-7	2-4	3	3	2	8
Smrek	0-0	0-0	0	0	1	0
Gervin	0-0	0-0	0	1	1	0
Paxson	1-3	2-2	0	0	3	4
Totals	47-102	37-46	44	15	34	131
Boston						
McHale	10-22	7-8	15	4	4	27
Bird	14-27	6-7	12	8	5	36
Parrish	4-11	5-6	9	0	5	13
Johnson	4-14	7-9	4	8	6	15
Ainge	8-13	7-9	4	5	5	24
Walton	4-8	2-2	15	2	6	10
Sichting	4-5	0-1	0	4	1	8
Wedman	1-3	0-0	0	0	0	2
Carlisle	0-0	0-0	0	0	0	0
Totals	49-103	34-42	59	31	32	135

Three-point field goals: Bird, 2, Ainge 1

Chicago	33	25	33	25	9	6 -- 131
Boston	25	26	37	28	9	10 -- 135

Officials: O'Donnell & Middleton

31

FIVE MILLION POINTS

January 25, 1988

Utah
vs.
Cleveland

The record belonged to a lot of people . . . several thousand, in fact.

But Ricky Green of the Utah Jazz got the credit for scoring the NBA's 5 millionth point when he sank a desperation, period-ending, 3-point shot without ever realizing when he heaved the ball toward the basket that he had an opportunity to make a little ("a little" 5 millionth point?) history.

Wilt Chamberlain helped out . . . 31,419, including 61 of the NBA's top individual scoring feats . . . his 100-point game against the Knicks . . . his record 4,029 in the 1961-62 season . . . 118 games of scoring more than 50 points.

This was one of those records that had a chance to be established by players on six different teams in three cities—the Philadelphia 76ers at Washington beginning two hours before Utah played the Cleveland Cavaliers in Salt Lake City, who started an hour before the Milwaukee Bucks played Golden State in Oakland, California. When the game in Washington began on the evening of January 25, 1988, some 4,999,550 points had been scored since the NBA began its first season in the fall of 1946.

Joe Fulks of the Philadelphia Warriors chipped in with 1,389 that first season and 8,003 of that 5 million belongs to him . . . 7,990 to Max Zaslofsky . . . 11,764 to George Mikan, and another 10,063 to his teammate Vern Mikkelsen . . . 16,266 to Paul Arizin and 10,023 to his teammate Neil Johnston, both of whom played with Fulks . . . and Dolph Schayes chipped in with 19,249 points.

The NBA had been charting this milestone since the 1987-88 season began, thanks to the intrepid bookkeeping of Philadelphia statistician Harvey Pollack. Not only did he alert the NBA late in the summer of 1987 that it would happen—he even pinpointed the date, based on the average number of points scored in each game. When the season began, 4,906,649 points had been scored in the first 41 years of play—meaning 93,351 points were needed for No. 5 million.

Five Celtics in the fifties—Bill Russell, Bob Cousy, Sam Jones, Bill Sharman and Tom Heinsohn—chipped in with more than 70,000 points . . . Bob Pettit added 20,941 . . . Jack Twyman has 15,840 . . . Johnny Kerr contributed 12,480.

There was no doubt after the games of January 24 that the magic number would occur the next night, at either Salt Lake City or Golden State. So an elaborate communications network was established between the NBA office in New York City and courtside at both arenas. The radio hookups for both home teams were cut into the NBA office, and running tabula-

Bob Pettit, 20,941 points.

tion was kept under the direction of Terry Lyons, the league's assistant public relations director, and some of the interns in the NBA office who kept the running count as the points began to accumulate. The 76ers-Bullets game went into overtime and Philly won 118-117, leaving just 215 points to be scored in the other two cities.

Oscar Robertson added 26,710 points . . . John Havlicek had 26,395 . . . two centers, Walt Bellamy and Nate Thurmond, got over 35,000 betweeen them . . . and Jerry West and Elgin Baylor of the Lakers had nearly 50,000 . . . two Knicks teammates, Dave DeBusschere and Jerry Lucas, each added 14,053 . . . Billy Cunningham contributed 13,626 . . . Lenny Wilkens got 17,772, just 2 more than Bailey Howell.

Utah and Cleveland cut the number by 103 during the first half of their game, and playing just a quarter ahead of the Cavs and Golden State, it then became a bit of a race to see who would hit the finish line first . . . and like any great race, there had to be a contribution from Lady Luck.

In the Golden State game, the Warriors called time out early in the second quarter, while in Utah, Cleveland's Mark Price was in the process of making a pair of free throws after being fouled by—who else but Ricky Green? Price's two points brought the figure to 4,999,998. But there were only a couple of seconds to play before the end of the third quarter, when the Jazz and Cavaliers would have their mandatory two-minute break between periods, and the Golden State-Milwaukee game would be resumed.

Sam Jones (below) and Bill Sharman (below left), two of the five Celtics who added over 70,000 points.

Of course, neither team was aware of the countdown, and neither were the spectators in either arena, though everyone had been alerted before the game that the magic moment could happen at either game. But in any game, once the action begins and points start accumulating, point-by-point tabulations are soon forgotten. Besides, who really can fathom the meaning of 5 million points?

Pete Maravich had 15,948 of them . . . Tiny Archibald added 16,481 . . . Elvin Hayes contributed 27,313 . . . Julius Erving got 18,364 . . . Easy Ed Macauley put in 11,234 . . . Carl Braun played before the 24-second clock and scored 10,625 . . . Wes Unseld and Gene Shue, who both coached the Bullets, had over 20,000 points . . . Bob Lanier added 19,248 . . . and little Calvin Murphy scored 17,949.

Mark Iavaroni certainly wasn't thinking about it when he quickly inbounded the ball for the Jazz following Price's second foul. He threw a long pass to Green, who stood with his back to his basket. The clock hit :01 as Green caught the ball, and in the same instant he turned and shot a 20-footer. It left his hands before the clock hit 0:00 and the official raised his hand, signalling the shot would count if it went in.

It did—Green's only field goal of the game. The near-sellout at the Salt Palace went wild . . . not because Ricky Green had just raised the NBA all-time point total to 5 million and 1, but because they had been stunned by a spectacular shot.

As soon as the teams went to the sidelines, a between-the-periods fans' shooting contest got underway and still no one—players, coaches or fans—was aware of the history that had just been made. However, at the scorer's table, Jazz public relations director Bill Kreifeldt, who had been in constant contact with the NBA office during the third quarter, got an excited question.

"Was that last shot good?" he was asked.

"Yes, it was," Kreifeldt replied.

"Then you got it, you got the 5 millionth point!" Lyons shouted into the phone.

"I immediately told our owner, Larry Miller, who sits at courtside, and he went racing down to our bench and began hugging all of the players and coaches," Kreifeldt recalled. "Now, the shoot-around still was going on, and the fans were buzzing about Ricky's shot. Then they saw all the celebrating going on, and I believe they thought we were still going crazy over the last shot. It wasn't until the fan promotion ended that we could make the announcement, and then the place really went wild."

Below: Wes Unseld, over 20,000 points. *Opposite:* Moses Malone, over 21,000 points.

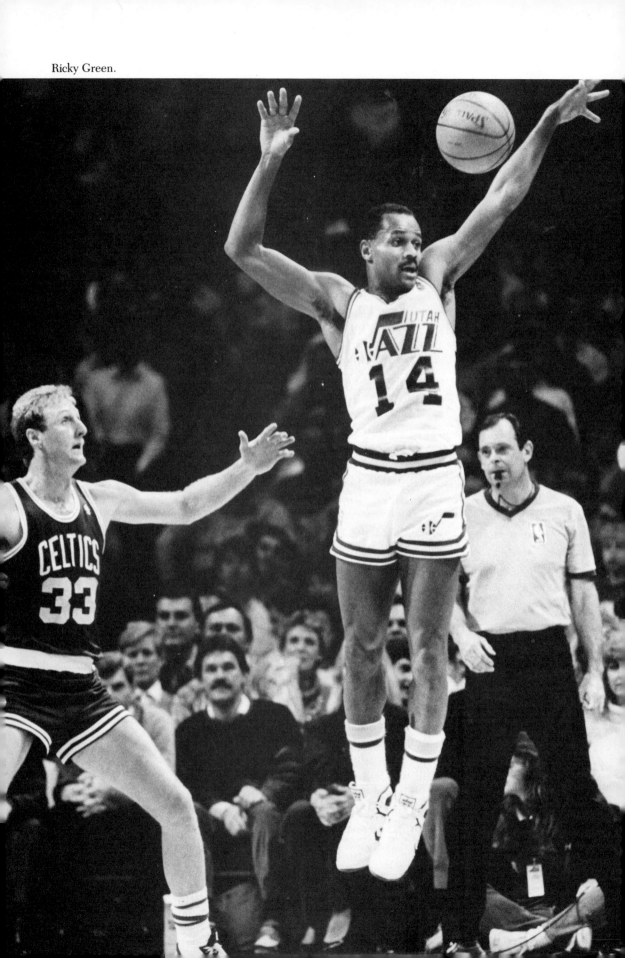

Ricky Green.

The game was halted for a midcourt ceremony in which Green autographed the basketball "Ricky Green #14—Utah Jazz"; it was then shipped to the Basketball Hall of Fame in Springfield, Massachusetts, for permanent display.

"All right!" Green exclaimed, before Utah went on to a 119-96 victory. "I'm in the Hall of Fame!"

Ironically, Green was once a No. 1 pick of Golden State and had been rediscovered by Utah coach Frank Layden during a ceremonial visit to throw out the first ball for a Continental Basketball Game in Billings, Montana, a few years earlier.

There were are evenings when Kareem Abdul-Jabbar added to his all-time point lead of over 37,000 points . . . and Larry Bird continued to add to his 16,000-plus points . . . and Adrian Dantley to the 20,000 or so that he'd scored . . . and Moses Malone continued to build on the more than 21,000 he had accumulated . . . and Magic Johnson built on his 13,000-plus . . . and all of them can say they contributed to the night when the NBA celebrated 5 million points.

But only Ricky Green can say that he scored it.

January 25, 1988, at Salt Lake City			
Utah	FG-FGA	FT-FTA	Pts
Malone	15-22	6-6	36
Iavaroni	1-4	2-2	4
Eaton	3-5	1-2	7
Tripucka	4-7	0-0	9
Stockton	9-11	2-2	20
Bailey	7-14	1-2	15
Green	1-3	3-3	6
Turpin	3-7	4-4	10
Hansen	0-1	0-0	0
Griffith	5-7	0-0	12
Kofoed	0-1	0-0	0
Totals	48-82	19-21	119

Three-point field goals: Griffith, 2; Green, 1; Tripucka, 1

Cleveland			
J. Williams	4-8	5-6	13
Hubbard	1-2	1-2	3
Dougherty	6-17	2-4	14
Harper	3-15	0-0	6
Price	4-8	6-6	14
West	7-12	0-1	14
Curry	2-8	0-0	4
Ehlo	1-3	0-0	2
Johnson	3-8	5-6	11
Corbin	3-8	2-2	8
Dudley	2-5	1-2	5
Rogers	.1-4	0-0	2
Totals	37-98	22-29	96

Utah	28	24	40	27 --	119
Cleveland	27	24	16	29 --	96

32

THE GIRLS CAN PLAY, TOO

August 7, 1984

United States
vs.
South Korea

February 5, 1985

Wayland Baptist
vs.
Schreiner

"You've come a long way, baby!"

While that seemed to become a rallying cry for many of the advances in women's sports during the seventies and eighties, nowhere was it more appropriate than in basketball. Consider:

(1) The United States lost the first women's basketball game ever sanctioned in Olympic medal competition, in 1976—an 84-71 decision to Japan—but came back and won three of the next four games to earn a silver medal behind Russia; and eight years later, the U.S. won the gold medal at the Los Angeles Olympics.

(2) Women's basketball on the intercollegiate level was not much more than an extracurricular activity in many areas of the country until the seventies. It then blossomed in 1982 when the NCAA finally sanctioned a post-season national championship tournament that, by 1988, had attracted national attention, including nationwide television coverage.

(3) In 1988 Wayland Baptist University's Flying Queens, which began its basketball program in 1948, became the first women's team to win 1,000 games.

The surge in the women's game, spurred by its sanctioning in Olympic competition and the recognition of NCAA championship competition, was a long time coming considering that women's basketball began its own Amateur Athletic Union (AAU) championship series back in 1926, and it continued right into the seventies with the Wayland Flying Queens and the Nashville Business College winning most of the titles.

The 1976 Olympics in Montreal really touched off a surge in women's competition and provided an impetus for colleges throughout the nation to improve existing programs and build new ones under the guidelines of Title IX government regulations that stipulated schools receiving any government aid must provide women proportionate facilities and resources for intercollegiate sports programs. At one point a separate governing body sought to shelter all women's collegiate sports, but it disappeared after the NCAA recognized the necessity of including women's teams in championshp competition. Soon, major conferences, which had featured competition between the men's teams, now had similar competition for women's teams. And small schools attended almost exclusively by women, such as Immaculata College outside of Philadelphia, were building excellent basketball programs.

From the large and small colleges alike came more talented players who were able to match their skills against teams from nations around the world, as the U.S. proved in its

Missy Fisher cans 2 of her 6 points as Wayland Baptist defeats Schreiner College to record a record 1,000th victory.

first medal competition at the Montreal Olympics. The U.S. team came down to needing a victory over Czechoslovakia in the final game to earn a medal—and remember, no American women's team had ever finished higher than eighth in any form of international competition. Lusia Harris, who had helped Delta State University of Mississippi win the national title competition before it became organized under NCAA tournament play, sparked a 15-0 run in the second half against the Czechs and led the team with 17 points and 9 rebounds. Ann Dunkle of La Habra, California, had 14 points, and three other players scored 10 apiece in the 83-67 victory.

"We were so high in the second half I thought we were going to fly through the roof," said Mary Anne O'Connor of Fairfield, Connecticut. "After a few of our earlier games, we had things to show people."

After that U.S. team had lost to the Japanese, they were embarrassed by the gold medal-winning Russian team,

Right: *Two-time All-America and leading scorer Sharla Harrison, gets as easy two in regular season game.* Opposite: *Coach Pat Summitt is carried off court after USA beat Korea for gold medal.*

112-77. But six years later, in 1982, the USSR's 24-year winning streak as world champions was ended by an American team, 85-83 in Budapest. The Russians won a 2-point game in 1983 and the long-awaited rematch in the 1984 Olympics was scrubbed when the Russians boycotted the Games (the U.S. had boycotted the 1980 Games in Moscow). But in 1986, the American women came to Moscow and crushed the Soviets in the finals of the Goodwill Games, 83-60, and did it again, 108-88, five weeks later in the same arena in the finals of the world championships.

But it was in the 1984 Olympics that American women's basketball really hit the top as a team led by Cheryl Miller won all six of its games by 28 points or more. Miller led the U.S. team with more than 16 points per game, and she sparked a 14-0 burst that chopped down an attempt by South Korea to beat them for the gold medal. The Koreans had closed a 20-point deficit to 10 points with 15 minutes to play before the U.S. exploded, led by Miller's three assists and a field goal that gave her team a comfortable cushion en route to an 85-55 victory.

The scope of the advances made in the game was demonstrated by the fact that Pat Head Summitt, coach of the U.S. squad, had been a member of the 1976 Olympic team, along with Nancy Lieberman, who became the first woman ever to play in a men's professional league when she was a member of the Springfield (Mass.) team of the United States Basketball League.

In the collegiate ranks, Louisiana Tech won the first women's NCAA tournament in 1982 and then repeated as national champions in 1988. Louisiana was twice beaten in other tournament finals, once by Southern Cal (which won back-to-back titles in 1983-84) and by Tennessee in 1987. The women's sport by 1988 was no longer directed only by women, as Louisiana Tech's head coach, Leon Barmore, became the first male to coach a national collegiate titlist.

Barmore's Louisiana Tech team staged a brilliant second half comeback against Auburn to win its 1988 title, coming from 14 points down in the second half. Erica Westbrooks scored 16 of her 25 points in that time, and Teresa Weatherspoon, burned for 16 points by Ruth Bolton of Auburn in the first half, held Bolton without a point in the second half.

"Any other game when we'd be behind by 14 points we'd be all upset," Westbrooks said. "This time we kept thinking that it had to be us. We had to keep digging and finding it within ourselves."

That began on defense, and here Weatherspoon led the

Flying Queens frosh Glyn'a Masters poses for an early publicity photograph.

Cheryl Miller and Anne Donovan (7) head downcourt after taking possession in first-half action against Korea. USA won gold medal in 1984 Games.

charge. "I love playing defense," she said. "If somebody scores on me like Ruth Bolton did in the first half, I'm out there to shut them down in the second half."

Weatherspoon also took over the direction of Tech's offense and dished out seven assists during the second-half comeback while Westbrooks came up with six steals and did a good job on defense herself, limiting Auburn's All-American forward, Vickie Orr, to just 11 points. But it was Weatherspoon who flicked a pass to Angela Lawson, whose jumper tied the score, 51-51. Forty-nine seconds later, Weatherspoon scooped the ball away from Bolton and set Westbrooks up for a layup that gave Tech its first lead of the game, 53-51, and with about a minute-and-a-half to play, she fed Lawson again to put Tech on top for good at 55-53.

Earlier that season in Plainview, Texas, Wayland Baptist was host to its Gold Rush Invitational Tournament, and that was the perfect platform from which to unveil a watershed mark in women's basketball—1,000 victories. The Flying Queens defeated the Schreiner College Mountaineers 75-45 and then celebrated the event with 15 former Queens players who came in just for the occasion. Among them was Glyna Harrison, an All-American player during the 1961-63 seasons. Her daughter, Sharla Harrison, was the team's leading scorer

Right: *Cheryl Miller runs into Korea's Aie-Young Choi.*
Opposite: *Sharla Harrison. The Flying Queen's mother was also an All-American.*

President Reagan congratulates 1984 NCAA champs, USC Women of Troy.

and a two-time All-American player.

Wayland's team got its nickname in the early fifties because of its willingness to fly across the country to play all available competition, and the school became one of the first to give women basketball scholarships. All of this helped to build up probably the most dynamic basketball tradition of any school competing in the women's game. And á la the Boston Celtics, it hung all of its championship banners from their gym's ceiling.

But the record also tells a good part of the story. Since beginning the sport in 1948, Wayland has:

• Won more than 82 percent of its games and averaged 25 victories a year.

• Made 37 playoff appearances and participated in 31 national tournaments, winning 10 national championships and finishing second 10 times.

• Put together the longest winning streak in women's basketball—131 games from 1953-58, including three consecutive unbeaten seasons and three AAU championships.

All of this tradition and excellence was evident in Wayland's landmark 1,000th victory because the Flying Queens used a 14-2 burst early in the game to get a 20-10 lead, and then held the Mountaineers without a point for six-and-a-half minutes to increase their lead to 39-24 at the half. A 9-2 run at the start of the second half clinched the victory . . . and left little doubt that the other 999 wins were clear evidence that, indeed, women's basketball had come a long way.

August 7, 1984, at Los Angeles

United States	FG-FGA	FT-FTA	Pts
Edwards	1-2	0-0	2
Henry	2-3	0-0	4
Woodard	3-9	1-3	7
Donovan	3-7	0-0	6
Boswell	2-3	0-0	4
Miller	7-10	2-4	16
Lawrence	6-11	2-2	14
Noble	3-5	4-5	10
Milkey	2-4	2-2	6
Curry	2-5	2-2	6
McGee	2-7	2-2	6
Menken-Schmidt	2-2	0-0	4
Totals	35-68	15-20	85

South Korea	FG-FGA	FT-FTA	Pts
A. Chol	9-15	2-2	20
E. Kim	0-1	0-0	0
H. Lee	2-4	2-2	6
K. Chol	0-1	0-0	0
M. Lee	0-1	0-0	0
H. Kim	6-13	3-5	15
Jeong	0-2	0-0	0
Y. Kim	0-1	0-0	0
Sung	5-10	1-1	11
Park	1-10	1-1	3
Totals	23-58	9-11	55

Halftime: United States, 42-27

February 5, 1988, at Plainview, Texas

Wayland Baptist	FG-FGA	FT-FTA	Reb	Ast	PF	Pts
Shelton	1-2	0-0	3	1	0	2
Burns	0-1	2-2	3	2	0	2
Remington	2-5	2-5	4	1	3	6
Harrison	5-10	4-6	7	4	4	14
Fisher	3-10	0-0	3	3	1	6
Wilson	0-1	0-1	3	0	1	0
Utterback	1-2	2-2	2	0	1	4
Schonerstedt	5-8	1-3	0	4	2	11
Morris	2-2	0-0	0	0	1	4
Scott	0-1	0-0	2	0	0	0
Stewart	5-9	5-6	13	2	2	15
Potts	0-0	0-0	0	0	0	0
Shippy	2-9	5-5	8	1	0	9
Zedlitz	1-6	0-0	2	0	1	2
Totals	27-66	21-30	50	18	16	75

Schreiner	FG-FGA	FT-FTA	Reb	Ast	PF	Pts
Ortega	0-0	0-0	0	0	1	0
Martinez	0-1	0-0	1	0	0	0
Etheridge	5-6	7-8	4	0	2	17
McAllister	3-5	2-4	0	0	3	8
Lagleder	1-7	0-0	2	1	2	2
Gamble	1-6	2-2	2	1	4	4
Griffith	0-0	0-0	2	1	1	0
Ledford	0-2	0-0	4	1	1	0
Haglund	0-0	1-2	0	0	0	1
O'Neill	2-11	0-0	5	0	4	4
Wilson	0-3	2-2	5	0	4	2
Lusinger	3-5	0-0	0	0	0	7
Totals	15-46	14-18	25	4	22	45

Three-point field goal: Lusinger

Halftime: Wayland Baptist, 39-24

33

JAY-HAWKS RUN— AND WALK— TO A TITLE

April 4, 1988

Kansas
vs.
Oklahoma

"**N**ot in my wildest dreams."

Larry Brown, the coach of the Kansas Jayhawks, certainly wasn't alone in that assessment after his team stunned the heavily favored Oklahoma Sooners and won the NCAA's 50th basketball championship in 1988. Millions around the nation watched in disbelief—and Sooners coach Billy Tubbs was one of them—as the once-woebegone Jayhawks placed themselves on the list of "incredible victors," along with such past NCAA champions as Texas Western (1966), North Carolina State (1983) and Villanova (1985).

The way the experts saw the scenario lining up was for Oklahoma's roadrunners to grind up their Big Eight rivals and leave them gasping in the dust as they named whatever final score suited them—and usually that was something over 100 points.

Okay, said Brown's players, we'll play your game—and note, they had lost twice already to the Sooners in Big Eight competition—and we'll run as fast and as far as you can. Mark that as surprise No. 1. Then, added the Jayhawks, after we do that for a half and you haven't shaken us, then we'll make you play our deliberate game and get you into the last five minutes with a chance for us to win, and we'll see how you handle that kind of unusual pressure.

And who would ever have believed this possible earlier in the season when Kansas lost 8 of its first 20 games and saw a preseason second-place national ranking go up in smoke? The backbone of their team disappeared—center Marvin Branch fell to academic problems, forward Archie Marshall to a knee injury and four other players to a variety of academic, physical, and disciplinary problems. Matters got so severe that defensive back Clint Normore was recruited from the football team because he had been an outstanding high school basketball player, and Brown was just about out of guards.

Kansas had moved deliberately through the playoffs, seeming to miss the better teams, which fell ahead of them to the usual rash of upsets. But in the Final Four, they earned their championship berth by blowing out to a 14-0 lead over favored Duke and playing to a very pat, comfortable victory that did little to impress the experts after they watched Oklahoma pulverize a disciplined Arizona team. What the experts overlooked was that in both Oklahoma victories over Kansas, the Sooners offense was no better than ordinary because it couldn't shake the pesky Kansas defense . . . and they also lost sight of the axiom that "offense wins games but *defense* wins championships."

Jayhawk Danny Manning led his Kansas team to upset over Oklahoma with a 31-point, 18-rebound performance.

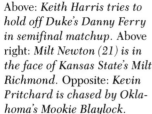

Above: *Keith Harris tries to hold off Duke's Danny Ferry in semifinal matchup.* Above right: *Milt Newton (21) is in the face of Kansas State's Milt Richmond.* Opposite: *Kevin Pritchard is chased by Oklahoma's Mookie Blaylock.*

Brown incorporated a bit of both in his game plan, and then turned matters over to a brilliant forward named Danny Manning to bring it all together on the court. Manning had declined an opportunity to join the NBA after the 1987 season, but it wasn't until Brown placed some responsibility for the team's success squarely on his shoulders that he really became the difference for this Kansas team.

And in no game throughout the season did he flash his true credentials more convincingly than in the biggest contest of his life. He played an almost perfect game in directing his teammates and producing 31 points, 18 rebounds, 5 steals and 2 blocked shots.

Manning integrated himself into the Kansas roadrunning strategy which, in the first half, did a better job of roadrunning than the Sooners, who had made their living with this style of play. Only the long-range shooting of Dave Sieger, who canned 6 three-pointers, and 15 Kansas turnovers kept the Sooners close. The Kansas defense had responded well to the

Jimmy Dunlap didn't score a point for the Kansas Jayhawks during their upset of Oklahoma in the NCAA championship game. He didn't pull down a rebound . . . or have any assists . . . in fact, he didn't even don a uniform.

He drove the team bus.

Better still, he's not even from Kansas. He's from Detroit.

Dunlap was the driver of the Jayhawks' chartered bus that took them from their hotel to the Pontiac Silverdome when they won the Midwest Regionals to get into the Final Four.

Kansas coach Larry Brown liked Dunlap so much that he arranged to get him from Detroit to Kansas City so he could drive the team's bus to Kemper Arena on the night of the game . . . an over-the-road good luck charm.

"He's a great person and very caring," Brown said. "I could see the way he treated our players that he really cared about every one of them."

They obviously cared about him, too, because when he took them to the airport in Michigan for their return to Kansas, he gave them all high fives and then was told by Brown that the coach wanted him in Kansas City to drive the team again.

"Until I got there, I took that with a grain of salt," Dunlap said, "because I've never heard of a bus driver flown nowhere."

transition game and kept the Sooners from easy run-and-gun baskets.

Brown did his part, too. Because his team would not bend to his pleas to slow down the tempo, Brown substituted freely. Tubbs, meanwhile, used only two substitutes during the entire 40 minutes. At the end the Jayhawks had much the fresher legs and Oklahoma could not generate any sustained push.

Free substitution might also have contributed to Kansas's shooting percentage—71 percent—in the first half as the teams battled to a 50-50 tie—the most points ever scored in a first half of an NCAA final. Led by Manning, the Jayhawks controlled the boards for most of this time, helping their transition game avoid even more problems from Oklahoma's constantly pressing defense.

In the second half, Brown pulled another surprise and clamped a suffocating defense on the Sooners. The nation's highest-scoring collegiate team stumbled along at a 35 percent shooting rate. Harvey Grant and Stacey King had combined for 23 Oklahoma points in the first half, but they got just 8 in the second half as Kansas cut off the inside passes. Manning, playing what looked like a lazy denial defense in the post, time and again lured Oklahoma into foolish inside passes to guards Mookie Blaylock or Ricky Grace and either knocked the ball away or picked it off. Finally, the Sooners, with no running game and no inside game, rested their offense outside and conceded the game's tempo to Kansas.

Still, Oklahoma broke out to a 5-point lead in the first ten minutes of the second half before Manning scored 7 straight points, the last giving his team a 69-68 lead. Kansas never again trailed, though the score was tied at 71 before Kevin Pritchard's baseline jumper put the Jayhawks ahead for good. Manning took over again, snapping down a couple of rebounds and canning a left-handed runner. His team took a 6-point lead on Keith Piper's score with three minutes to play.

At this point, Oklahoma was in disarray. The Sooners, too eager to close the gap with single plays, saw long-range shots bounce off the backboard or clang off the front of the rim and into the hands of Kansas rebounders. Their stamina spent, they allowed the Jays to hold the ball for long periods and let the clock tick down to where it seemed too late to save the game.

Only Kansas helped to bail them out and give Oklahoma a last-minute reprieve when, smelling the upset, the Jayhawks briefly lost their cool and threw up some foolish shots. Blaylock's spinning one-hander at the left of the key ended a

4-1 Sooners run that brought Oklahoma to within a point, 78-77, with 40 seconds to play.

Clearly, the Sooners had a chance, but unaccountably, they again allowed Kansas to use the clock. It took 24 seconds for Oklahoma to foul Scooter Barry to force a change of possession with just 16 seconds to play. Barry's father, Rick, one of basketball's all-time free-throw shooters, watched from the stands as his son made one of two shots for a 79-77 lead. More importantly, in the scramble for the missed second shot, Manning was knocked down and then awarded an opportunity to make a couple of more foul shots.

He did—with 14 seconds to play, and Kansas was home with its 83-79 victory.

Manning was more concerned with how his team's victory was viewed. It's a great feeling and something we deserved," he said. "A lot of people said we were lucky.

"But what's luck? Luck presents an opportunity, and we were prepared for that. We capitalized on all of the opportunities we got."

April 4, 1988, at Kansas City						
Kansas	FG-FGA	FT-FTA	Reb	Ast	PF	Pts
Newton	6-6	1-2	4	1	1	15
Piper	4-6	0-0	7	2	3	8
Manning	13-24	5-7	18	2	3	31
Pritchard	6-7	0-0	1	4	1	13
Gueldner	1-2	0-0	2	1	0	2
Barry	0-2	1-2	0	2	1	1
Normore	3-3	0-1	1	4	3	7
Harris	1-1	0-0	1	0	2	2
Minor	1-4	2-2	1	1	1	4
Maddox	0-0	0-0	0	0	1	0
Totals	35-55	9-14	35	17	16	83

Three-point field goals: Newton, 2; Pritchard, 1; Normore 1.

Oklahoma						
Sieger	7-15	1-2	5	7	2	22
Grant	6-14	2-3	5	1	4	14
King	7-14	3-3	7	0	3	17
Grace	4-14	3-4	7	7	4	12
Blaylock	6-13	0-1	5	4	4	14
Mullins	0-0	0-0	1	0	1	0
Totals	30-70	9-13	30	19	18	79

Three-point field goals: Sieger, 7; Blaylock, 2; Grace, 1.

Halftime: Kansas 50, Oklahoma 50
Officials:

34

BASKET-BALL'S ULTIMATE SHOOT-OUT

May 22, 1988

Boston
vs.
Atlanta

"It was like two gunfighters
waiting to blink."
—*Celtics forward Kevin McHale*

Nothing that Larry Bird ever achieved, nor any duel he
ever fought during his career with the Boston Celtics,
matched the *mano-a-mano* battle he had with Dominique Wilkins of the Atlanta Braves in the final
game of the NBA's 1988 Eastern Conference semi-finals at Boston Garden.

"The fourth quarter was like two people standing at arm's
length and punching each other," Celtics forward Kevin
McHale said after Bird had made 9 of 10 shots and scored 20
points in the last ten minutes of the fourth quarter while
Wilkins was scoring 16 of his 47 points over the same period of
time.

Mere figures don't tell the tale, as millions of national
television viewers who watched on that May Sunday in 1988
will attest. Seeing it was best, because only then could anyone
truly appreciate the awesome individual battle waged by both
men in search of a victory for their team.

"They each put their team on their back and said, 'Let's
go,'" Atlanta coach Mike Fratello said afterward.

They did that—but they also did a lot more that made a
ten-minute stretch of basketball a priceless sequence in the
game's history because it showcased the very best that two of
the game's greatest players had to offer under excruciating
pressure. When it was over, they shook hands and walked off
the court, fully satisfied that they had carried their own teams
as far as they could go.

"It was like Larry was playing on Mt. Olympus and we
were down on the Greek islands," said Boston guard Dirk
Minnifield.

"He wanted it," Atlanta assistant coach Don Chaney,
himself a former Celtics player, declared so emphatically. "He
wanted the ball and he came through. That's what superstars
are made of."

"I tell you there was one four-minute stretch there that
was as pure a form of basketball as you're ever going to see,"
McHale added.

Actually, all ten minutes of this shootout were marvelous.
Bird had thrown down the gauntlet two nights previously
when the Celtics scrambled to tie the series at three games
apiece after Atlanta had gone ahead 3-2 with a stunning upset
at Boston Garden. "They had their chance," Bird said. "They

*East All-Stary Larry Bird tries to work ball around
West All-Star James Worthy in the 1986 All-Star game
in Dallas.*

244

had a big chance . . . now we'll be at home and the shots will be falling. I think Sunday will be a big win—for the Celtics."

For about three quarters of that game, it was nip and tuck, and Bird didn't have much influence one way or the other. Bothered by Wilkins's tough defense, he couldn't get into the flow of the game. Wilkins, though, was into it with both feet, despite some tenacious defense by McHale. He had scored 31 points in the first three quarters, and during that time it had been a McHale-Wilkins scoring matchup as Kevin had 21 points and 9 rebounds in the first half in his battle against Kevin Willis. The whole job was an energy drain on McHale, who worked hard enough on offense to shoot 13 fouls (and make all of them) and then tried to keep up with Wilkins.

"That's as hard as I've ever worked to guard a guy who wound up with 47," he said afterward. "I was draped on him

Below and opposite: *East All-Star Larry Bird tries to work ball around West All-Star James Worthy in the 1986 All-Star game in Dallas.*

three or four times and he still made the shot. I wouldn't have been surprised if they had called fouls."

There really is no telling what turns on Bird and Wilkins in crunch time, except that like all great players, something within them kicks off a hidden engine that just seems to put all the right wheels into motion. That's how it was when Bird and Wilkins began their game-deciding duel.

Boston held an 84-82 lead going into the fourth quarter, but Atlanta tied the game at 96 with 10:26 to play, and it was evident from the mood of the crowd that they were waiting for Bird to do something.

As if Bird sensed the time was right, he got a screen from center Robert Parrish and popped home a 16-foot jumper at 10:03 to play, and with 9:26 to play, following a Glenn Rivers field goal, Bird swished in a 13-foot turnaround rainbow from the right side.

"Funny," he said later, "I never particularly liked that side, but ever since I got here, we've run most of our plays from there, so I just picked it up. It also helped in this game that Atlanta had dropped off some of their double teaming because D.J. [Dennis Johnson] had burned them in the third quarter with some outside shots, and they had a man watching him."

Next, after Atlanta had again tied the score (90-90), came the most electrifying play of the game. Bird started from the right corner and came across the key to try to bank a runner, drawing Antoine Carr's contact. In the same instant that Bird heard an official's whistle signalling the foul, he threw up a shot, a straight-up, underhanded heave as he fell downward, just hoping it *might* go in—and it did! Then he made the foul, with 8:56 on the clock.

"After that shot went in," Bird said, "I wanted the ball the next time down, just to see how hot I really was."

He had to wait, though, because Wilkins answered the challenge and hit a 3-point shot from the sideline to tie the score again, 93-93 with 8:39 on the clock. But 19 seconds later, with 8:20 on the clock, Bird launched a jumper from the left side that went in and spun out again. It was the only shot he missed in that fourth quarter. Within 15 seconds, he came right back and stole the ball from John Battle, then found he was as "hot" as he had imagined when he nailed a jumper from the corner. On the clock: 8:05 . . . so in the course of 1 minute and 58 seconds, Bird had scored 11 points, and Wilkins had gotten 3, and Boston's lead still was only 2 points . . . and it was yet several minutes later when the real Bird-Wilkins shootout began. Here's how it went:

Celtics president Red Auerbach, who has witnessed all of his team's greatest moments during nearly four decades with the club, missed the Larry Bird-Dominique Wilkins shootout at Boston Garden. He was 70 miles away in Springfield, Massachusetts, receiving an honorary degree from American International College.

"A commitment is a commitment," Auerbach said without any apology. "I said yes to them a long time ago and I never go back on my word."

However, he did alter his procedures a bit, foregoing the academic procession to watch the finish of the game on television. He then walked into the ceremony and took his place among the honored degree recipients, but not before flashing a thumbs-up signal.

The crowd erupted with a huge cheer . . . and Auerbach got his honorary degree.

Kevin McHale (behind Bird) said of the Celtic superstar, "I'll remember games like this and what it was to play with him."

5:57—Wilkins hits a 20-foot sideline fallaway from the deep left corner and ties the score, 99-99.

5:42—Bird sinks a 10-foot left-handed leaner. Boston is ahead 101-99.

5:25—Wilkins's jumper from the top of the key, after a neat stutter-step move on McHale, ties the score 101-101.

5:25—Bird cleanly swishes a 17-foot turnaround from the left side. Boston, 103-101.

4:38—Wilkins ties the score 103-103 as he banks home a 10-footer from the left side of the lane.

4:24 to 3:34—McHale hits two free throws and Randy Whitman gets a jumper to tie the score for the tenth time in this quarter.

3:34—Bird nails a 14-foot turnaround in heavy traffic and Boston retakes the lead, 107-105. They never relinquish it.

But neither Bird nor Wilkins was finished as the teams battled to the very end. They continued to make big plays, with or without the ball, such as when Bird stuffed Carr at 1:48 with the Celtics ahead 109-105. In a flash, he headed downcourt, and that began another incredible sequence:

1:43—Bird, from the left corner, and well behind the three-point line, sticks a shot directly over Wilkins's arms, and no one was more amazed than Dominique.

"He hit that three-pointer with my hands dead in his face. What can you do?" Wilkins asked afterwards, shrugging his arms. "He just stepped back and shot it. He's a hard guy to guard."

1:31—Wilkins hits a turnaround shot in the lane and trims the Celtics' lead to 112-107.

0:45—Wilkins sinks two foul shots, and Boston's lead now is 112-109.

"I felt when he scored, I had to come back on the other end and keep our rhythm up, keep the tempo going," Wilkins said. "Our guys were pitching the ball to me off screens and my bank shots were going in—jumpers, bankers, top of the key."

0:26—Bird vs. Wilkins going across the middle again, and Larry goes hard to the basket for a left-handed running scoop shot, and a 114-109 lead.

0:20—Wilkins, after an Atlanta time out, follows up his own miss of a dunker and sticks in the rebound. Boston, 114-111.

0:17—Bird quickly retrieves the ball after Wilkins's basket and puts it in play with a long downcourt pass to Danny Ainge, who gets two points on a goal-tending call. Boston leads 116-111, but Rivers's two free throws and Rollins's hook shot, sandwiched around a couple of foul shots by Dennis Johnson, bring Atlanta to 118-115.

0:01—Wilkins hits the first of two foul shots (118-116) and then tries to bounce the ball off the rim, hoping for a two-point desperation shot. But Parrish gets it first and taps it to Johnson as the game ends.

Wilkins had his own perspective.

"This was one of the greatest two-man shootouts I've ever been involved in, but what can you say?" he noted without the slightest trace of remorse. "I thought I did everything I possibly could do on the offensive end. Defensively I was all over people. He hit the big shots. I hit the big shots."

Still, he wouldn't concede it was a Wilkins vs. Bird battle.

"I don't think of it as me vs. Bird. It was the Hawks vs. the Celts, and whoever was executing best down the end would win."

McHale had the last word.

"Sometimes after Larry plays a game like this, it makes me think ahead," he said. "I'll be retired in Minnesota and Larry will be retired in Indiana, and we probably won't see each other much.

"But a lot of nights I'll just lie there and remember games like this, and what it was like to play with him."

May 22, 1988, at Boston Garden						
Boston	FG-FGA	FT-FTA	Reb	Ast	PF	Pts
Bird	15-24	3-3	4	6	2	34
McHale	10-14	13-13	13	0	4	33
Parrish	6-10	2-3	5	4	2	14
Ainge	5-10	1-1	1	10	4	13
Johnson	6-11	4-6	4	8	2	16
Lewis	2-2	0-0	0	0	1	4
Acres	1-1	0-0	0	0	0	2
Roberts	0-1	0-0	0	0	1	0
Paxson	0-1	2-2	0	0	1	2
Gilmore	0-0	0-0	0	0	0	0
Totals	45-74	25-28	27	28	17	118

Three-point field goals: Bird, 1; Ainge, 2.

Atlanta						
Wilkins	19-23	8-9	6	4	0	47
Rivers	7-17	2-2	4	17	6	16
Willis	5-11	0-0	15	0	5	10
Wittman	11-13	0-0	1	1	5	22
Webb	0-1	0-0	0	1	3	0
Carr	6-8	1-1	3	2	1	13
Levingston	0-1	0-0	0	0	4	0
Batle	2-4	0-0	2	4	0	4
Rollins	2-3	0-0	2	1	0	4
Hastings	0-0	0-0	1	3	6	0
					2	
Totals	52-81	11-12	34	33	27	116

Three-point field goal: Wilkins.

Boston:	28	31	25	34 -- 118
Atlanta:	30	26	26	34 -- 116

Chronology of the Game

1891—In December, after being ordered to develop a game to provide indoor exercise and excitement between the football and baseball seasons for students at the International YMCA Training School in Springfield, Massachusetts, Dr. James Naismith directed the first game played with nine men to a side, and two peach baskets tacked to balconies which were 10 feet above the floor of the school's auditorium. The peach baskets were in lieu of two boxes which Naismith originally had designed, but which a janitor could not find. A soccer ball was used. Nasmith set up 13 rules for the game.

1892—Naismith's game was officially called "basketball" after he vetoed "Naismithball."

• First outside competitive game was played in February in Springfield between Central and Armory Hill YMCAs. It ended in a 2-2 tie.

• A round-robin tournament between teams in Albany, Troy, N.Y., Schenectady, Providence, Newport, R.I. and New York City was played.

• Women began to play the game at Vassar and Smith Colleges

• Amos Alonzo Stagg introduced the sport at the University of Chicago.

1893—Cone-shaped baskets replaced peach baskets.

• Field goals were worth three points, fouls one point.

• First collegiate competition when Vanderbilt defeated the Nashville YMCA and Hamline (Minn.) lost to the Minneapolis YMCA.

1894—First backboards, 6 by 4 feet strips of screen, were used.

1895—Fred Cooper and Albert Bratton of the Trenton (N.J.) YMCA introduced the short pass to get the ball closer to the basket.

• First intercollegiate competition: Haverford beat Temple 6-4 and Minnesota Aggies defeated Hamline 9-3.

1896—Wood backboards were introduced ten feet above the floor, and open nets were allowed on the baskets.

• First pro game was played by YMCA teams in Trenton, N.J.

• A YMCA tournament in Brooklyn was deemed the "Basketball Championship of America."

1897—Field goals were set at two points.

1898—First professional league, National Basketball League, established in Philadelphia.

1901—Columbia, Cornell, Harvard, Princeton, and Yale establish the Eastern League.

1905—Teams officially set at five players per side, regardless of the court size.

1906—Rules committee okays painting backboards white.

1910—Rules committee okays use of plate glass backboards.

1915—AAU, NCAA and YMCA standardized rules to remove violence from the game.

1916—Dribbling the basketball is allowed.

1917—Baskets are moved two feet inside the court, allowing shots from anywhere within the playing area.

1920—10,000 fans watch CCNY and NYU play in a New York City armory, the largest crowd to see a game to that time.

  • National High School Federation is formed in Chicago and 20,000 schools adopts its rules

1921—New York Celtics and New York Whirlwinds play a two-game "championship" series before 11,000 in New York City and each wins one game. Third game cancelled for fear of fan violence.

1923—No longer will fouls be awarded for running with the ball or double-dribbling, only loss of possession.

1925—Passaic (N.J.) High Schools ends 159-game winning streak.

1926—Abe Sapperstein forms the Harlem Globetrotters.

1927—Now the Original Celtics, team wins first of back-to-back American Basketball League titles.

1934—First college doubleheader in Madison Square Garden draws 16,180 to watch NYU beat Notre Dame and Westminster defeat St. John's. Event was the brainchild of sportswriter Ned Irish.

1936—U.S. wins first Olympic basketball title, defeating Canada 19-8 at Berlin Olympics.

1937—National Basketball League formed in 13 midwestern cities and Akron Goodyears win first championship.

1938—National Invitation Tournament (NIT) is begun in New York City, and Temple beats Colorado for title.

1939—Oregon defeats Ohio State in first NCAA championship game, in Evanston, Illinois.

1940—Harlem Globetrotters win world professional title.

1945—Oklahoma A&M first team to win two NCAA titles.

1946—Basketball Association of America is formed in 11 Eastern and midwestern cities and Philadelphia wins first title, beating Chicago in six games. Joe Fulks of Warriors wins scoring title.

1948—Minneapolis Lakers, with George Mikan, and three other NBL teams, join BAA.

1949—BA and BL merge to form National Basketball Association. Lakers win first NBA title.

1950—First black players, Sweetwater Clifton of the New York Knicks, and Chuck Cooper of the Boston Celtics, play in NBA.

1951—East defeats West 111-94 in first NBA All-Star Game, in Boston Garden.

  • NBA reduced to ten teams

1953—Bob Cousy of the Celtics sets playoff scoring record with 50 points against Syracuse in four-overtime game.

1954—NBA adopts suggestion by Syracuse owner Danny Bissone and adopts 24-second clock, and establishes a bonus foul after a team accumulates six during a quarter.

  • Frank Selvy of Furman becomes first collegian to score 100 points in Division I competition vs. Newberry.

1957—University of San Francisco ends 60-game winning streak, longest in major college competition to that time.

  • Boston Celtics win first NBA title in second overtime of seventh game.

1959—Boston Celtics win second NBA title and begin run of eight straight championships.

  • Elgin Baylor scores record 64 points for Lakers versus Celtics

  • Bill Russell of Boston sets record with 71 points against New York.

  • Wilt Chamberlain sets single game rebound record with 55 vs. Celtics.

1962—Wilt Chamberlain scores 100 points against Knicks in Hershey, Pennsylvania, and finishes season with record 50.4 points per game.

  • Philadelphia Warriors move to San Francisco.

1963—J. Walter Kenndy named to replace Maurice Podoloff as NBA commissioner.

Syracuse Nationals move to Philadelphia and become the 76ers while Chicago Packers move to Baltimore and become the Bullets.

1964—NBA widens foul line from 12 to 16 feet.

  • UCLA wins first of 10 NCAA titles under John Wooden

1966—Bill Russell becomes NBA's first black coach, with Celtics.

1967—American Basketball Association is formed and Pittsburgh Pipers win first title.

1968—52,693 persons, most ever to see a college basketball game, watch Houston defeat UCLA in the Astrodome.

1969—UCLA becomes first team to win three straight NCAA titles en route to record seven in a row.

• Celtics era ends with 11th NBA title in 13 years and Bill Russell retires as player and coach.

1970—NBA celebrates Silver Anniversary season and realigns into two-conference, four-division league.

1972—U.S. loses first Olympic title on disputed basket by Russian team at the buzzer.

• Lakers win record 33 games in a row

1974—UCLA record winning streak ended by Notre Dame at 88 games.

1975—John Wooden retires after winning 10th NCAA title for UCLA

• Lawrence O'Brien becomes third *NBA* Commissioner.

1976—NBA and ABA merge

• U.S. Women's Olympic Team wins Silver Medal in Montreal 1982—Louisiana Tech wins first woman's NCAA title.

1983—Detroit and Denver score 186 points, most ever in NBA game.

1984—U.S .Women's Olympic team wins gold medal as does men's team in Los Angeles Olympics.

• David Stern named fourth NBA Commissioner.

1986—Michael Jordan of the Chicago Bulls set a playoff record with 63 points vs. Celtics.

1988—NBA recorded its 5 millionth point.

Photo Credits